Also available at all good book stores

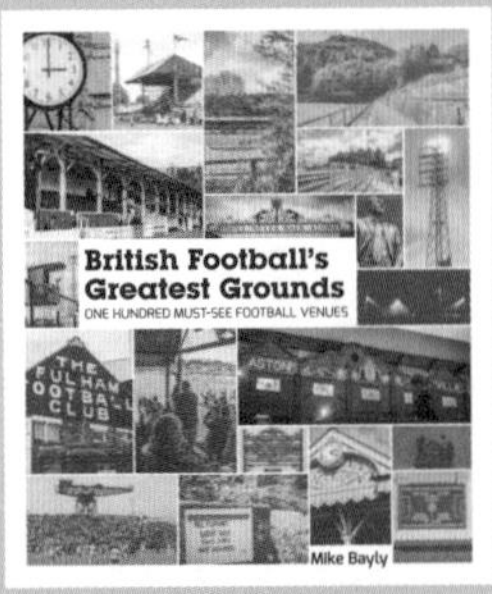

9781785316470

9781785313929

9781785315466

9781785316548

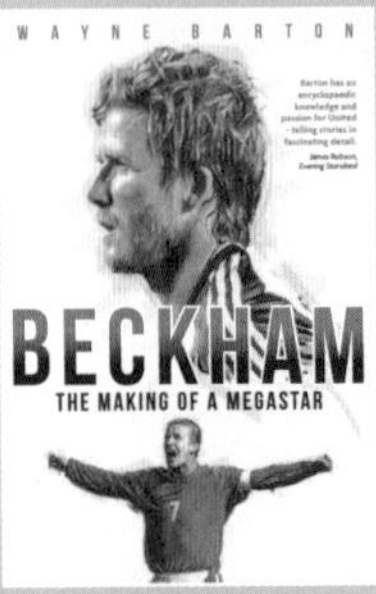

9781785316760

9781785314995

9781785316685

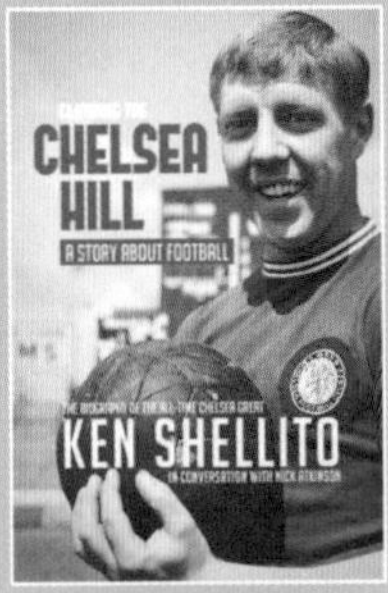

9781785316807

9781785315008

Never Give Up

The Graham Buster Tutt Story

GRAHAM TUTT
with MATT EASTLEY

pitch

First published by Pitch Publishing, 2021

Pitch Publishing
A2 Yeoman Gate
Yeoman Way
Worthing
Sussex
BN13 3QZ
www.pitchpublishing.co.uk
info@pitchpublishing.co.uk

A CIP catalogue record is available for this book from the British Library.

ISBN 978 1 78531 848 1

Typesetting and origination by Pitch Publishing

Printed and bound in India by Replika Press Pvt. Ltd.

Contents

Foreword
by John Motson

LIKE GRAHAM Tutt himself, I also distinctly recall Saturday, 21 February 1976. Roker Park was like a cauldron that day for the match between Sunderland and Charlton Athletic, two great old clubs with fine traditions. It was my fifth season working for the BBC and I'd already seen a lot but the events of that day have always stayed with me. The devastating injury which ended Graham's career in this country came very early in the game which is always challenging for a commentator. He was highly rated in the game and who knows what he may have gone on to achieve. I'm able to replay the moment the injury happened in my mind. The lob from Tony Towers, the header from Joe Bolton and the ball breaking free. I saw Graham rushing out and then … the terrible collision with Sunderland's Tom Finney. It happened so quickly and looked like excellent goalkeeping which is why I said on the commentary that day, 'Good save by Tutt who got the bang on the head. What a brave piece of goalkeeping that was.' The next thing I knew was that Graham was being carried off and, on my monitor, I could see the blood pouring from a wound. It was obvious then he would take no further part that afternoon but what nobody realised was that he would not play another professional game in this country.

I was obviously concerned for Graham's welfare that day and can recall being anxious that he had gone to hospital. I followed reports in the newspapers and was relieved that he made a recovery of sorts.

What I didn't know was what happened next and it is only since being asked to write this foreword that I have found out. I am delighted that Graham has gone on to live such an interesting and varied life. This is a unique story which spans three continents and provides a fascinating insight into the life of a professional footballer, not just in Britain, but in South Africa and the United States. Graham's experiences in each country make compelling reading. Perhaps none of it would have happened were it not for the incident at Roker Park on that chilly February afternoon. There are life lessons for all of us in the book and the title 'Never Give Up' is very apt indeed.

The story also has a really happy ending with a fascinating reunion but you'll have to read the book to find out what that is.

PART ONE

LONDON AND THE UK

Chapter 1
The Boot

EVERYBODY SAID I shouldn't have returned, even though the place had been silently luring me back for years. While my head told me they were right, my heart protested. I felt I had to. Closure, they call it. To eradicate the dull ache in the pit of my stomach that wouldn't shift. Nevertheless, I was here; the street names gave it away even though houses now stood where the football ground had once been. Clockstand Close, Midfield Drive, Turnstile Mews. They were my compass and map.

Otherwise, I never would have known that the regulation houses on this identikit estate in the north-east of England rested at the scene of the terrible moment my life changed forever.

It was quiet when I returned, save for the occasional shout of children playing on their bikes. I could feel the chill wind blowing in from the North Sea, like razor blades on my cheeks. I live in another country now, a much warmer one, but it reminded me of how cold England could be in winter, taking me back to my childhood. The bracing sea air kick-started my memory and, like fragments of a half-remembered dream, took me back to that fateful day more than 40 years ago.

I closed my eyes and saw throngs of people heading to a famous old football ground. Red and white scarves, donkey jackets, trench coats and parkas. I could smell the tobacco and beer in the late winter air, the waft of frying onions, burgers and hot dogs and hear the distinctive brogue of England's industrial north-east.

You see, I'm a lot older now. But I used to be a professional footballer and I had returned to the site of Roker Park, the former home of Sunderland Football Club. I never played for this great old club, but I will always have a connection with it. For the life of me, with no disrespect whatsoever to their brilliant followers, I wish I didn't have.

Because it was here that my soccer career finished prematurely. Suddenly, shockingly and in a pool of blood.

As I stood there, so many years on, quietly absorbing my surroundings, I felt a lump in my throat and my eyes filling with tears – the physical manifestations of a gnawing sense of injustice about what might have been.

I dug my hands – my big goalkeeper hands – into my pockets and, with the stoicism for which my countrymen are renowned, stole one final look. Where *exactly* had it happened, I wondered? Could I work out where that penalty box had been? I moved hesitantly towards the spot. There had been nothing hesitant about my actions on that other chilly afternoon. On the contrary, I had been bold and decisive. Because that was the way I had played. No half measures. It was what I had been paid to do.

As I reached the imagined spot, I stopped in my tracks. And then I saw it. The boot. *That* boot. The one that did the damage. I could see it coming towards me, almost frozen in time. It had taken on hideous proportions in my memory. It was just a standard boot but it had wrought so much damage, both physically and emotionally. I felt another freezing gust blow in from the bleak coast and I knew I had seen enough. I had returned, which was all I needed to do. It had been upsetting, yet cathartic. I turned to leave this old proud city which had unwittingly played a part in my fate.

I decided there and then I would never return.

Before I left for good, I stopped briefly outside Sunderland's fantastic stadium – the Stadium of Light, constructed around the turn of the Millennium just a stone's throw from Roker Park.

While I admired its imposing presence and modern grandeur, something grated. It felt alien. Perhaps it represented how far the sport I loved had come since my world fell apart. It symbolised the new. And I wasn't part of it. As I headed back towards the station, I saw it again. The boot.

Chapter 2

A Stolen Dream

I REMEMBER 21 February 1976 as if it were yesterday. How could I ever forget it? It was a life-defining day.

For two years up to it, perhaps more, my life had been on a seemingly endless upward trajectory, propelled by the exuberance of youth. I thought anything was possible.

I was progressing rapidly in my chosen profession and my family and friends were bursting with pride at my achievements.

'Is this the real life, is this just fantasy?' That's what Queen's Freddie Mercury sings in the opening line of 'Bohemian Rhapsody', which had been number one for what felt like an eternity. To me, that was spot on. I was 19 years old and my life *did* feel like a fantasy. I was a professional footballer, a goalkeeper playing for a proud London club that, after years in the doldrums, was on the way back.

I was the established first-choice keeper playing with and against some top players. Yes, I was young but, from the moment I'd crossed that white line for my first-team debut in March 1974, aged just 17, I knew I belonged.

Perhaps I could be forgiven for occasionally getting carried away with my dreams. But why not? I was hungry for success and bursting with the fearlessness of youth. I loved playing for my club, but I was ambitious too and knew I could play at the top level – the first division. Then, who knows? I'd heard whispers big clubs were watching me. In more tranquil moments I dreamt of FA Cup medals, league championships, European football and then, the ultimate, pulling on the yellow jersey worn by England goalkeepers at that time. I watched the likes of Ray Clemence and Peter Shilton on television and dreamed one day I would emulate their success. And why not? I had time on my side.

Then, just like that, my dreams were shattered in that famous old ground, many miles from home. My fate was witnessed by millions on national television and, in the next day's papers, the horrific photograph of my battered and bloodied face would induce winces from even the least squeamish.

My professional football career in Britain was ended in a flash and my life would never be the same again.

Chapter 3
On the Up

IT IS time to introduce myself. My name is Graham Tutt, a born and bred Londoner, and in the mid-1970s I was the first-choice goalkeeper for Charlton Athletic Football Club. First choice that is until my career ended, abruptly and devastatingly.

Things had been going well not just for me but the club as a whole and we had our eyes on the top division, where we'd meet the real big guns of the game – the likes of Liverpool, Manchester United, Arsenal and Spurs. Then, who knows?

Just under a year earlier, in April 1975, on an incredible night at our cavernous bowl of a ground, aptly called The Valley, we'd clinched promotion to Division Two. No Charlton fan who was there will forget it. On a sticky, humid night we came from a goal down to beat Bobby Charlton's Preston North End team 3-1 to claw our way out of Division Three. There was no doubt about it, we were on our way back and confidence was soaring. Mine was, definitely.

Promotion brought greater exposure and publicity. There was genuine optimism in our corner of south-east London. Things were also taking off for me personally and I just went with it.

I gladly accepted a lucrative advertising deal from a high-street bank. It was money for old rope.

I simply had to do a short voiceover for a radio advert, say a few lines about 'making a great save' and opening a new account and I was paid £500, which was decent money back then.

Even so, I wasn't letting anything go to my head. I knew we would have to prove ourselves all over again in the higher division.

After the euphoria of promotion had died down, we knuckled down into some hard graft. Pre-season training that summer was tough and relentless.

But there was no choice. If we slacked at all, we'd have our arses kicked. I had to pinch myself when I thought of some of the international-class players I'd be coming up against, like Peter Osgood, Johnny Giles, Alan Mullery and even the king himself, Bobby Moore. Make no mistake. This was a strong division with some big-name teams in it, like West Brom, Chelsea, Southampton and Nottingham Forest. You could add Sunderland to that list, managed by former Charlton boss Bob Stokoe. Two years earlier, they had stunned the football world by lifting the world-famous FA Cup, overcoming the might of Don Revie's Leeds at Wembley in the final. They were a powerhouse in our league, attracting huge crowds to Roker Park. But we weren't frightened of them and we reckoned on our day we could beat anyone.

After a shaky start to the 1975/76 season, we had found our feet and began adjusting to life in the second division. I was loving my football. We were on television regularly. The leading football highlights show in the UK, *Match of the Day*, visited The Valley for the first time in seven years to cover our match against Blackpool. It was quite strange to see myself on telly, but it was a sign we were on the up. We were on again a couple of months later when Brian Moore and *The Big Match* team rolled up for our match against, ironically, Sunderland. We were also televised at Wolves and again by *Match of the Day* cameras when we travelled across south London to play Fulham at Craven Cottage.

Little did I know that the next time the *Match of the Day* cameras filmed us would be my last match as a professional footballer in the UK.

But all that could wait. In the League Cup third round we gave London rivals Queens Park Rangers a run for their money. They were then riding high at the top of the first division and had a fantastic side including the likes of Stan Bowles, Gerry Francis, Dave Thomas and Don Givens. We played brilliantly at their West London ground, Loftus Road, holding them to a 1-1 draw.

More than 32,000 packed into The Valley for the replay. We held our own for more than 70 minutes before their class finally told and we conceded three times late in the game. But we'd gone toe-to-toe with one of the best clubs in the country at that time.

Back in the league we were starting to turn heads. Two days after Christmas we beat Chelsea 3-2 at Stamford Bridge and our form going into 1976 was good. The media were now calling us the 'New Charlton'.

I was supremely happy. I was fulfilling my boyhood ambition. It was everything I had ever wanted. If you had told me then that it was all going to end in a split second I'd have laughed in your face.

My boyhood dreams were coming true. Dreams that had been cast ten years earlier on a patch of wasteland in southeast London.

Chapter 4

The Bombsite Was Our Wembley

LET ME take you back to the mid-1960s. April 1965 to be precise.

A ragged group of young kids, with grazed, dirty knees are playing soccer on a small patch of wasteland where 30 family houses once stood, before they were obliterated by a wartime bomb.

Just 20 yards from the makeshift pitch stands a modest council house. Discreetly peering through the curtains of an upstairs window, Reg Tutt is smiling proudly, as he watches his eight-year-old son, Graham, that's me, performing heroics in goal.

The house, 75 Revelon Road, was rented from the council and was in a working-class area of south-east London called Brockley. It was a tough, no-nonsense area with a reputation for spawning boxers, footballers, the occasional ne'er do well and some thoroughly good working-class people.

Although my name was Graham, no one ever called me that except my teachers and my mum when I was in trouble. The rest of the time I was Buster. This cheerful moniker came from the day I was born. I weighed in at more than ten pounds and my puffy face looked like a boxer who'd gone a few rounds. My dad said I looked like a real Buster and the name stuck.

At eight years old I was already football-mad and the bombsite was my Wembley. It felt a little eerie knowing so many people had died there. The damage had been done late one night by the German flying bomb known as a doodlebug. It killed more than 30 people and flattened as many homes. We were told most victims had probably been killed instantly in their beds.

By the mid-60s, everyone was doing their best to put the memories of the war behind them. London and her suburbs were slowly recovering. Nevertheless, our makeshift football pitch served as a permanent memorial to those who had perished.

Saying our playing field was makeshift is actually an understatement. Our goalposts were a pile of broken house bricks. Our pitch had broken rubble emerging from the dirt providing unpredictable bounces and causing regular cut knees, twisted ankles or worse. It was all we had but what really mattered was that it was ours.

Even now I can see myself as a little ragamuffin, still wearing my school shirt, necktie round the wrong way, holes in my trousers and scuffed, dusty shoes, making a full-length diving save. I never wanted to be a goalscorer like Jimmy Greaves, Bobby Charlton or Denis Law. No. I wanted to be keeping goals out not scoring them. Gordon Banks, Ron Springett or the great Russian keeper, Lev Yashin were my heroes.

We didn't have referees in our games. The occasional push, shove or over-the-top tackle were all part of the game. However, our mums ruled the roost and when they spoke, we listened. All the mums were attuned to our game times and worked to the same dinner schedule. Six o'clock was dinner time and it never lasted more than 15 minutes, so we could get back to our games.

On this particular day I found a gas mask while clearing off a pile of bricks from the back of my goal area. It looked very strange and was a stark, sinister reminder of the past.

Chapter 5
My Family

MUM, DAD and my sister Julie, who was 17 months older than me, were nearly always halfway through eating when I arrived at the table. Every day, without looking up from her meal, Mum would instruct me to wash my hands.

I hung my new-found gas mask on the back of my dining chair.

My older brother, Jim, had already wolfed down his meal and was on his way out, probably on a date. He was 20 – 12 years older than me – and my hero.

He looked like Elvis Presley with his slicked-back hair, long, wide sideburns and white ironed shirt with the collar up. His winkle picker boots and dark drainpipe trousers completed the look.

He ruffled my mop of hair before dashing out, rattling the front-door knocker with his hefty slam.

The dining room table always groaned with Mum's great food. My favourite was roast lamb, roast potatoes and veg. We may have been a traditional working-class family, not wealthy by any means, but Mum fed us like kings.

Talk turned to the gas mask which Mum said was for a baby and had been issued to families during the war as protection from a German gas attack. There was rarely, if ever, a time when the word 'German' was not followed by the word 'bastards' from any adult member of our family. Though everybody wanted to move on, the bitter memories of World War II were still raw.

The discovery of the mask had piqued my curiosity again and sparked another conversation about the night our neighbourhood was bombed. I was spellbound as Mum said the bomb had landed at about 11 o'clock one night. The general consensus was the bomb had probably veered away from its intended target, most likely the London dockyards.

And now, for the first time, I learned that my mum had been incredibly lucky not to have been killed herself.

'I hadn't wanted to go to the bomb shelter that night because I had just got comfortable in bed,' she told me. 'But when the siren went off your granddad, as always, demanded we all run to the bomb shelter at the bottom of our garden. He was a stubborn, lovable old fart.'

Mum told me that my nan and granddad and my uncle Bill and aunt Pat just managed to close the shelter door before hearing the flame of the rocket stutter to a mid-air stop indicating it was going to drop from the sky and would explode on impact just a few seconds later.

Nearly 60 years on, I can still see Mum's serious face and hear her urgent voice as she continued: 'Seconds after hitting the houses across the road, the blast blew off most of our roof and a big slab of concrete landed on my bed, right smack in the middle of my pillow. It landed exactly where my head had been only five minutes earlier.'

She sighed deeply before whispering: 'Thank God we listened to your granddad that night.'

Mum looked up slowly and gazed lovingly at Julie and I before telling us quietly that neither of us would have been born if she hadn't listened to our granddad. It was a poignant moment which has always stayed with me.

I learned so much from my parents' war stories. It taught me about resilience, and never giving up, words that would come to mean so much to me personally in later life. Mum and Dad's philosophy had always been to stay calm and try to overcome anything life threw in their direction. It was a mindset that rubbed off on myself, Julie and Jim, maybe without us even knowing it.

Mum and Dad were both hard workers and would do anything to put food on the table for us. Dad was a toolmaker and made bombs in a factory during the war while Mum worked on the checkout counter of our local Co-op. I'm not asking that you get the violins out, but money was very tight.

Chapter 6

A Special Talent?

I KNEW Dad had been watching me play on the bombsite but didn't appreciate just how closely he'd been monitoring me. Dad knew his football and one day over tea he told me what a good goalkeeper he thought I was. He was impressed by my confidence and courage. Even though I had only just turned eight, Dad thought I should make a concerted effort to win a place in my under-11 school team.

I can still remember his words:

'You know, Buster,' he told me, 'I think you have a special talent for football but it will take much more than that. I notice your concentration, composure and passion for playing in goal. If I'm right and you have what I think you have, you could go far.'

Dad was no mug with a ball at his feet. He played on the right wing in his army days and by all accounts was pretty useful so he knew what he was talking about.

Dad continued: 'Every person has a special gift and I think yours is football, son. Trust in your abilities. It's inside you son, I can see it.'

Fast forward 11 years to 20 February 1976. I woke early and, just as I did every morning, smiled broadly as I reminded myself how lucky I was to be a professional footballer. Things were going well, the team was winning, I was playing well. Everything was good and I allowed myself an extra five minutes in bed. I had a long coach journey in front of me.

I got myself ready, had some breakfast, packed my bag and headed off to The Valley. I felt on top of the world as I made my way through the south London traffic. I was determined to enjoy every moment of being a professional footballer.

Chapter 7

A Swig of Brandy

A FEW weeks after Dad's proud endorsement of my abilities, I tried out for the Turnham Road School under-11 team on a bitterly cold day. I was on my game that day, right in the thick of the action, diving this way and that and dealing with shots from every angle. After 40 freezing minutes of showing what I could do, a teacher we called Coach Pigden, or Coach P for short, announced his selection. I had done enough. I had made the under-11 school team.

Coach P was also our maths teacher. This actually proved very useful because he would talk to me about goalkeeping angles and where I should position myself to make it as difficult as possible for the other team to score. Coach P always wore a tartan flat cap, matching tie, a tweed jacket, nicely pressed trousers and starched white shirt. His sharp attire never changed from the classroom to the football field. He looked more like a racehorse owner than a football coach.

Coach P was special. He was constantly giving encouragement. Even when I let a goal in, I would hear him chime: 'Unlucky, Tuttie, next time you'll stop it.'

My best mate was called Pigeon and he also made the team at right-back. We were excited to be together on the same team, which had some really good talent in it.

Just a few days after the under-11 trial match, we played our first official game at a ground called Ladywell Park, near Lewisham. The weather had deteriorated and there was almost two inches of bright white snow on the ground, meaning we played with a heavy orange leather ball to make it easier to see. We were cruising to victory, crushing our opponents 11–0. I had enough time on my hands to read a comic. In fact, I hardly touched the ball in the second half at all and felt almost frozen. Very few goalkeepers wore sweat bottoms or gloves back then. You just had to blow on your hands to keep them warm or shake them around to get the blood circulating. It was at that point I saw Mum heading my way.

As inconspicuously as possible she walked around to the back of my net-less goal, and surreptitiously beckoned me towards the goalpost: 'Here you go son, have a swig of this. It'll warm you up.' I recognised it immediately as my granddad's silver flask and it contained brandy. Of course, I took a quick swig and soon felt a warm glow and a relaxed state of mind which made the last ten minutes bearable.

I don't think any parent would dare do that today. Not at all appropriate in the modern world. They would probably be arrested and charged with irresponsible behaviour towards a minor or something. But that was Mum. She always had her own, unique way of dealing with things. No doubt it seemed the right thing to do in her eyes at the time. Her boy was near freezing and she wanted to help.

I arrived at The Valley in good spirits. The lads were in great form and the jokes were flying around. We knew that unless we had a catastrophic loss of form, we were staying up. Ten minutes later I was settled at the back of our new luxury team bus, with both feet up, resting my calves on a card table. Even before heading north, several of our senior players like Peter Hunt, Jimmy Giles and Phil Warman had begun a game of poker a few rows down the aisle. Most of the younger lads like myself and the curly-haired Mark Penfold were not interested in cards. In fact, Mark lost no time in curling himself up and trying to sleep. Mark and I had come through the club ranks together and were good mates. We were both 19 and felt we had years ahead of us to make our mark in the game. As the coach set off, I heard a roar of laughter from the card school and a raucous cry of 'you lucky bastard'. I smiled to myself as we negotiated our way through the tight streets around The Valley at the start of what would prove to be a fateful journey.

Chapter 8
Mum

MUM WAS stubborn with a capital 'S' and would never change her mind once it was made up. I suppose that was good in many ways because you knew exactly where you stood with her. There were no surprises or grey areas in her world. Whatever she said was always followed through. That particular attribute seems rare in today's world.

Having good manners was very important to Mum. 'Please' and 'thank you' were automatic. I'm glad she raised us that way because it instilled my own family values.

You certainly did not want to get on the wrong side of Mum and I saw her stand up for herself on numerous occasions, but she was not mean. She had a caring and passionate way with her, especially when it came to neighbours and the people in our neighbourhood. I used to get highly amused when walking around the block with her and our three-legged dog, Sadie. It would usually take us two hours or more to do a 20-minute dog walk. This wasn't because of Sadie but because Mum would insist on popping in to see how people were. She would stop at an old friend's house just to see if they needed anything. Or maybe they had been unwell and she was checking how they were. She had a good sense of humour too and made me laugh one day when an old lady asked her to pick up a bottle of milk from the shop. Smiling away, Mum said: 'Now don't you die on me before I get back, because you are not looking so good and you haven't paid me for the milk yet.' She said things in such a way that she could get away with it and people would laugh along with her. Her sense of humour was different. People listened when she spoke because her message was always conveyed with a dash of wit.

Mum loved bingo and on Tuesdays and Thursdays she would go to a club called the Rivoli Ballroom at Crofton Park, with her mum, my nan. One night the pair of them walked into our living room and threw 200 £1 notes up into the air while we were watching telly. Julie and I were only young and we both thought we were millionaires when the pound notes began raining down on us. Then Julie and I rolled around on the money for the fun of it. Nan and Mum divided up their win, giving Julie, Jim, myself and themselves equal amounts. That's how we worked. Sharing came naturally to the Tutt clan.

If ever Julie or I fancied an apple or banana we would automatically cut it in half to share with one another. When we were growing up, an apple or banana was a luxury. We felt extra special when we had an apple, banana or orange stuffed in our Christmas stockings. It felt good to share no matter what it was.

Mum claimed she got married because my dad would help support her immediate family. Mum had a younger sister by ten years called Kitty, who had severe health problems. Kitty was a very pretty girl with dark curly brown hair, big brown eyes and a beautiful smile like Vivien Leigh in *Gone with the Wind*. Kitty needed to be cared for on a daily basis so Nan would look after Kitty during the day and Mum would take the evening shift.

Mum left school at 14 to look after Kitty and a blind neighbour. With Kitty being very young and needing constant attention and the blind lady close by, it must have been a trying time.

Kitty died when she was only 14, just before the end of the war in 1945. I'm sure it nearly broke Mum's heart. Mum never brought her up in conversation without having some tears, especially on Kitty's birthday. Mum would always talk about how beautiful she was inside and out. She would always close the conversation with: 'It wasn't fair what happened to sweet Kitty.'

Mum loved to reminisce about the war years. She was 18 when war broke out and some of her stories were funny while some were extremely sad. She loved going out dancing in London with her friends. She said the Yanks were always trying to give her nylon stockings, candy and cigarettes, which she didn't accept because she'd feel obliged to see them again.

Mum lost her older brother Jim to tuberculosis a year after the war ended. He was just 30 years old. Mum thought Jim came back into this world through me as she said Jim and I looked almost identical. We were both 6ft 4in, with similar personalities and were both football-mad. Unfortunately, Jim had been unable to play because of his illness but participated as a linesman. Mum would want to hold my hands sometimes simply because they reminded her of Jim's.

She also loved telling stories about her half-brother, my uncle Bill. She knew he was my favourite uncle so I would be all ears. Her best story was about when he was staying in our house when the living room windows were blown out by an exploding bomb at the bottom of our garden.

At the time Uncle Bill was laying down, half asleep, on the couch. Mum said if it hadn't been for his thick wool trench coat, which he had pulled over his head and body in the nick of time, he would have been gashed to pieces. 'The coat looked like a glass porcupine,' laughed Mum.

In later life, Mum worked in the heart of London in an area called Holborn where she was a sausage packer at Sainsbury's three days a week. Her hands would be constantly in ice and cold water while she worked on the conveyor belt: 'Stack 'em, pack 'em and push 'em on,' she would say. That's what she did for some extra income while we were growing up and never complained but I'm sure it's why she developed severe rheumatism in her hands and arms as she got older.

Our state-of-the-art luxury coach was the best you could get in 1976. It was beautifully appointed and even boasted a toilet with washing facilities at the back. We were heading for the Blackwall Tunnel to take us under the Thames. It was the start of an eight-hour coach journey towards what would surely be our toughest game of the season. But we were pros and these were the games we lived and worked for. Sunderland at Roker Park was as good as it got in this division and I for one was determined to enjoy every moment.

The Sunderland fans were known for their passion and demanding nothing less than the very best from their team. They were also not above giving some serious stick to opposing teams, especially those from the south who they considered soft and easy meat. This was all passing through my mind as we emerged from the tunnel into east London. I looked out of the window. 'Bring it on,' I thought. 'Bring it on.'

Chapter 9
Wisdom from a Hero

DAD WAS one of quite a few people who would go to The Den one week and The Valley the next but I found myself rooting for the men from The Den. Both clubs were equidistant from our house in Brockley and it was only around 20 minutes to either stadium. Because the two clubs were so near to each other, their home games were alternated so as not to clash.

I found myself asking Dad lots of questions about the goalkeepers and I loved to hear about the young Millwall goalkeeper Alex Stepney. I don't know why but the name 'Alex Stepney' intrigued me and I wanted to know more about him so I badgered Dad for more information. Dad told me that Alex had it all. His positioning was brilliant, meaning he rarely had to dive. He also had great hands, hardly ever dropped a ball, and was tremendously brave when diving to collect the ball off an oncoming forward's feet. Dad said he made goalkeeping look easy. Without actually seeing him play, Alex Stepney became my hero. Little did I know that, very soon, I'd be meeting him.

On the way to school one rainy morning, my best mate Pigeon told me that Millwall occasionally practised at Deptford Park which had an all-weather cinder pitch. It was just a ten-minute bike ride from my house.

I took a chance the very next day and skipped the morning off school. It had rained heavily the previous evening, was still a little drizzly in the morning and my instincts told me the Millwall squad would be using the all-weather pitch. So, I cycled to Deptford Park hoping they would be there.

I was genuinely excited at the prospect of seeing Alex Stepney and the Millwall team. I couldn't get there fast enough, dodging in and out of the red double-decker London buses and black taxicabs.

My instincts were right. When I got to the edge of the park, I could see from the top of the hill approximately 20 players. They were lightly jogging in pairs and Alex was leading the pack. His light-green padded goalkeeper jersey made him stand out.

I hid behind a huge oak tree and suddenly became painfully shy, though I told myself this was not the time. So, with a great deal of hesitation, I edged closer by sprinting from tree to tree until I could hear what was happening. It sounded like a shooting practice was about to begin.

I took my chance to edge closer until I was only about 20 yards away from the entrance to the pitch. I felt my heart beat faster when I heard Alex telling the coach he was ready for action.

With everybody preoccupied, I felt confident enough to move half behind a final tree, which was closest to the entry gate and just behind Alex's goal.

The shooting session went on for nearly 45 minutes and I watched spellbound as Alex worked his proverbial backside off. He was diving everywhere and exchanging good-natured banter with the players, saying things like 'Is that all you've got?' or 'Come on, my grandma would stop that with her handbag.'

While it was all good fun, it got increasingly lively as the players tried everything in their power to get one past him.

The intensity had lured me out from behind the last tree and I stood with my hand on the gate latch without really realising that I was mesmerised. The strikers were now blasting the ball with real ferocity and shouting banter like 'Pull this one out of the net, you cocky bastard.' But it was all done with a smile. Try as they might they could not get their shot past Alex Stepney.

It was brilliant, intense and totally unforgiving. The shots on goal were now relentless. They were peppering him. And all the while Alex stood strong and unflinching with a wry grin on his face.

Finally, it was over and the coach instructed the players to do some quick ball work before congratulating Alex for his excellent keeping and telling him he was done for the day.

By now I was right inside the gate and standing by a drinking fountain on the inside of the fence.

The next thing I knew Alex Stepney was walking towards the fountain. He looked exhausted but happy, even with a little blood coming from his lip where a ball must have smacked him in the mouth. He was now just a few feet away from me as I instinctively stepped back.

Then he spoke to me: 'Shouldn't you be at school, son?' he asked as he squirted a jet of water across his face before taking several large gulps.

I couldn't believe I was talking to Alex Stepney. I moved a little awkwardly towards him and said nervously: 'I skipped school to watch you practise.' Then I did something which, looking back, seems a little odd but it was an instinctive move for a nine-year-old boy. I tugged gently at his sleeve and stammered, 'Mr Stepney, I want to be a pro just like you.'

He stared at me for a moment before replying with words that would change my life: 'You will, son. Just practise every day, do your very, very best. Never give up and you'll be a pro someday too.'

That was it. The briefest of exchanges but one that had me walking on air. From that day on, I began practising as hard as I could every day. I even adopted his style of banter, joshing with my mates when I saved their shots: 'Is that the best you can do?' and 'My granny can shoot harder than that.'

It wasn't long before England's top teams were vying for Alex's signature and, in May 1966, Chelsea snapped him up for £50,000. Apparently, Chelsea intended playing Alex and the also-brilliant Peter Bonetti on alternate weeks, but Alex merited a regular first-team place in his own right and within three months he was on his way to Manchester United. He went on to have a glittering career, winning the First Division Championship in his first season at Old Trafford and the European Cup in 1968. Little did he know how that one piece of advice he offered me that morning changed my life.

'Practise every day, do your very, very best. Never give up and you'll be a pro someday too.'

After meeting my hero, I raced back to school, making some feeble excuse about why I hadn't been in that morning. When I got home, I asked Jim to take me to our local park, Peckham Rye, to fire some shots at me. I was inspired after watching Alex perform so outstandingly that morning. I also wanted to show Jim I was as good as Mum and Dad were saying I was.

Jim had recently bought an impressive Ford Consul Convertible. It was a real eye-catcher with light-blue bodywork contrasting perfectly with the white interior and matching soft top neatly folded into the back of the car. It looked like the kind of American cars we had seen on telly. Jim loved it and cruised along with his elbow resting on the open window. With his long, dark sideburns and slick combed-back hair, he looked every inch the mid 60s hipster. We both felt like a million dollars as we cruised. We entered Peckham Rye with all eyes on us and even some kids trailing behind.

I'll never forget that day. We weren't often together like that because Jim – being 12 years older than me, remember – was always out with his mates or a girl. At first, he kicked the ball gingerly towards me, testing the waters to try me out. After a few minutes he could tell I knew what I was doing. At this point our sibling rivalry kicked in, especially when I started to imitate Alex Stepney's banter I had heard that morning. I started with, 'Is that the best you can do, Jim? Julie [our sister] can kick harder than that.' That seemed to do it. Before I knew it, he was blasting the ball from about 15 yards away with all his might.

Jim was a useful player and could put both power and a decent swerve into a shot with either foot. That day we went at it hammer and tongs with neither of us showing any mercy. After an hour we collapsed together in a brotherly heap after Jim tried to dribble around me but I recovered enough to block his shot and we landed on top of each other, both exhausted. We then agreed our shooting session was a draw on the saves to goals ratio.

We both gained respect for each other that day because Jim could really strike a ball cleanly and I genuinely surprised him with my goalkeeping ability. We laughed all the way home until a policeman on a motorbike pulled Jim over and threatened to give him a speeding ticket. Fortunately, any notion of speeding was soon forgotten after they started chatting about Jim's car. That day I also saw what a smooth manner Jim had as he talked the officer out of giving him a ticket. Jim engaged the officer in such an enthusiastic way that he forgot why he had stopped us and wished us well.

My brother Jim was, and still is, my hero. He looked like Elvis, had a convertible, and carried the Elvis swagger perfectly. He also showed me he had the gift of the gab.

That spring day in 1966 made a deep and lasting impression on me. It started with watching my sporting hero Alex Stepney performing goalkeeping heroics before giving me some invaluable advice and ended with a terrific fraternal bonding session. Different elements of both my heroes' characters rubbed off on me that day and that was invaluable. Now all I needed was to see an actual football match!

Chapter 10

Tenth Birthday Treat

MY DAD was starting to feed off my passion for football and it was rekindling his love for the game. Our enthusiasm was ignited further when England won the World Cup in July 1966. It helped that England beat the 'German bastards', as my parents called them, 4-2 in extra time. We watched that historic, never-to-be forgotten match on our old black and white TV. I was transfixed by England's goalkeeper that day, Gordon Banks. It cemented my desire to be a professional goalkeeper. I was now almost ten and getting taller all the time.

A few weeks after that special afternoon, Dad was working in the back garden when he beckoned me over for a chat. I knew he had something important to say as he dug his shovel into the soft dirt, and rested on it. He told me the first-ever professional football match he had seen was in November 1927 when he was taken by his dad. It was his tenth birthday present and it was at Charlton's huge ground, The Valley.

I thought I knew what was coming next but let Dad continue as he was in full nostalgia mode: 'I distinctly remember the game,' he said. 'Charlton were playing Norwich. It was a humdinger. During the first half Charlton's keeper Tom McKenna went off for treatment for about 20 minutes because he got a bad whack on the shin. Back then there were no substitutes so the left-back Edwin Herod had to play in goal for a while.

'It meant Charlton were playing with ten men and they went a goal down. But being a man down seemed to galvanise them. The atmosphere was fantastic and, with the fans going mad, Charlton roared forward and went on to win the game 3-2. From that day on, I was a Charlton supporter. I think it was the way they responded to going down to ten men that impressed me so much. They just never gave up.' There was that phrase again. 'Never give up.'

Dad then grinned a little and continued by saying that my tenth birthday was coming up and it coincided with a Millwall v Charlton match at The Den. His grin broadened into a fully fledged smile: 'Will that be a decent birthday present for ya, Buster, son?'

Dad knew exactly what he was doing and I had a lump in my throat as I looked deep into his smiling eyes, which were glistening with tears. He was reliving the time his dad had treated him to that match against Norwich almost 40 years previously. I said nothing but gave him a long, grateful hug. This gift from my dad to me would ignite something of real significance within me. Something bigger and more special than either of us could have ever imagined.

Hatfield. I found myself smiling at the band name Hatfield and The North. The players had settled into the journey with several dozing. I chose not to, though I was happy to be left alone with my thoughts. We had seven hours to go. Thankfully we would be spending the night in a five-star hotel near Sunderland to prepare mentally and physically for the match.

I took a deep breath and told myself: 'Be cool, confident, make quick decisions and enjoy it.' To me the mental preparation was as important as the physical. Nowadays sports psychologists call it 'being in the zone'. To me it was simply about getting my head straight.

Chapter 11

The Lions' Den

WORLD CUP fever was still in the air as Dad and I arrived at The Den, Millwall's famous ground, situated deep in the working-class area of Bermondsey, surrounded by railway lines, narrow streets and wasteland. We took our seats ten rows back, perfectly in line with the 18-yard penalty box. The pitch looked beautifully green. Though the stand was showing its age, it had lost none of its atmosphere. Buoyed by World Cup success, more than 20,000 fans were jam-packed in the stadium. It was the best birthday present ever for me. I looked around me with wonder. I looked to my left to the Ilderton Road End and then straight across towards the open North Side banking. Finally, I looked to my right to see the Cold Blow Lane terrace which, unusually, housed the tunnel from which the teams emerged. The atmosphere was brilliant. Both teams were massive south-east London rivals, separated only by a 20-minute bus ride on the number 53.

On the way to the ground Dad had told me all about Millwall's incredible home record. They were in the middle of an astonishing unbeaten run at The Den which stretched back to 1964. The fans were exceptionally proud of this record and in no mood to see it broken. In the stand I looked around me and studied the faces of some of the fans. They looked hard and not to be messed with. I could smell beer and tobacco in the air. It was a boisterous atmosphere and I absolutely loved it.

As the clock ticked towards three o'clock, I sensed the tension rising to fever pitch. And then, out they came. Millwall were wearing blue and white striped shirts and blue shorts. They were shortly followed by the red shirts, white shorts and red socks of Charlton who were given a hostile reception.

I knew that Dad was supporting Charlton but I liked the look of the blue and white striped kit.

'Sorry Dad, I like Millwall's team uniform better,' I said innocently.

He smiled and turned towards me and said: 'Well it looks like we have some in-house team rivalry then, son.'

It was a brilliant game of football with both teams going for it from the off and there was some great end-to-end action. That was just what I wanted too, because it meant plenty of work for the two goalkeepers.

To people who don't understand the game, a 0-0 draw might not sound exciting at all but that was a reflection of the excellence of Charlton's keeper Mick Rose and Millwall's Lawrie Leslie.

Rose made a succession of different acrobatic saves. He was a real crowd-pleaser.

Lawrie Leslie, meanwhile, had a very different style. He was rough, tough and fearless. 'He's built like a brick shithouse,' my dad said, without mincing his words.

I looked on in awe as Leslie showed courage time and again. One moment he was diving head first at a Charlton striker's feet to retrieve the ball, the next he was palming away fierce shots from multiple angles. He stood strong, defiant, like a gladiator doing battle in the Coliseum. The Millwall fans loved him and chanted his name over and over again and I found myself chanting along with them.

Looking back, that game was a pivotal moment in my development. I started to think about becoming a goalkeeper all the time and, as the months and years passed, I'd look back on that match at The Den and also hear Dad's words in my mind: 'Study their movements and habits, son. Watch and learn.' I started to create mental images in my mind about cutting down the angle of a striker's shot and coming assertively off my line to take a high cross. I knew from that day at Millwall that there was only one thing for me. I was going to be a goalkeeper. Period!

As our team coach powered up the A1 highway, I reflected, with satisfaction and pride, on how far my career had come. I had established myself as Charlton's first-choice keeper. Our season was going fine, we were sitting comfortably in mid-table and our current form was excellent. For me personally, things were on the up. There was open talk in the game that I was one of the best up-and-coming goalkeepers in the country. Just that week I'd been delighted with a public endorsement in London's evening paper, The Standard. *It contained a quote from the highly respected former Manchester City coach and one-time interim England manager, Joe Mercer. The sub-editor cleverly referenced my height in the headline, which highlighted Mercer's opinion that I had the potential to claim a shirt in the England under-23 squad. The headline read: 'Tutt Walks Tall Towards an England under-23 Cap'.*

Mercer must have fancied me to take over from the near age-graduating and highly talented QPR goalkeeper Phil Parkes as well as the excellent Mervyn Day at West Ham. The quote had made me feel really good. It was a real confidence boost that someone of Mercer's stature would offer such a compliment. That said, I knew I had to keep my feet on the ground. I knew all the praise in the world would not keep the ball out of the net. You are only as good as your last game, especially as a goalkeeper, where you constantly have to prove yourself and people will only tolerate one or two bad games. The match against Sunderland was just another chance to prove myself. Nevertheless, Mercer's quote had done me no harm at all.

Chapter 12

I've Found You a Team, Son … They're Rubbish!

WE COULDN'T play on the bombsite anymore because the council had cleaned it up and erected temporary housing called 'prefabs'. Prefabs (prefabricated homes) were a basic box but served a great purpose and housed many families in need of accommodation throughout south London.

We now had to play football in the street, which in many ways was safer than the bombsite. A Jamaican family had moved in three doors down with five brothers who were all very good footballers. We had some great matches and being just kids we never thought there was any racial element at all about one team being all black and the other all white. No one thought twice about saying 'blacks versus whites'. We were lads in a kids' world without prejudice. I would witness true prejudice several years later in the adult world.

By now I had graduated to junior club football, playing for a team called Heathland Celtic under-12s. We played at Plumstead Common or Sutcliffe Park near Blackheath and other areas around south London on Sunday mornings. On Sunday afternoons Dad and I would watch *The Big Match*, with Brian Moore, on London

Weekend Television (LWT) together. Straight after, I would rush out to play football with my mates, trying to emulate what we had just watched.

We'd rise early on those Sundays. One day, after breakfast, Dad was reading the paper at the table with his second cup of tea. I could tell he was on a mission. He was studying the men's amateur leagues.

It was 1969 and I was quite happy playing for my school on Saturday mornings and Heathland Celtic on Sunday mornings. But Dad wisely saw things slightly differently. He was not so keen that I played for such a good team because it often meant I wouldn't touch the ball for long periods during a match. Most of the time, I was picking my nose and feeling bored.

With a huge grin on his face, Dad suddenly folded his paper and piped up: 'Son, I have found you the worst possible men's team to play for. They are called London Irish and they look rubbish.'

He continued, smiling before saying: 'They need you, son. Boy, do they need you! They're rock-bottom of the fifth division in the London League and have only scored four but let in over 60 goals in eight games.'

The poor team did appear quite useless and lo and behold, they needed a goalkeeper. Dad showed me a small advertisement which said: 'GOALKEEPER WANTED, London Irish Football Club' followed by a telephone number.

But all this was for show because Dad was ahead of the game. Not only had he already spoken to the London Irish coach, he had fixed me up a game that same day, as Heathland Celtic were without a match. 'Do you fancy it, sonny boy?' said Dad, barely able to conceal his glee. 'You'll be busier than a one-armed policeman directing traffic at Trafalgar Square.' That was a typical Dad comment. Two hours later Dad and I were standing on an all-weather cinder pitch with no goal nets, close to the Oval Cricket Ground in Kennington, south London, anxiously waiting for the London Irish team to show.

The other team had already warmed up and looked very much ready to go. Then just a few minutes before kick-off time, a beaten-up, hand-painted, bright-green van pulled up and ten half-dressed blokes spilled out. They were doing their best to tie up their boots and get ready for kick-off, which was now only one minute away. Then a glowing, red-faced, rather overweight chap waddled quickly towards Dad and me.

'Hello lads, I'm Paddy, the coach,' he said, panting for breath. 'My real name is Mick but the lads call me Paddy for some unknown reason. Sorry we're a bit late but I could not find the keys to the van. We had a wee team party last night.'

Dad and I exchanged sidelong glances and wondered what we had let ourselves in for. As Paddy spoke, we both became enveloped in alcohol fumes, with the predominant odour being what I would later discover was Guinness.

Paddy was clearly still drunk from the previous night's party by the look and smell of him. It did not take Dad or I long to realise that the rest of the team was also still hammered. Some of them were dragging a quick couple of puffs of a fag before the game started even though everyone else was ready to kick-off.

'No warm-up necessary, ref,' Paddy shouted towards the bemused official who was looking on in bewilderment.

Paddy then yelled 'let's play' before lifting up one leg and letting rip a loud fart that made everyone laugh. Maybe it was a kind of team war cry!

After less than two minutes, we were 1-0 down. My beer-bellied, left-back simply stopped running in mid-stream while trying to catch their nifty right-winger. He abruptly halted his chase and threw up near the halfway line. My three other defenders stopped running to guffaw at their team-mate chucking up on the pitch. This left three of their strikers unmarked and bearing down on me. General Custer probably had more chance at the Battle of the Little Bighorn than I did in that situation.

I knew from that moment it would be a long game but I absolutely loved it. In the first half, before our team could sober up, I had made around 15 saves. It was great fun. Eventually the final whistle blew and everyone celebrated that we had only lost 9-0, which almost represented a victory compared to their usual results.

'We lost 18-0 last match which means we played twice as good this week,' said Paddy while cracking open a beer and sucking on another cigarette which he held between his thumb and nicotine-stained forefinger.

'Can you join us for the rest of the season, son? There's only four games left,' Paddy added between huge gulps of ale.

I looked at Dad uncertainly before answering. We then both smiled, nodded our heads and laughed, 'Why not?'

It proved an inspired move by Dad. Playing for a poor men's team was considerably better than playing for a very good youth team. I knew with this lot I was going to get 20 to 30 touches per half.

It was a tremendous experience and great fun playing for the London Irish team. Miraculously, we ended up second from bottom of the league. You would have thought we had won the World Cup when we drew 2-2 in my second game. In fact, we drew two consecutive games before winning our last match of the season.

Playing for such an inept team taught me a huge amount, especially in terms of the crucial goalkeeping skills of decision-making and knowing when to come off or stay on my line. I also loved learning how to come off my line for corner kicks and crosses. There were big, gnarled strikers every game hungry to score against me in this league. It also made me really appreciate winning. But, in truth, whatever the result it was never less than enjoyable and a really good laugh. The London Irish Football Club was a genuine education for me and certainly helped toughen me up for my next challenge in the game.

We flashed past the sign for Welwyn Garden City. No player likes these long journeys, I reflected, but, in some ways, it was providing a chance for a useful rest as we'd gone toe-to-toe with our London rivals Fulham the previous Tuesday. We'd fought to the end and squeaked home 3-2 with an injury-time winner from our unstoppable striker Derek Hales, completing his hat-trick. What a player Derek was. I looked across the coach at him. He seemed to be chewing gum while he slept, slouched in his seat.

I loved watching him play. He was rough, tough and deadly in front of goal. Often, especially after a home game, Derek and I would have a few beers together and he would drop me off at my sister's place in Sittingbourne, Kent, close to his own home. Derek was called 'Killer' not only because of his killer instincts in front of goal but also because his family were butchers. He was an old-fashioned goal machine and his thick beard gave him a swashbuckling, piratical look. I'm glad he was on my side and not playing against me, that's for sure.

Chapter 13

Jeff Astle and Malcolm Allison

AFTER MY last game with London Irish, completely out of the blue, I was invited by a Millwall youth scout to come and practise with their under-16 team. As a Millwall fan, this was a dream come true. Evidently, one of the London Irish players knew one of the Millwall scouts and asked him to come along and watch our last London Irish game. I was almost 14 years old in 1970 when the scout called me at home.

The Millwall training sessions took place at a miserable location next to a gin distillery. The area smelled awful – like rotten eggs – and the facility itself was not much better than the bombsite we used to play on. After a few training sessions I heard from one of the coaching staff that the head coach thought I was not tall enough to be a goalkeeper, which I thought was odd as I knew I still had a lot of growing to do.

I later found out that the head coach wanted another goalkeeper who was related to his family and got his assistant coach to tell me the bad news.

It broke my heart but the knock-back made me even more determined to prove myself because I knew I should have been treated better than that. Though I was extremely upset, I dusted myself down and decided to find another club that would appreciate my efforts.

I was a pupil at Roger Manwood High School in Forest Hill where one of my English teachers was called Mr Andy Rogers. It transpired Mr Rogers had some influence at West Bromwich Albion and said he could fix me up for a trial if I wanted, which I immediately accepted. Albion were in the English First Division (equivalent to today's Premier League) and a couple of years earlier had won the FA Cup, beating Everton in the final, courtesy of a goal from their star striker, Jeff Astle. It turned out Mr Rogers was good friends with both West Brom goalkeepers, Jimmy Cumbes and John Osborne.

I went along and it was simply a brilliant experience. Mr Rogers and I watched West Brom lose at home to Manchester City 2-1, after which we went into the players' lounge. I was completely starstruck as I captured the autographs of some world-class players like Francis Lee, Mike Summerbee, Asa Hartford and Jeff Astle himself.

Though I was still only 14, I stayed in a five-star hotel, on my own, for four nights and practised with the youth and reserve team, all of whom were three or more years older than me.

On my second day Jeff Astle wanted some extra shooting practice and it just so happened I was the only goalkeeper around and I was more than happy to take on the challenge.

It was another incredible education and an experience I will never forget. Jeff could strike a ball very hard indeed with both feet. He was also able to put the ball exactly where he wanted it.

To give myself a chance of stopping one of his shots, I quickly realised I had to read his shooting foot, anticipate where he intended to plant the ball, and then dive before the ball left his foot, to cover the area he was aiming for. I then had to adjust in mid-flight to make the save, otherwise I would have found myself rooted to the ground watching the ball rebound out of the net.

I learned a lot that week. The coaches liked what I had to offer and said I was a year away from making the colts under-18 team. I was still five months shy of my 15th birthday. The youth coach asked me to keep in touch for the following season.

My experience at West Brom was reported by a London newspaper and attracted the attention of the Charlton Athletic chief scout, Les Gore. Mr Gore had also got wind of my dissatisfaction with the below-par training facilities at Millwall and the unsatisfactory manner of my departure. Mr Gore's phone call to invite me for practice at The Valley with the Charlton Colts team could not have come at a better time. Dad was as excited as I was. After all, Charlton had been Dad's one and only team for the past 40 years.

Because I was determined to make the grade, I wanted to double my chances so I also began practising with the under-18s at Crystal Palace. I was at Charlton on Monday and Wednesday and Palace on Tuesday and Thursday.

Malcolm Allison was Crystal Palace's head coach at the time. He was flamboyant and a little too flashy for me. I felt uncomfortable being around him. Allison must have sensed my vibe and dismissed me after three weeks. He bluntly announced to me, directly after training, in earshot of the other lads, 'You're not good enough son, gotta let you go.'

Allison's offhand and rather public rejection upset me deeply. As is often the way though, in the long run it ended up as a good thing because my total focus went towards winning my place in Charlton Colts under-18 team.

By this point, I was coming to the end of my final year at school. 'Afro' hairstyles were in and I was beginning to look like a member of The Jackson 5. You have to remember it was 1973 and sideburns were all the rage, especially if you were wearing a pair of bellbottom trousers. I cringe when I think about it but I even wore a pair of wet-look patent leather black zip-up boots. What was I thinking? I thought I looked good at the time!

During my last few weeks at Roger Manwood High School, I got in trouble with a very strict technical drawing master. I had drawn what I thought was a rather good series of goal designs using the teacher's expensive art poster boards. The teacher was furious. I wriggled out of trouble by saying, 'But Sir, all the goals are exactly to scale at one inch to one foot and the angles are all perfectly measured.' I went on to proudly show him about 20 more poster boards with all the goals of various first division clubs drawn to precise scale. The previously irked teacher was now so impressed by how I'd worked out the angles of my 3D drawings that he gave me an A. Thank goodness I had paid particular attention to the goals at Upton Park, home of his favourite team, West Ham United. The teacher kept that one for himself.

Our journey continued. I thought back to the midweek Fulham game and reflected on what a privilege it had been to be on the same pitch as Bobby Moore. He was definitely another of my childhood idols, growing up with the 1966 World Cup Final sealing his reputation as a Boy's Own hero.

Bobby Moore was always super-cool under pressure; he never looked anxious, he just did his job simply and effectively. He made the difficult look easy. To me Bobby displayed James Bond-type characteristics on the football pitch. He never got flustered or rattled, hardly ever missed a tackle or, for that matter, looked out of position. His reading of the game and knowing where to be, when, was exceptional. I closed my eyes and visualised him being carried shoulder-high around Wembley by his victorious team-mates, and holding the Jules Rimet World Cup trophy aloft framed by a beautiful blue sky. It was an emotionally moving and inspiring experience for the nation. It was the first time I had cried with joy along with my mum and dad. The game was exhilarating. Beating West Germany 4-2 after extra time had helped to inspire me to be a professional footballer right there and then. It felt like yesterday but I realised it was nearly ten years ago. Now I'd played against the man in the middle of that story. I pondered what might happen to me in the next ten years.

Chapter 14

Banks? No Thanks …

TO MY delight, soon after leaving school, Charlton offered me an apprentice professional contract. To my surprise and that of my family and friends, I turned them down. Obviously, I had my reasons. Even though I desperately wanted to turn professional, I did not want to be an apprentice professional. That would have meant cleaning two huge player baths, polishing boots and being a general dogsbody who picked up litter after home games. I backed myself and took a stand, which was, quite simply, if they valued me enough, they would offer me a full-time professional contract. So, I gambled a little on my football future. I had to hold tight, keep my mindset right and continue playing for the colts team. My firm belief was to keep improving and that good things would follow.

But it did mean I had to get a 'proper' job. So, during the summer, and a month before my 17th birthday, my best mate Pigeon and I applied for positions at Lloyds Bank in the heart of London's financial district. Looking back, it seems incredible how easy it was to get a job back then. After a brief interview we were accepted and asked to start the following Monday. From the moment I walked through the bank's revolving glass doors,

I hated it with a passion. Every morning Pigeon and I had to squeeze on to a packed double-decker bus and then rush to catch an equally crammed train to reach our new office.

I was supposed to be studying accountancy but it was far from it. Pigeon and I worked through hundreds of cheques from the previous day's business, sorting them in alphabetical order. It would take us over four hours and was an exceptionally tedious task. Then after a 30-minute lunch break I had to be on the customer enquiry desk for two hours.

I didn't enjoy this at all and found myself constantly asking more experienced co-workers how to answer different customer enquiries. I did not like disturbing my colleagues. I felt like I was being a nuisance to everyone who worked at the bank. It didn't help that there was one particularly irritating supervisor who was always on my case.

This went on for nearly two weeks until one midweek morning I got a call at the bank from my mum. She was terribly excited and explained that Colin Murphy, the Charlton reserve team coach, was desperately trying to contact me to play in a behind-closed-doors, reserve team friendly at The Valley at 3pm. Was this my lucky break? The other more experienced keepers had all been incapacitated in some way. The third-choice goalie Mickey Franklin was in bed with flu, the reserve keeper Derek Forster was injured and the first-team goalkeeper, John Dunn, was nursing a sore knee. Breathlessly, Mum advised me to call Colin immediately before he found someone else.

Without hesitating, I called Colin and said I would be there. I needed to tell my supervisor. In many ways he was the archetypal 'Little Englander' – the kind of person found all over the workplace who had achieved a modest amount of authority and built a small empire of people who he thought he could control. Physically, as I found was so often the way, he was unimposing, a short, skinny individual. I regret to say he reminded me of a mini Adolf Hitler as he sported a somewhat greasy comb-over with thin black hair and a carefully manicured, Hitler-styled moustache. Not a good look.

The telephone call had emboldened me and I decided there and then that I wouldn't be returning to the bank again. I told my supervisor I was off to play football and wouldn't be back. He was suitably stunned and clearly not used to being spoken to so directly by an underling like myself. Behind him I could see Pigeon and half a dozen or more staff members giggling uncontrollably.

'Good luck, Buster,' Pigeon said laughing. I gave Pigeon a high-five and left the bank forever. I had to pick up my boots on the way home before heading to The Valley. I learned one very valuable thing from those two weeks at the bank, which was that football meant everything to me and was all I really wanted to do in life. I knew too that the next few hours would be make-or-break time.

As we approached Cambridgeshire, I did what I did in the lead-up to every big game. I reminded myself what my dad had drummed into me as a young goalkeeper, replaying his words in my head: 'Keep your feet on the ground, study the game, do your best and stay humble son. And, of course, never give up.' The irony of telling a goalkeeper to always keep his feet on the ground was not lost on me. But I knew what Dad meant and it was good advice as, even with only a couple of years as a pro behind me, I knew the game could be fickle to the point of brutality. If a coach or manager likes you, there's no problem, but if he doesn't – well you had better start packing your bag. Consistency of performance was everything. Just one or two average games and you could quickly find yourself out of the picture. I had witnessed it myself a number of times already. This was a dog-eat-dog existence.

Chapter 15
Theo

THAT RESERVE match proved pivotal for me. Our opponents, Southend United, were a decent team and they peppered my goal constantly. There were shots coming from all angles, followed by crosses whipped in at all heights. I was forever coming off my line to smother the ball and needed to foil several one-on-one moments. The game could not have gone any better. In terms of my burgeoning career, it was a defining match.

At one point, I felt like I was back playing for the London Irish team as the opposition kept coming at me. They were relentless and should have killed us. Without wishing to sound immodest, it was by far the best game I had ever played. Fortunately for me, it had been witnessed by the Charlton manager, Theo Foley. After the game he entered the dressing room with great gusto and made straight for me. We instantly made eye contact and he congratulated me warmly before saying: 'Come and see me tomorrow at 2pm in my office, okay?' He winked, shook my hand, slapped me affectionately on the back then walked towards the physio's room to get an update on his injured players.

The next day could not come quickly enough. I got to The Valley at 1pm where I was greeted by Mrs Jean Doble, the club's lovable and highly efficient assistant secretary, who guided me to the boardroom, telling me that's where Theo wanted to meet me. When she asked me if I wanted a cup of tea, I shook my head left and right and nodded up and down not knowing whether I meant yes or no. I was so excited I didn't know how to answer a simple question.

'I'll bring you a cup of tea,' she smiled. Mrs Doble knew that I was a little dizzy with it all.

She then quietly slipped out of the boardroom.

As soon as I was on my own, my thoughts turned to my dad. He had been a Charlton fan for the best part of 50 years. He would be so proud if he could see where I was. The boardroom was huge and dominated by a very long mahogany table with six chairs on each side and a larger chair at one end that looked like a throne. Trophy cabinets lined both sides of the room containing silver cups, shields and plaques. At the far end of the room was a framed newspaper article reporting Charlton's famous FA Cup Final victory against Burnley in 1947.

I had butterflies in my stomach and could feel my heart quickening so I told myself to calm down. I always found it helpful to talk aloud to myself. I must have inherited it from my dad who always thought out loud on important issues before reaching a decision.

It wasn't long before I started thinking mischievously. I sidled over to the biggest chair – the throne – and plonked myself down in it. It then dawned on me the chair must belong to Michael Gliksten, the club chairman and owner. Dad had once told me that when Mr Gliksten was 23, he had been the youngest chairman in the English Football League. He inherited the position from his father who was also the club's chairman and original owner through the 1930s, 40s and 50s.

Dad told me the Glikstens made their millions in the timber business. He also mentioned that the original owner, Michael's father Albert, and his brother Stanley, also a board member, had spent more money on players than Michael had.

That sounded a distinct possibility because Charlton had had some genuine glory years either side of the Second World War. In fact, if it wasn't for the outbreak of war, they may well have been Division One championship contenders. As it was, they had had to be content with being runners-up but, after the war, they reached two consecutive FA Cup finals, winning the second in 1947. Back then, 60,000 crowds were regular occurrences at The Valley which, for many years, boasted the biggest capacity of any league ground in the country.

But after being relegated from the first division in the late 1950s, the club declined and the 60s and early 70s were periods of famine, culminating in relegation to the third division in 1972.

Yet, as is so often the case in football, relegation was the catalyst for an upturn in fortunes and, from around 1973/74, things began to look up.

In my opinion, a lot of the credit was due to Theo Foley, who brought sunshine back to The Valley. He had been a tough but skilful defender, well versed in the playing, coaching and administrative aspects of the game. Theo had earned a well-deserved reputation for developing young talent, bringing them through the ranks and introducing them to first-team football. He strongly believed that homegrown players would repay his efforts with loyalty to him and the club, therefore providing stability and giving the club their best years. In keeping with many other 'smaller' clubs, this was not a philosophy Charlton fans were used to and they had watched on helplessly as top players such as

Eddie Firmani, Billy Bonds, Lenny Glover and Alan Campbell had been traded in to Sampdoria, West Ham, Leicester and Birmingham City respectively. Yet the current squad of players recognised that Theo's strategy was to develop local talent and combine them with some very experienced senior players.

I was pondering all this and getting comfortable in the 'throne' when I heard Theo's voice outside the imposing double oak doors. I jumped up quickly, but not quickly enough as Theo caught me halfway out of the chairman's seat.

'You're alright son, sit down,' he laughed. 'I've always wanted to sit in that chair myself.'

He had a way of immediately relaxing you and making you feel a million dollars. It was difficult not to warm to him.

After giving me what I came to recognise as his trademark wink, which suggested he might be about to deliver good news, he came straight to the point. It was music to my ears: 'Tuttie, I want to sign you as a full-time professional. You'll get £22 a week plus regular win bonuses and other incentives. Is that okay?'

He then slid a pre-prepared contract in front of me and produced an official Charlton Athletic pen from his top pocket. I felt a moment's hesitation. Was this all happening a bit quickly? 'Shouldn't I read this first and take it home for my mum and dad to look over?' I asked nervously, immediately fearing I was sounding a bit wet behind the ears.

Theo was quick to reassure me and what he said next, and how he said it, has stayed with me forever. It spoke volumes for the man: 'You could do that, son, but one thing's for sure. If this club and myself don't treat you right and you feel cheated it will show in your game. So, I will make you this pledge. I will look after you properly as long as you do your job, keep your nose clean and perform to the best of your ability. Then all will be good.' He smiled again, gave me another wink and sealed any doubts by adding with total sincerity: 'I'll treat you right, son.'

Theo Foley had confirmed exactly what I had thought about him. He was top shelf, the very best to my young eyes. I could do nothing but look up to him and trust him. He exuded an air of total trust and paternalism. To me he was more like a father figure than the manager. He moved his chair closer to me, clearly still tickled that I was sitting in the chairman's chair.

'You have just turned 17 and you have a tremendous amount of potential,' he said. 'I want you to work your arse off for the next three months. Okay?' He smiled and winked for the third time. 'If you do what I ask, we will be signing a better contract three months from now.'

With that I took the pen and signed on the bottom line. I trusted him in the same way I would my parents. I also felt he was showing me as much respect as I was showing him. It was a two-way thing. Laughing, he then told me I should get out of the chairman's seat before I got caught.

With my deal done I couldn't wait to get to training the next day.

Training sessions quickly fell into a thoroughly enjoyable routine. In the afternoon, Theo would take me and a few strikers to the 'shooting box' for some extra work. The shooting box was a large sandy area in front of a full-size goal. The sand was thick and deep and, in no time at all, your thighs started to feel like lead weights. Sometimes it was just Theo and I up there. He would shoot at me from every angle for well over an hour. Then, for fun, I would start an 'Alex Stepney' routine on him, which he loved: 'Is that the best you've got, boss?' and 'My granny could shoot harder than that,' and 'Come a bit closer Theo and give yourself a chance.' When he got really determined to score, I would put one hand behind my back to goad him a little. Sometimes, in either excitement or frustration, he would smack the ball high and wide over the bar and I would yell 'Taxi!' meaning his shot was so far off target he'd need a taxi to retrieve it. We had a lot of fun … and yes, true to his word, he worked my arse off.

The way the ball moved when clipping the sand was challenging to say the least. A shot from 20-30 yards would skid along the surface before taking an awkward bounce as it crossed the sand. The unpredictable bounces sharpened my reflexes and pushing off the heavy sand strengthened my legs. After this training I found that, with a side skip, I could dive and reach the top corners of either side of my goal. I can still remember the physical feeling of diving and reaching for the top corners. I felt like I was flying in slow motion, hanging in the air for a short time then extending my body and arms to their limit and getting enough of a touch to guide the ball over the crossbar. It was common knowledge in the game that not too many keepers had this ability. Theo was pushing me through the necessary barriers to prepare me for first-team football. After working on the sand, I found diving on normal grass a cinch.

I loved those sessions with Theo. He seemed to enjoy it as much as the rest of us. There were whispers he trusted certain players too much and they took advantage but I didn't see that. I saw him as mentor, father figure, trusted friend and respected coach. I loved the guy and continued to do so until his passing in 2020. He saw something in me and was determined to draw it out. I also knew he craved success as much as I did.

True to his word, three months later, he asked me to join him in the boardroom again after practice. I was confident I was going to sign another, improved contract. But that morning I noticed his demeanour was not as cheerful as usual. I immediately thought I must be doing something wrong, that I was not progressing as he had hoped. I started to get a little paranoid that I'd upset him and he was going to let me go.

Theo kept me waiting for over 30 minutes, which was unlike him. By this time, I had convinced myself I was on my way out and, when I finally heard his voice through the double doors, I had made up my mind he was delaying telling me I would not be figuring in his future plans. Eventually Theo entered the boardroom. He seemed very serious and as though the weight of the world was on his shoulders. I jumped up nervously and stuttered: 'Good afternoon, boss. Is, er, everything, er, alright?' I really wanted to know what was going on.

This time it was Theo who sat in the chairman's seat, very slowly. His face remained deadly serious. Then, after a lengthy pause, he started to speak: 'Remember when we were in here before and I asked you to work your arse off for the next three months?' My head was bobbing up and down like a chicken, as I answered, 'Yes boss,' three times. He then cleared his throat, like he was ready to pronounce a sentence. I gulped hard and struggled to compose myself. I was waiting for the hammer to fall. Instead, his words changed my world in the most fantastic way:

'Well, you have done all that I asked and more. Tomorrow we travel to play Shrewsbury and I want you to start in goal. I'm also doubling your salary.' Finally, Theo cracked a huge smile.

He was an old pro who had seen it all but I swear he started to well up as he continued: 'I have never seen anyone work as hard as you have, Tuttie. You have performed very well indeed in the reserves and the colts. You fully deserve this opportunity and to be perfectly honest I am totally delighted for you, your parents and our club.'

He walked around the table to hug me. I don't mind admitting that I was shedding tears of joy. This was everything I had wanted since I was a boy and Theo was wise enough to know it. In that moment, I started thinking back: Dad giving me my first real leather football when I was five on Christmas Day 1961; the football matches on the bombsite; witnessing Lawrie Leslie playing brilliantly for Millwall and Mick Rose performing heroics for Charlton on my tenth birthday; and Alex Stepney patting me on the back and saying, 'Practise every day, do your very, very best. Never give up and you'll be a pro someday too.' Now I was here. My opportunity had arrived. And it was going to happen tomorrow against Shrewsbury Town.

Theo had both hands on my shoulders and was looking straight into my eyes. His eyes were glistening and I remember thinking to myself: 'Wow, tears of joy, from Theo Foley to me.' He was an emotional old sod.

'Boss, I really thought you were going to let me go,' I said.

Theo was now back to his old self: 'No son, I just wanted to get you back and wind you up the way you have been winding me and the rest of the lads up for these past three months. Remember those comments at the shooting box, like, "Is that the best you can do?" and shouting "Taxi!" when I or someone else ballooned the ball over the goal? Well, I thought it was time to wind you up a bit.'

We both began to laugh. Then he hugged me again and we shook hands. I walked out feeling even taller than my 6ft 4in. All that effort and hard work was coming to fruition. I felt confident, strong, proud and privileged to be playing for such a great club, managed by someone with the class and decency of Theo Foley. And you can only imagine how proud my dad was. It was March 1974, I was only 17½ years old and my dream and opportunity of a lifetime had at last arrived. I felt ready for it.

We were at Peterborough and I was still lost in my own thoughts. I looked through barely open sleepy eyes around the coach and a sudden, comfortable feeling coursed through my veins. 'I'm a professional footballer,' I thought to myself. 'I'm doing what I love and getting paid for it.'

I couldn't help but smile and felt an overwhelming sense of gratitude deep in my soul. I was half dreaming but I found myself thanking God that everything was turning out so perfectly. I actually whispered 'Thank you God' and hoped no one else heard me. I was feeling so grateful, happy and fortunate. 'I've made it,' I thought to myself. I reflected on what the alternative might be and pictured myself two years earlier, sorting cheques in the bank. I settled even more into my seat, completely contented with my lot.

Chapter 16

Thrills at the Meadow

THE MIDWEEK game against Shrewsbury Town was brought forward a couple of hours to an odd-sounding 5.30pm kick-off. A strike by coal miners had affected the whole country and the government had banned the use of all non-essential electricity, which included floodlights at sporting events. I knew the attendance would be severely impacted because Shrewsbury were in the relegation zone and many fans would not be able to get away from work in time to reach Gay Meadow, Shrewsbury's ground. To me the attendance was unimportant. It was the match itself that mattered. And to me it was nothing less than a World Cup Final.

I can't recall much about the lead-up to the game but the match itself was a real humdinger that ebbed and flowed from the start. In the 13th minute I had no chance of stopping Shrewsbury's opener as the ball bulleted by me from seven yards, after a defensive scramble.

One minute later, the brilliant Mike Flanagan evened the score with a typical 'Flanno' rocket from 20 yards which ripped into the top-left corner of the net. Then, on the half-hour, the talented Welsh midfielder Alan Durban got lucky when I was wrong-footed after his fierce shot deflected off one of our defenders to put Shrewsbury 2-1 up.

I wasn't sure what to make of my own performance so half-time was interesting. Theo slammed our defence for not getting the ball out of the box quickly enough for the first goal and told them they had 'put Tuttie in the shit'.

But Theo was a man who always tried to find some positives and he went on to praise Flanno, Keith Peacock and Paddy Powell for their efforts.

The second half was a different story altogether. Keith Peacock sneaked in a beautiful diving header at the near post from a pinpoint low cross from Paddy to equalise.

We went 3-2 up just over 15 minutes later when Flanno scored again with a scrambled tap-in. Unfortunately, that did not last long, as one of our defenders slipped on a failed back pass, I was left helpless and they scored in an easy two-on-one situation.

With the score locked at 3-3, the last 20 minutes was harum-scarum stuff. I had to make two crucial one-on-one saves, block two close-range shots and then catch or punch away a barrage of crosses in the final few minutes. But we hung on for a point. It had been a great match and I felt that I had held my own.

Even though there were only 1,200 or so fans to witness the game, every one of them must have gone home feeling royally entertained. *The Sun* newspaper gave me a guarded compliment the next day with a story headlined 'Tutt Gets Little Help From Mates'. This was based on Theo's comments to reporters afterwards so I did not feel too bad. However, I'd seen Theo rip into a couple of our defenders about their lack of marking which is a side of him I hadn't seen previously.

In that Shrewsbury game, I instantly learned there was no margin for error whatsoever at this level. You would be punished there and then if you screwed up.

Three days later we came up against Cambridge United at The Valley. Theo wisely rested me, for reasons which would soon become apparent. Charlton's long-serving goalkeeper, John Dunn, was in the twilight of his career and was struggling with his knees. John had enjoyed a successful career with Aston Villa and Chelsea and Theo felt, rightly in my opinion, that it would have been unfair to freeze him out permanently.

Theo told me after the Shrewsbury game that he wanted to give me a taste here and there, not overtire my body and burn me out, which playing three first-team games in seven days would have done. Instead, John Dunn generously began to pass on his vast experience to me, knowing that his first-team days were numbered. So, we had an understanding. John played the next home game against Cambridge and I would play in the following home game against promotion favourites, Oldham Athletic.

I will never forget that game against Oldham, played at The Valley on Tuesday, 26 March 1974. Not only was it my home debut but it was an important day in the context of my family because my hero brother Jim, his wife Pat and their three children were emigrating to live permanently in South Africa the following day. I loved my brother very much and looked up to him as one of my heroes. I did not want to disappoint him on what would probably be the last time he watched me play in a very long time.

It proved an emotional night. Especially when I made my first decent save and I picked out Jim's voice above the applauding crowd, shouting, 'Well dun', Buster.' It was comforting knowing it came from my brother. I felt I was not out there on my own.

We were not expected to beat Oldham simply because they were in a rich vein of form and strong contenders for promotion, which they went on to secure a few games later. Conversely, we were in the middle of the league and treading water. But that night everything came right, the soccer gods were on our side, and with two goals from Arthur Horsfield and one each from Paddy Powell and Mike Flanagan we blew Oldham away in a 4-1 win. The result put us on the map and gave us some real credibility in the league. It was on the back of the Oldham result that people started talking about the 'New Charlton', which in truth was a little premature.

There were 12 games left, of which John Dunn and I were scheduled to play six each. Theo was blooding not just me but other youngsters like Mark Penfold, Richie Bowman, Ray Tumbridge and Les Berry by giving us all a taste of first-team experience. Everyone could see Theo was building for the future.

I was not a particularly religious person but during the coach journey north I felt the need to thank some kind of higher power. I wanted to show my gratitude for the progress I had made over the past three seasons. I had reached my goal and was relishing every moment. Physically, I felt 100 per cent and emotionally I was balanced. I was bang in form and exuding confidence. I felt I had proved my worth by stacking up quite a number of first-team games for someone still in their teens. The Sunderland game would be my 75th first-team appearance. I knew I had more in me. I was not the finished article but was ready to push on to learn the advanced specialist techniques required to become a really top goalkeeper. I was over 6ft 4in, and starting to fill out. With the exuberance of youth, I felt like Superman.

Chapter 17

Heartbreak

AFTER OUR sublime performance against Oldham, one of those strange footballing things occurred which defies logic. Our form fell off the proverbial cliff. The next Saturday we got tanked 4-0 at Wrexham which was quickly followed by a 2-0 defeat at Huddersfield. I played in both. John was then recalled for the next game, a fortunate 0-0 draw at home to Bournemouth, before we turned in a Good Friday horror show at Grimsby, losing 5-0. We beat the Mariners 2-1 in a return fixture on Easter Monday but then went down again at Plymouth the following evening by a single goal. Suddenly, after this slump in form, the pressure was right on Theo and, after Watford turned us over 3-1 at The Valley on the Saturday, the directors, and more importantly the chairman Michael Gliksten, decided they'd seen enough and, with just three games of the season remaining, Theo was sacked.

I was heartbroken, as many of the younger players were. Whispers started circulating that a senior player or players had thrown Theo under the bus and had a quiet word with the chairman that things weren't going well. It felt especially harsh to me as we were mid-table, in no danger of relegation and, though we'd had a few bad results, it was not exactly a crisis.

Nevertheless, the chairman obviously felt it was better for the club if Theo moved on.

It seemed obvious to everyone, except the owner, that Theo was planning for the following season. Four or five youngsters were starting to bloom and proving they could make the step up. All Theo needed was another season under his belt and I was convinced success would follow. We had simply not quite gelled as a team yet.

It was an awful blow to take for me personally, almost like a bereavement. I wrote Theo a letter expressing how much I admired him and how grateful I was that he had shown faith in me and given me my big chance. I told him I thought he had been treated badly by the club. It was such a shame. Theo had so much to offer us younger lads, the club and the game. It was painful!

We finished the season with chief scout, Les Gore, taking the reins. I was grateful that Les selected me over John to finish the season and, although we lost our first game under Les at Port Vale, we once again turned over champions-elect Oldham at their place in front of over 18,000 fans, before ending the season with a 2-0 victory over Aldershot at The Valley. We finished in 14th place, not especially good but not too bad considering the young team that Theo had been developing.

Things were about to change, with a new manager coming on board. He was quite the contrast from Theo Foley. He was a 39-year-old no-nonsense Londoner. On 17 May 1974, Andy Nelson, lured away from Gillingham where he had spent three years in the hot seat, was unveiled as the new manager of Charlton Athletic.

I looked down to the front of the coach where our boss, Andy Nelson, was staring grimly ahead. He had been our manager for nearly two years and we all knew how he operated. There was simply no room for excuses. You performed or you were out. Simple as that. Nelson took no prisoners and every single player at Charlton knew it. I thought back to Theo and how much he'd looked after me. I missed him.

Chapter 18

Workington ... Where's That?

BEFORE HIS untimely sacking, I heard Theo had been trying to fix me up with a loan deal to get more games under my belt. When Andy Nelson came in, I assume the club Theo had been talking to had got back in touch. Andy must have agreed it would be a good idea and mentioned it in passing one day after pre-season training.

I wasn't sure where I was heading but it's fair to say I didn't expect to be on my way to a struggling, industrial town in Cumbria in the very north-west of England next to the Irish Sea. If the town of Workington had seen better days, then the football club certainly had as well.

It seems that Theo was a good mate with the Workington Town manager, George Aitken, who had been in the game a long time as a player and coach. Two things shocked me when I quickly checked up on Workington. Firstly, where the town was located, which to me looked like the back of beyond. And secondly, where they had finished the previous season – 23rd out of 24 with only Stockport County below them. I wasn't sure what I was letting myself in for. Having said that, I thought I might be getting plenty of practice if their league position was anything to go by.

Before I had time to say 'Accrington Stanley' I was on my way to Workington for a month's loan.

I will never forget getting off that small, two-carriage train at Workington station. A few years later there would be a band called Wet Wet Wet and I'm certain they must have named themselves after Workington. It was pouring down with rain which seemed to be the default weather conditions for the town. In fact, the rain was driving down so hard that I could barely see the town. There was no one getting on or off the train except me. In fact, there was nobody around whatsoever, not even a ticket collector. I found myself standing on the platform like the proverbial drowned rat, clutching my large kit bag as the train lurched slowly away. All of a sudden, I felt very much on my own in this strange north-western outpost.

It was not the most auspicious of starts but it turned out to be an experience which I can only describe as invaluable in so many respects.

Yet that felt a long way off as I ambled somewhat disconsolately out of the station.

There were no taxis, no one to greet me and even the public phone was not working. I felt even more alone as the rain continued to pour. In the far distance I saw the telltale silhouettes of four floodlight pylons.

I assumed this was where I would be plying my trade for the next month. With my heavy bag I started the trek towards the stadium using the darkened floodlights as my compass. By the time I got there I was totally drenched, with squelching shoes and my saturated bag weighing twice as much.

It was a relief when I found George Aitken in his office squirrelled away under the stand at Borough Park. George looked like he could sink a few pints and boasted, if that's the word, a beer belly and flushed face. But then again, who could really blame him, considering the stress he was under, managing a side fighting for its very survival.

All these years later, I still recall his opening gambit: 'Welcome to Cumbria laddie, where it don't stop raining.' This was my first human interaction for several hours.

Shivering with cold I expressed my thanks and called him Mr Aitken.

'Call me George,' he said. 'I'll take you straight over to your landlady. Mrs Galley. She's just around the corner,' he said, grabbing his keys.

'Yes, great, it would be good to get something dry on,' I said, smiling through gritted teeth.

Slapping me on my sodden back, George told me that training started 'around ten' and that I should report to his office beforehand to collect my kit.

Mrs Galley was a lovely old widow in her mid-70s. She really did live just around the corner too, in a two-up, two-down miner's row house. It was a dark home with a few glowing oil lamps which I assumed were to save electricity. Yet it smelled good, homely, the way my old home smelled when Mum had something tasty cooking on the stove.

Following Mrs Galley's advice, I hung all my wet clothes up to dry on several string lines above an old-cast-iron claw foot bathtub. I then had a good long soak to ease the aches of a ten-hour day of travelling. London seemed a very long way away.

When I came downstairs to the kitchen, I found a large plate of beef stew, a pile of buttered bread and a tall glass of milk sitting on the table with a note which read: 'Gone to bingo, make yourself at home. Be back at 11pm, Mrs Galley.'

After feeding my face, I watched about ten minutes of telly on Mrs Galley's black and white flickering set and then wrote her a thank you note. I couldn't wait to get into the feather bed which reminded me of my old nan's bed where she had told my sister and me war stories as young kids. Within seconds I fell into a deep sleep.

The next thing I knew, there was a knock on my bedroom door and Mrs Galley was standing with a cup of tea suggesting I come down for breakfast before I went to training.

This was all very pleasant, I had to admit, and was helping me settle in nicely.

When I arrived at Borough Park, George Aitken was busy on the phone. He had my training gear rolled up in a towel, tightly tied together by long football socks with GT written in magic marker on each garment. George then gave me the 'one moment' sign as he started wrapping up his phone call. He was looking exasperated.

Shortly afterwards, he slammed the phone down and uttered, with thinly veiled contempt, in his thick Scottish brogue, 'Fuckin' excuses, I've heard them all.' Shaking his head he shared a piece of homespun philosophy with me: 'In my book, there's no excuses when you do what you're supposed to do.' George revealed it was one of his senior players excusing himself from training because his dog had got loose and he was on the hunt for it.

Then, like a switch had been flicked, his mind moved on. 'Graham, let's introduce you to the lads,' he said more optimistically with a glint in his bright blue eyes.

I actually found the atmosphere in the dressing room was pretty good considering the team's plight. All the lads seemed pleased to see me, even their current goalkeeper, Mike Rogan, whom I was replacing for a month. Mike was a great keeper but I would soon discover that he was burned out and needed to rest. Even so, he was genuinely supportive of me from the outset and all the while I was there. Mike went on to play another 400 league games after I left so my one-month stay certainly must have been good for him too.

The team had some good players, like Tony Geidmintis, Ronnie Walker, veteran favourite John Ogilvie and a new striker called Dave Murray. They were decent, experienced pros and fun to be around. I couldn't understand why their results were not better. It wouldn't be long before I found out.

Two days later, we had just finished our Friday training session and, as I was preparing to go back to my digs, I was shocked when the lads invited me to go out drinking with them. This was completely against my usual philosophy and, even as an 18-year-old, I thought it was unprofessional. But the sad truth was the team as a whole didn't seem to care and looked like they had simply given up.

Being somewhat naïve, through a combination of peer pressure and wanting to be accepted, I broke my golden rule and went for a beer. I had two swift pints before making an excuse to go somewhere while most of the lads continued to drown their sorrows.

The season had started inauspiciously with a draw against Scunthorpe followed by defeats to Cambridge and Rotherham. However, I'm pleased to say that in my debut for Workington, we beat Stockport 3-1 and, though we would lose to Southport and Rochdale, we did beat Swansea 2-0, so in my four games, we won two and lost two.

When I left the team, we were occupying the heady position of 20th in the league, which represented something like progress. We could now boast that we were second from bottom.

To be honest, it reminded me of my time with London Irish so it meant rolling with the punches and keeping my chin up.

One definite plus point was that Borough Park had one of the best playing surfaces in English football. Obviously, all the rain was doing it good. The playing surface was perfect, with its short, lush grass making it play slickly for a quick-passing team. I soon found out this was great for our quick strikers but not so good for our back four defenders who were, in footballing terms, starting to knock on a bit.

Throughout the month it rained for several hours every day. And I mean every day. It did become rather depressing not seeing any sunshine. We practised for only 90 minutes each day; because George had so many injuries, he did not want to risk any other lads getting hurt. He even asked me not to come back in for extra afternoon training in case I got hurt. Instead, I went on long-distance runs in the beautiful Cumbrian hills to improve my stamina.

During the home game against Swansea there was an amusing incident when one of our less mobile defenders, under a good deal of pressure from an over-aggressive striker near my right corner flag, was panicked into hoofing the ball wildly out of play. He simply walloped the ball under the cover of the overhanging stand. Unfortunately, the cover was so rusty that the ball went straight through the overhang and made a cannon ball-sized hole, causing bits of rust and debris to fall on a small group of fans below, who were desperately covering their heads to protect themselves from the falling shrapnel.

Both teams stopped play for a few seconds as officials made sure no one was hurt. Then everyone, including the referee and both teams, had a good laugh at the hole it had created. It was a perfect metaphor. No wonder the club was voted out of the fourth division a few seasons later. The stadium, like the team, was falling apart.

I knew it was Theo who had put the wheels in motion for my loan stay with Workington before he was sacked and he was 100 per cent correct when he said the experience would do me good. When I returned to Charlton, I came back a better goalkeeper and confident enough in my own abilities to know that I could cement my place in the first-team football. It was just an awful shame that Theo was no longer my boss.

We were at Stamford on this interminable journey, not even half way. I looked around the coach at my team-mates and could see they meant business. There were no slackers in the team. We weren't carrying anyone. This match was vital for both teams as Sunderland were going for promotion. To add extra edge to an already important game, BBC1's Match of the Day *was covering it, meaning millions would see edited highlights on Saturday night. Not that I needed extra motivation, but that just made me doubly determined to do well and impress.*

Chapter 19

We're Going Up

WITH THEO gone, I had to get used to Andy Nelson, who was now our team manager and head coach. He had a big, quite intimidating physical presence and his first pre-season team talk with us consisted of a lengthy list of dos and don'ts. Straight off the bat, we all knew that Andy would be ruling with an iron fist. It was going to be his way or the highway and he had no room for questions. Both on and off the field, any excuses from players would not be tolerated.

He was old school through and through which was fine in itself but he combined it with a touch of the playground bully. It was his way of dealing with players. He was capable of scaring certain players to death on match days. Anyone who didn't abide by his instructions was threatened with being dropped or even transferred. His approach did not accord with my way of thinking. We were all adults and I did not think instilling fear into us was the right way to motivate players or the team as a whole.

From the outset, I had little time for his methods and thought it was, at best, unnecessary and very disrespectful. I realised early on that his ruling-by-fear approach would not last long. At some point I knew that respect would go out the window and that no decent player would want to play for him. Yet he could point to the fact that his methods had worked at Gillingham, where he had won promotion to Division Three.

I was still only 18 and often wondered to myself if one of our senior players would ever have the balls to stand up to Andy and ask him to lay off a bit, but no one ever did. They were probably too scared of the consequences. With Theo, every player was shown respect and could ask questions. Andy was the total opposite.

Here's how he operated. If we had lost the last game, he would ignore any cordial greetings like 'Good morning, boss' as he entered the dressing room. There would be no response at all from him save for an aggressive, intimidating glance. If we had won the last game, he would at least respond with a 'Good morning' and half smile back at you.

I found this inconsistent behaviour very unsettling but, at times, found myself smirking, or shaking my head when I should have been looking serious.

In later years, we'd hear about Alex Ferguson's famous 'hairdryer' treatment. Well let me tell you, Andy Nelson was employing this tactic long before Fergie did. Sometimes he would threaten players with detailed instructions at the top of his voice and within a very short distance of their face, sometimes virtually nose to nose. He would get so worked up over something that seemed trivial to most of us that his screaming would produce flecks of spit that would land on your face. If it was my turn for a bollocking – which thankfully was not too often – I would look him straight in his eyes and try not to show I was intimidated. I think he knew that many of us wanted to say something back to him but wouldn't dare. His own conduct never seemed to bother him.

Every Charlton fan of a certain age knows what a great winger Paddy Powell was and how he'd die for the Charlton cause. But that didn't stop Andy Nelson trying to instil fear into him. He would say to Paddy, 'If you don't take on the defender on the outside, by dribbling past him, seven out of ten times I will hook you off.' Thankfully Paddy had the ability to deliver. So maybe Nelson's tactics worked for some but they did not motivate me or make me want to play for him. I was playing for the team and myself. Andy Nelson and Theo Foley were like chalk and cheese.

Behind his back the players were starting to nickname the new boss 'Andy Hitler'.

Theo genuinely nurtured his players with constructive, positive coaching. Andy's way was to machine gun you to death verbally, like a sergeant major. What irritated me most was that he had inherited over 80 per cent of Theo's team and was now receiving all the credit for our change in fortune. I don't wish to sound churlish and I must give credit where it's due because the new boss did bring in a few decent players like David Young from Sunderland and Harry Cripps from Millwall, but the other side of the coin was that, ultimately, he crushed the spirit of many lads during his tenure.

Physically Nelson was pretty scary too. He was about the same height as me – 6ft 4½in – but he was heavier set with what could be politely described as a boxer dog face. He came from Custom House in London's East End and had enjoyed an impressive playing career with West Ham, Ipswich, Orient and Plymouth Argyle. At Ipswich he had played under the great Sir Alf Ramsey and was part of the team which surprised the footballing world by winning the league championship in the early 1960s. He was a tough, uncompromising centre-half who took no prisoners, dished it out and took quite a lot back by the looks of things. He was an old warhorse and his nose had been flattened a number of times, giving him an unfortunate habit of snorting like a pug dog because his nasal passages were blocked.

Whereas, under Theo, I'd been staking my claim for a first-team place, Andy did not play me over John Dunn or Mickey Franklin until early November. That 16-match period killed me, not being out there, as I'd already got a taste of first-team football and had come back from Workington chomping at the bit. When he did finally bring me back, for a midweek game at Watford, I was able to prove myself, become ever-present for the rest of the season and a large part of the next, playing over 60 consecutive games. Andy Nelson had made me angry enough to show him that I deserved to win the shirt and keep it. Maybe he was doing a good psych job on me and I should give him some more credit. Unfortunately, his brutal actions rubbed me up the wrong way.

Even when I played exceptionally well, I never felt Andy offered me the encouragement or praise that Theo or any reasonable coach would have done. I can only recall a grudging, semi-compliment from him when we played Chelsea at Stamford Bridge just after Christmas in 1975. We won 3-2 and I had played out of my skin, especially in the last 20 minutes, to keep the Chelsea strike force at bay. After the game, he said: 'You did alright tonight Tuttie.' And that was it. He couldn't say 'well done'. He just didn't seem to have it in him to praise any of the players.

After winning back my place in November 1974, we started to string a few decent results together, including an excellent win at Wrexham and a 4-1 drubbing of Colchester United on

New Year's Day, after which we went second in the table behind Blackburn Rovers.

In mid-January, we had a huge game against our local rivals Crystal Palace. I must admit I saw it as a chance to get my own back on Malcolm Allison, who had dismissed me in such a brusque way when I was younger. In front of over 26,000 fans at The Valley on a Friday night, we beat Palace 1-0, courtesy of a Derek Hales goal. It was a pivotal game in our promotion bid with Palace hot on our heels in the league table. In truth, I had very little to do for most of the game until right at the very end. Then, in the last two minutes of the game, I pulled off two really classy full-length saves to preserve the full points. Both saves came from corner kicks. The first was a bullet header from the penalty spot that was heading to my top left-hand corner and the second saw me diving full length towards the bottom right of the goal from a volley just inside the edge of the 18-yard box. I was particularly pleased with that save because I had to take two quick side steps to my right then make a full stretch dive to push the ball away for another corner. I knew it was a good save by the reaction from the crowd. My team-mates were equally generous.

When the final whistle blew, I felt like I had proved myself twice over to Malcolm Allison. His insensitive brush-off a couple of years previously had stayed with me and it was in my mind as I shook his hand after the game.

Years later, I can see it was just Big Mal's style. I doubt very much it was personal, it was just his way of dealing with an awkward situation. Yet I cannot deny that victory over Palace gave me huge satisfaction.

The game had been given added spice because Mal had boasted that Palace would finish higher in the league than

Charlton that season and was confident enough to have a £300 bet with Andy Nelson. Unfortunately, his prediction was shot to pieces when we not only finished higher than Palace but won promotion too. One thing Big Mal did teach me was that predicting you were going to beat a local rival was not a sensible thing to publicly boast about.

'Stay modest and say nothing,' was a mantra my dad drilled into me as a kid, telling me it was a much safer route. Why put unnecessary pressure on yourself by shooting your mouth off? It bewilders me why some players and coaches still do that. All they achieve is winding up the opposition to really want to beat the heck out of you.

When I saw the back page of *The Sun* newspaper the next day, the headline read:

'Tutt, Tutt Palace', and then, just below, a sub-head said: 'Charlton keeper stuns Mal'.

The report included a headshot and my name, with a one-word caption underneath which read 'Brilliant'.

Allison probably saw it the next morning and may well have choked on his cornflakes.

After the Palace game we really kicked on and by the end of March we were still in second spot with promotion in our grasp. We then had a blip in April, losing successive home games to struggling Bournemouth and mid-table Bury.

It all meant we had to win our last game of the season to secure promotion to Division Two. The game took place on a humid evening at the end of April, against Preston North End, coached by the legendary Sir Bobby Charlton. The Valley atmosphere was electric with nearly 25,000 fans going nuts. The game was a rollercoaster especially after we went 1-0 down in the first ten minutes and then our right-back Bob Curtis missed a penalty. We went in at half-time still losing 1-0 and concerned it wasn't going to be our night.

After an old-fashioned bollocking from our lovely boss we stormed out in the second half with an early equaliser from our big, blond centre-half, the likeable Bobby Goldthorpe. We continued to rally with the crowd roaring behind us and Derek 'Killer' Hales scoring two great goals to deliver a 3-1 victory and seal promotion to Division Two.

However, there was a hilarious, almost circus-like, moment with just 15 minutes to go which has stayed with me because it was so bizarre. We were holding on to our 3-1 lead and getting ready to party with the crowd. Suddenly a Preston defender delivered an enormous long-distance clearance from their goal area. The ball quickly sailed over the head of David Young, our captain, who was my last defender at the back.

Suddenly with a Preston striker closing in on David, I immediately knew it was up to me to sweep up by coming quite far out of my area to clear it. I raced at full speed about 15 yards outside of my 18-yard box. My plan was to simply wallop the ball back up the pitch and out of danger. Just as I attempted to do so, my non-kicking left foot slipped slightly on the muddy surface and, though I still made contact with the ball at near maximum power, it changed the direction of the ball. Unfortunately for David Young, who was also galloping back at full speed, my clearance of the ball caught him with maximum force in his 'crown jewels'. The ball cannoned off David's 'jewels' and started rolling at a fair pace towards our goal.

I heard the crowd gasp as they sensed an extraordinary own goal could well be in the making.

Then I heard David scream an unprintable obscenity and briefly clutch his groin while still in stride; after putting his pain aside, my captain bravely continued to chase the ball before it crossed the goal line. To reach the ball in time he had to slide kick it away for a corner. However, in the process of sliding and lunging down to clear the ball off the line he slid, open-legged into the foot of the goalpost. He had successfully been walloped in the nuts twice in a matter of five seconds.

The Charlton fans collectively winced a second time. Everyone rushed to congratulate David for his most valiant effort to avoid an own goal. Still grimacing with pain and clutching the body parts in question, he looked at me and said: 'Tutty I took TWO whacks in the nuts for the team. I deserve two promotion medals to replace my goolies.'

It was one of the most heroic, funny and frankly absurd things I ever witnessed in my career. All these years on, I still wince and feel David's pain and then laugh every time! David Young was my hero that night. I offered to give him my promotion medal for saving my bacon. He said no because he wanted me to keep the medal and to remember what happened! We had all played our hearts out. If we had lost that last game Crystal Palace could have nudged us out of a promotion spot. But they didn't!

The celebrations on the field and the bumper crowd, including my proud parents, made it an unforgettable night for all of us. My dad's favourite team was going up and I had played my part in them doing so. Dad didn't have to say a word when I walked out of the players' entrance. He just hugged me and cried, along with thousands of fans celebrating around us. What was magical was the fans chanting my name, which I know made Dad even more proud. You never forget moments like that.

Another bonus came a week later when we won the *London Evening Standard* 5-a-Side Knockout Competition at Wembley Pool. We had to beat some top London clubs to reach the final including Arsenal, Chelsea and Spurs, before beating my boyhood favourites, Millwall, to win the tournament. It was brilliant watching the highlights that evening on television with my parents. It was really something special and almost surreal to share it with Mum and Dad. It capped off our season. Things could not have been going any better. Charlton were the talk of London and good times had returned to The Valley. I felt on top of the world.

We passed Newark. I had not spoken to anyone for the entire journey. Not because I didn't want to, but I had simply been lost in my own thoughts since London. It had been an interesting period of reflection, quite cathartic. I smiled to myself because I had always been told that as a goalkeeper it did not pay to think too much. In many ways it was an instinctive art. So, I told myself to relax a little, enjoy myself and not put myself under any unnecessary pressure. 'Enjoy the ride son, because it won't last forever' echoed in my head – more pearls of wisdom from my dad when I first started my career at 17.

Chapter 20

Sunderland, Here We Come

WE TOOK a bit of time to find our feet in Division Two and began with two straight defeats to Notts County at The Valley and Plymouth Argyle at Home Park. The good news was that I was now firmly established as the number one choice. John Dunn had gone to Tooting and Mitcham and Mickey Franklin had gone back to Yeovil Town. The shirt was mine. Once we'd settled, the results started to come, as we knew they would. In September, the BBC1 *Match of the Day* cameras made their first visit to The Valley for seven years for our home game against Blackpool, which ended 1-1. We had an excellent following week, grabbing a 1-1 draw at West Bromwich Albion and then travelling to the East Midlands where we beat Brian Clough's Nottingham Forest 2-1. We had a blip at the beginning of October when we lost 5-0 at Bolton and 4-0 at Bristol City in successive weeks but I didn't let even that get to me. I felt totally secure in my ability.

Andy Nelson then realised he needed some back-up for me in case I got injured or to rest me occasionally. Playing three games per week would wear on you. So, the boss moved in for a young unknown goalkeeper playing for Harlow Town, called Jeff Wood. I immediately got on with Jeff but there was no way he was having my shirt. I was determined to hold on to the number one spot.

We played brilliantly on the last night of October, beating a Southampton team containing Mick Channon and Peter Osgood 4-1 on a Friday night at The Valley. We then found ourselves on television again two weeks in succession. The *Match of the Day* team was there for our trip to Fulham, and the following week our home match against Sunderland was on *The Big Match.* We were all getting used to the increased media exposure with a smile on our dial.

As we neared Yorkshire, I reflected on our recent form. December had been an odd month, beginning with a heavy home defeat to Luton and ending with that excellent win at Stamford Bridge with two more goals from Killer helping secure a 3-2 victory. We then hit a fine run of form in the New Year, climbing up the league and reaching the fifth round of the FA Cup before losing to Wolves at Molineux. Goals were flying in for us with Killer, inevitably, spearheading our attack. Unfortunately, his brilliant strike partner Mike Flanagan wasn't on the coach after sustaining an injury.

But we still felt we could score every time we went forward with summer signing from Newcastle, George Hope, and the highly rated midfielder-cum-striker Tony Young just signed from Manchester United.

I looked around the coach and assessed our midfield which was up there with the best in the division. At its heart was the long-serving and highly experienced schemer, Keith Peacock. Keith's all-round play and leadership were top drawer and he also had a great sense of humour which he used to relax us at crucial times. It was a pleasure to play with such a class player who was already established as a Charlton legend. Either side of him, Keith had some great ball-winners with Londoners Peter Hunt and Richie Bowman. Both were 110 per centers who could create chances for our strikers and also chip in with much-needed goals themselves.

In defence, we were solid with my friend, the highly skilled and still sleeping, Mark Penfold playing right-back. Manchester United had thought enough of Mark to invite him for a one-month loan a few weeks back. Even though things did not work out for him at Old Trafford it demonstrated what a great player he was becoming.

The athletic, quick-thinking Phil Warman was our left-back. Phil was a good all-round sportsman, very fast off the mark, a great tackler with a tremendous leap. To me, Phil was most exciting when performing his trademark, overlapping attacking runs. He created regular opportunities for our strikers whipping his low crosses into the danger zone.

Our main defensive ball-winner was the no-nonsense and ultra-consistent Jimmy Giles. I liked Jimmy a lot. He and I had an excellent understanding which is crucial between a centre-half and goalkeeper. I always felt Jimmy and I had a telepathic link. We protected each other. I felt especially confident when I came out to the edge of the box to catch crosses. Jimmy would hold off and cover me while I took the high ball or was always there if I called 'Away Jimmy' and, nine times out of ten, would win the header to clear any danger.

I glanced across at Nottinghamshire-born Bob Curtis, our other central-defender. Though just 26, it felt like Bob had been at the club forever and he was as reliable as a Swiss watch. He could hit a dead ball harder than most, was a brilliant penalty-taker and was a long-range specialist. I loved watching his rising 30-yarders. His tackling wasn't bad either and it was a rare thing to see Bob lose a 50/50 ball.

As we entered Sunderland, I took one last look round the team bus. I was proud to play in this team. We were solid at the back, quick and skilful in midfield and had strikers who could score goals and turn a game on its head in a flash. We played fast, with intensity, always pressing forward without fear. We were gelling and becoming a team that Charlton fans could once more feel proud of.

All was good as the jolt of the bus and the hissing of the brakes startled me as we pulled in to our hotel. One of my superstitions was that I liked to get off the coach last and, as I climbed stiffly down the steps, I felt ready for a steak, baked potato and veg, a cup of tea and an uninterrupted night's kip. Like the rest of the lads, I was feeling travel sore and, not to put too fine a point on it, knackered. Little did I know that this particular night's sleep would be the last good night's sleep I would have for a very, very long time.

Chapter 21

I Miss the Moon

SOMETHING RATHER odd happened before I went to sleep. It was a little before midnight and just before curfew when all our lights had to be off. The ever loyal and dependable Bob Curtis was my regular room-mate. We were listening to a late-night phone-in on a local radio station. Bob and I were having a giggle at, to our ears at least, the radio presenter's almost incomprehensible accent. Though Sunderland fans recoil at the term 'Geordies' (they're called 'Mackems'), there's a tendency for southerners to call anyone from the north-east a Geordie. Though his accent amused us and we found it hard to decipher, it had a pleasant, undulating intonation, which was easy on the ear.

Bob and I had an agreement that the last person awake would switch off the light and radio. The lamp was inconveniently situated on the opposite side of the room next to an enormously long Victorian window.

Soon, I heard Bob snoring, so it was my responsibility to turn off the lamp and radio. I was halfway across the room when the panic-stricken voice of a woman cut through the DJ's banter and captured my attention. What she was saying was so unusual that it stopped me in my tracks. She kept repeating: 'I can't see the moon. I can't see the moon.'

The radio host was clearly confused. Then the mystery caller closed with a very sad, 'I miss the moon, I miss the moon.' It struck me as a really bizarre and slightly spooky thing to say on a phone-in. I found it unnerving.

As I turned off the radio and then the lamp, a shaft of moonlight cut across our room and on to the headboard of my bed. It was like a spotlight and dragged me back to the window. I drew the long curtains and there I saw the moon in its entire splendour. It was as full as it could be and as bright as standing under a streetlight. I stood in awe for several moments, taking in its beauty.

Then, inevitably, I thought about the woman on the phone-in. Now I had seen the huge, bright moon in all its glory, her words sounded even more odd.

I rested my head on the pillow, still gazing at the moon with the curtains fully open. Once again, I heard my inner voice: 'Come on son, you're going soft. You've got to get a good night's sleep because tomorrow is Sunderland.'

But the radio call and the other-worldly moon had unsettled me. Was it some sort of omen I wondered?

Chapter 22
Day of destiny

Saturday, 21 February 1976, 07:00

Saturday arrived as a typical north-east English morning with grey skies, mist and some rather melancholy drizzle which, unaccountably, was symptomatic of my mood.

After waking, I was immediately drawn to the window I'd peered out of last night when I had seen the moon. I thought back and recalled the peculiar voice on the radio. Put together, the moon and the disembodied voice seemed somewhat eerie, ghostly even. As I continued to look out, I realised, in the distance, I could see Roker Park. I found it rather surreal to think that some eight hours later, I'd be there in front of thousands of fans with millions more tuning in later to watch the highlights on *Match of the Day*. I'd never stopped to think of it before but I found it strange to think the person looking out of the window and the person who would be stepping foot on the Roker Park turf were one and the same.

It sent a shiver down my spine, a shiver of excitement and expectation. But it also slightly unsettled me. Briefly, I was once again lost in my thoughts and I pondered why I had been so prone to reflection in the last 24 hours. It was unlike me. I quickly snapped out of it and headed for the shower. It was match day and time to get my game face on.

09:00

I was more like my old self over breakfast, relaxed, chatty and carefree. The lads seemed in good spirits. Killer was full of it. Seven goals in his last five games had given him and everyone else confidence that we could score against anyone at any time. Only Andy Nelson appeared glum. There again, it took a lot to make him happy.

13:30

The rest of the morning had raced by and, before I knew it, it was half past one and our coach was pulling to a stop outside the official players' entrance. As usual, I let everyone else get off before me. It was normal for people to cluster by the coach; some of them were Charlton fans who travelled all over the country and who we all came to recognise. It was great to see them at away matches. As I disembarked, I noticed an unfamiliar man. He was short and rather chubby but well dressed in a tweed jacket, shirt, tie and flat cap. He extended his arm to shake my hand and said in a broad north-east accent: 'Welcome to the north-east, Graham.' I had no idea who he was but I replied politely 'Thank you, mate' and shook his hand. I was trying to place him.

I headed for the players' entrance but the man continued: 'I'll be watching you today, Graham.' I was getting an inkling that this man thought he could help me. It was a glint in his eye which suggested he might have the keys to the kingdom. But we were still in small-talk territory.

'I'll try not to disappoint you, sir,' I reciprocated as I strove to keep up with the rest of the lads who were now disappearing into the players' entrance.

Sensing I was in a hurry, the man decided to show his hand. Grasping my arm tightly, he moved in closer and, speaking more quietly so as not to be overheard, he told me he was Newcastle United's chief scout.

He paused and waited for my reaction.

'You're the chief scout at Newcastle,' I repeated somewhat unnecessarily but I felt I needed confirmation.

He nodded quickly and told me Newcastle were having some goalkeeping issues and that he had received some good reports about me from his London contacts. It's fair to say he now had my attention. I was happy at Charlton but Newcastle's home fan attendances were three to four times larger. With no disrespect whatsoever to Charlton, it would be a major step up for me. Was this my big chance in the game?

He then paused for a few seconds to let his words sink in. There and then I found myself juggling three different scenarios. Firstly, on purely professional grounds, I would be crazy to not at least consider any approach from a club like Newcastle. Secondly, I was alarmed by the somewhat surreptitious nature of the encounter. It felt slightly odd and ethically dubious. I knew enough about the mechanics of transfer dealings that any enquiries would usually be made directly to the club. Maybe the guy was simply doing his job by sounding me out before Newcastle made an official approach to Charlton.

Thirdly, a rather more paranoid thought entered my mind. He was a Sunderland fan, trying to put me off my game and affect my concentration for the next few hours.

He was clearly an astute guy and it dawned on me this might be the way he operated. Whatever the reason, he felt confident enough to carry on and reveal more of his hand: 'Do you like the north-east well enough to move up this way?' he asked me, with more directness. I knew my next answer was the one he had been fishing for. 'Well, who wouldn't want to play for Newcastle? They are one of the biggest clubs in England,' I said.

His face broke into a broad smile, revealing a set of nicotine-stained teeth. In fact, his round face briefly reminded me of the huge moon I'd seen last night. What a weird few hours I'm having, I thought to myself. Still beaming, he said, 'Good. That's good, Graham. Very good. We'll be in touch through Newcastle on Monday. Have a great game and beat this lot won't you, because they're our rivals. Good luck and cheers for now, Graham.'

'Thank you, I look forward to hearing from you,' was all I could muster. And with that he flashed me another yellow-toothed smile, tipped his cap and waddled off like an overweight jockey.

It was a most bizarre encounter. I stood, a little paralysed for a few seconds, and watched him as he melted into the crowd. I was the only one of the Charlton party not in the dressing room but I took some further time to reflect on what I'd just heard. I visualised St James' Park in my mind. I thought of Newcastle United and the players in their ranks: Malcolm Macdonald, Irving Nattrass, Alan Gowling, Micky Burns, Alan Kennedy. Then I thought of their manager, Gordon Lee, and their highly respected general manager, Joe Harvey. I was not the biggest fan of Andy Nelson and might prosper even more under a manager I had a good rapport with. They were a good side with massive support and their interest flattered me. It sounded like they were ready to move quickly and make an offer.

Weighing things up, I didn't believe it was a hoax. This corpulent fellow in the flat cap had clearly been interested in my reaction and, by saying Newcastle were having some goalkeeping issues, had revealed the rationale. 'Wow, what an opportunity,' I whispered to myself. A hundred things were swirling round my head but the fact I had a game to play in less than 90 minutes wasn't one of them.

I snapped out of it and signed a few autographs for a clump of Charlton fans who had made the trip up. Yet my thoughts kept returning to the mystery man. If he had been an imposter trying to unsettle me, then he had succeeded! The fact was, I was pretty certain he was genuine. I signed my last autograph and this time strode quickly to the players' entrance and headed for the dressing room. I felt a twinge of disloyalty for even entertaining thoughts of a move while I was still a Charlton player and I loved these blokes.

13:50

When I entered, most of the lads were already halfway through changing, which made me feel a little anxious, but nobody seemed to have clocked that I had been detained. I found my changing peg easily. It had a faded number one stencilled above it. My green goalkeeping shirt was hanging on the peg with my white shorts and long socks folded and placed neatly below next to my polished boots and shin guards.

14:15

I was still feeling rather reflective and found myself thinking about the top goalkeepers who must have hung their kit on this same peg. From Gordon Banks – in my opinion, quite simply one of the greatest goalkeepers of all time – to a menu of other greats I had admired as a young lad. Even my hero Alex Stepney must have used this peg at some point. I rubbed the upturned peg for good luck. It was mine today and I felt privileged to be using it.

14:40

Everybody was changed now and players were going through their pre-match routines. Studs were clattering on the dressing-room floor and the banter was flying.

Andy Nelson arrived with the Sunderland team sheet and went through it. There were some familiar names. In goal was the brilliant Jim Montgomery, a hero of the 1973 FA Cup-winning team, and other names from that memorable side included right-back Dick Malone and the little, moustachioed midfielder, Bobby Kerr. There were other big names including the Scottish centre-half Bobby Moncur, who'd made almost 300 appearances for Newcastle, and another ex-Newcastle favourite, the prolific Bryan 'Pop' Robson who'd also been a hero at West Ham before joining Sunderland. He would be starting up front, wearing the number ten shirt, alongside the rangy Scot, Mel Holden.

Striker Roy Greenwood had recently arrived from Hull but had dropped to the bench. His place was taken by Belfast-born Tom Finney, signed from Luton Town in 1974. Tom was a robust striker and no doubt he would be determined to prove he was worth the £100,000 transfer fee Sunderland had paid for him.

14:50

From our dressing room we could hear the shouts of encouragement and the clatter of boots as Sunderland left their dressing room and headed up the tunnel. Then we heard an enormous cheer as they emerged on to the pitch. Their home form was superb. I gathered my last bits and pieces together and tried not to think about the moon, the eerie voice on the radio and the bombshell that Newcastle United might fancy me. Andy Nelson drilled our roles into us one last time, Jimmy Giles pumped his fist and urged everyone to give 100 per cent and we began to file out. Just before we left the tunnel, we were halted by an official whose job was to give us the all-clear to go out. We could hear the crowd clapping and chanting. Then it was time to go. There was a steep incline to enter the field. I felt like a Roman gladiator entering an arena to do battle. The noise of our studs was now drowned out by more than 30,000 fans, the vast majority of who viewed us as the footballing equivalent of sacrificial lambs.

Our skipper Keith Peacock had a way of saying things in the right way at the right time. His tone was always spot on and he turned round, with a smile on his face, and shouted, 'It's show time lads.' He had a way of doing it which somehow reminded us we were privileged to be getting paid for doing something we loved.

I had learned to channel my nerves. Even though I felt my knees were knocking and I could feel butterflies in my stomach, I had turned this into a positive and I knew that soon I would feel lighter, more agile. It was times like this that every player lived for. Once more I looked at my team-mates. Each player would be lost in his own routine, talking to himself, getting focused on the job in hand.

Keith Peacock turned again and wished everybody luck before leading us out. We were wearing our away colours of yellow and black. It was deafening. As we trotted out, I glanced up and spotted the instantly recognisable figure of the top football commentator, John Motson. 'Motty' was wearing his trademark oversized earphones and his camel-coloured, sheepskin coat. Lip-mic to his mouth, he was perched like an eagle in its eyrie, under the rafters of the stand, level with the halfway line. I could just make out the BBC logo on the side of the cameras which made my heart beat a little faster.

This was actually the second week running we'd been on *Match of the Day* and the second week running we'd played in front of a 30,000-plus crowd. The week before, our FA Cup run had been ended by Wolves at Molineux thanks to a brilliant hat-trick by John Richards.

I was loving the big stage, the cameras and the atmosphere generated by so many passionate fans. I smiled to myself, remembering what my dad had told me, which was to drink it all in and enjoy every moment because it wouldn't last forever. Yet, at that moment, on the Roker Park stage, I felt that it would. Little did I know that in less than 15 minutes' time, my world would come crashing down around me.

Chapter 23
Roker Park

14:52

Straight away I noticed the grass was damp as a light rain had fallen. Parts of the pitch were muddy, especially in the goal area. I was well used to this and it gave me no concern. But I sensed it could be slippery underfoot and the ball could skid about a lot.

I had a little routine I went through before every match. My first priority was making sure the penalty spot was correctly centred to the inch, as it was my vital navigational point. It gave me my bearings and ensured I got my positioning and angles correct when there was no time to look back and check my posts. If the penalty spot was off by even a few inches it would disorient me. But all was good on the Roker Park pitch.

I felt great during the short warm-up. I was catching the ball well. I thought very briefly of the weird call to the late-night radio station and wondered if the caller was in the ground but I quickly dispelled this from my brain.

I glanced behind my goal and saw the massed ranks of Sunderland fans. It was a great sight. Thousands of fans were chanting again and again in a slow, almost tribal, three-syllable dirge, which was both hypnotic and infectious: 'Sun-der-land …

Sun-der-land' and so on. There were more than 30,000 in the stadium. They had come to see a Sunderland win. They were virtually unbeatable at Roker Park and the fans were fiercely proud of that record. They didn't want a bunch of yellow-shirted Londoners to break it.

The chant continued. It was almost primeval. I loved it and fed off it myself. Of course, there were one or two pleasantries exchanged too. As I faced the fans, I heard a north-east voice cry out: 'Tutt, you fucking cockney bastard.' And that in turn sparked a few more greetings such as, 'Fuck off back to London, you big fairy,' followed by hearty guffaws.

I loved it. It made me laugh. I greeted their cries with a double thumbs-up sign. It was their job to unnerve me and it was my job to rise above it. It inspired me even more. The toss was over, handshakes completed and we were ready to go.

I was now fully focused and took a deep breath as Keith Peacock turned to us all and urged us to die for the cause. Roker Park was now seething with anticipation as the referee, Ken Walmsley from Blackpool, blew his whistle, signalling the kick-off. The time had arrived. It was game on.

Chapter 24

Why Me?

15:00

The crowd were in a frenzy. There had been almost 50,000 in the ground the previous Tuesday to see their team beat Stoke City in an FA Cup fifth-round replay and the atmosphere felt like a continuation of that. They were incredibly pumped up and that seemed to be translating itself to the Sunderland players who had four league games to play in 11 days before a sixth-round FA Cup showdown with Crystal Palace.

Every goalkeeper, whether it's in a park game or the World Cup Final, wants to have an early touch of the ball. You'll often see a keeper 'cradling' the ball, bouncing it vigorously two or three times or putting both hands either side of it to get a proper feel. It's mainly a psychological thing, I think. In those days, every team played with their own choice of ball and this gave the home side a slight advantage until the opposition got used to the weight, flight and feel of it.

If teams had a couple of long-shot specialists in their line-ups, they often liked their match ball to be a little on the lighter side while others were pumped up to be hard and heavy to suit their game. Straight from the kick-off, I got the early touch I wanted after my room-mate, Bob Curtis, gave me a pass back. I felt the ball, gave it a good look, moved it around my hands, tossed it forward in the air, let it drop and picked it up again. I kicked it 70 yards downfield and immediately knew we were playing with a light ball. On that basis, I envisaged a busy day with plenty of testing, long shots. That didn't faze me one bit. I was ready for it.

I'd rarely played in a game of such ferocious pace. Everybody seemed pumped up and the crowd were baying at Sunderland to score. Nobody could get hold of the ball for any length of time.

15:06

There was a fierce 50/50 between the two highly competitive number fours, our own Peter Hunt and the talented former Manchester City man, Tony Towers. The ball broke loose to Pop Robson who hit a misdirected pass which was cut out by Bob Curtis. Bob found Derek Hales but his pass gave Tony Young too much to do and Sunderland regained possession.

I looked on, in rapt concentration. Little did I know that within a matter of seconds my life was going to change forever. Sunderland had a little space and Towers found Bobby Moncur moving forward on the left flank. My instincts sensed danger and I heard the crowd behind my goal urging their team forward. Moncur played it back to Towers who was now 30 yards out.

What Towers did next was brilliant but he had unwittingly played a ball that would determine my fate. With the outside of his right boot, he audaciously – and superbly – chipped the ball upwards, like a golfer putting backspin on the ball, right into our penalty area. The unlikely figure of Sunderland's Joe Bolton then glanced the ball on with his head. It fell to Sunderland's Mel Holden who was being closely shepherded by Jimmy Giles.

The ball spilled into no man's land and I knew it was mine to claim. I yelled 'keeper's ball' at the top of my voice and dived in head first gathering the ball on the six-yard box. A second later I felt like I had been hit by an express train. I felt an awful thud unlike anything I had ever felt before. It was as though I had collided at full speed with a bar, whipping my head back instantly. I went numb for a second and then dizzy and then felt extreme pain down the right side of my face. I was confused for a few seconds and lay motionless trying to figure out what had happened. I could not lift the side of my head off the ground. My neck had whiplashed back, straining my neck muscles and was not strong enough to support my head. All I could do was lie with the right side of my face on the muddy surface.

What the heck was going on? I believed I had timed the dive and gathering of the ball perfectly. And I still had it in my grasp. I wanted to jump up and release the ball back in play but I couldn't because my body could not move.

A second later I heard Jimmy Giles yelling, 'Fucking hell, why did you do that?'

It then occurred to me that I must have been kicked in the face by a Sunderland boot, which I later learned belonged to their number 11, Tom Finney. The 23-year-old had been bought from Luton Town and had been in and out of the starting line-up. With Roy Greenwood recently bought from Hull City, Tom had a point to prove. It is my opinion that he was late going for the ball.

My mind was trying to process what had happened because my body was unable to respond or move. Surely this was not happening to me. Was I seriously hurt or just stunned? I continued to cradle the ball in my midriff as I tried to take stock.

I then heard Jimmy Giles's voice screaming again but this time towards the referee, Ken Walmsley.

'Fucking hell ref, why did he do that? Send him off,' I heard Jimmy imploring. Jimmy was a first-class defender and a seasoned pro who always looked out for me, probably because of my age. I had a huge amount of respect for him and hearing him so animated and angry made me feel that I had been the victim of a reckless challenge.

I also heard Keith Peacock verbally lambasting Tom for his actions, which all my team-mates thought were reckless. Keith was another man I completely trusted and respected. He was measured and composed, so the fact he was fired up too carried a great deal of weight.

'Why me?' was a question that started running through my head. The Charlton fans had nicknamed me 'Gentle Giant' after getting to know my style of play. So, I was trying to think what I had done to deserve this.

As I continued to cradle the ball in my midriff, I became aware that blood was starting to pool on the mud below my head. The right side of my face and head felt completely numb, which was extremely alarming. I kept laying down. I was frightened and not ready to confront whatever had happened to me.

My neck had no strength. I couldn't lift my head off the mud because my neck muscles were strained. Tom's boot had struck me just under my right cheekbone, but my entire head was numb and blood was flowing so I did not know – and did not want to know – the full extent of my injuries.

When I did eventually find out, I was horrified. But that would come later. For now, I felt nauseous and like I was literally fighting for my life as I was having trouble breathing.

15:07

Charlie Hall, our long-serving physiotherapist, was the first medical person on the scene. I heard him panting urgently for breath as he put his hand on my shoulder – another sign that the situation was critical. I was still lying on my side cradling the ball almost for comfort when he tried to roll me on to my back to properly assess the damage to my face. Charlie confirmed things were dire with his utterance of a single word: 'Stretcher.' He then repeated gravely: 'I need a stretcher, right now … and get an ambulance too.'

Now my head was starting to spin; I had the kind of slightly sick feeling you get when you spin yourself in circles too many times. I did not know which way was up or down. I was disoriented and not really sure where I was. Even though there were more than 30,000 people in Roker Park that day, I could barely hear anything beyond my immediate vicinity and even that was muffled and vague.

Charlie grabbed my hand – which was still clutching the ball for dear life – and said: 'You'll be all right, Graham, you'll make it.' Charlie no doubt meant well but I found those words alarming and I began to wonder just how badly hurt I was. I was starting to feel the whole right side of my face throbbing and beginning to swell up. Blood was still coming from somewhere as well – I just didn't know exactly where. I felt hopeless and lost on a muddy field far from home. I couldn't lift my head up no matter how hard I tried.

15:10

Charlie now had the stretcher he'd requested next to me and a couple of St John Ambulance workers were assisting. I was barely conscious but I heard Charlie say I was about to be lifted as he put his hand below my head to support it as they started to gently raise me onto the stretcher.

Quite simply, I felt dreadful and very afraid. My head had started to pound at the same tempo as the blood that I could feel flowing from various parts of my head – my mouth, nose and eyelid. It must have been a sickening sight for those forced to witness it.

Now that I had been placed on the stretcher Charlie was attempting to stop the bleeding from my nose and told me to lay all the way back. He proceeded to do what he thought was best and gently squeezed my shattered nose in an attempt to stem the blood. It was a well-intentioned act by Charlie to stem the blood loss, not to mention sparing the fans inside Roker Park and millions of *Match of the Day* viewers from seeing the shocking sight. Yet when he squeezed my nose and tilted my head back, I felt my sinus cavities filling up with yet more blood which I could sense immediately running down the back of my throat. I don't think it's too dramatic to say at that stage I was genuinely in danger of choking to death on my own blood. I could not breathe in or out. I firmly pushed Charlie's hand away and my instinct told me to get back on my side in the hope that gravity would help me breathe. I was now in survival mode because I could hardly breathe at all, in or out. Charlie tried to squeeze my nose again but this time I made it clearer by pushing his hand away a second time more firmly. By propping myself up on my left side, I was finally able to take a short, shallow breath of air. It certainly felt like the right thing to do.

I started having a conversation with myself: 'Keep calm son ... get some air ... get some air from somewhere ... get an air passage open … mouth or nose … just get a clear air passage … otherwise you are going to die.' These were the very thoughts playing out in my mind and, even now, all these years on, I do not think they were misplaced.

15:12

They stretchered me into a first-aid room located just off the players' tunnel. It was then that I started to throw up. It felt like a pint or so of blood had entered my stomach through my nasal passages and down the back of my throat.

Looking back, I think it was my body telling me to throw up so I could take a decent breath. That was the longest half a minute of my life. I was still trying to figure out the best way to lie to create a natural air passage. I couldn't breathe at all due to the haemorrhaging. Suddenly, I coughed and then immediately gasped. It was the best gasp of breath I've ever taken. A partial piece of my cheekbone was expelled while I was throwing up into a large kidney-shaped bowl which had been placed beside me. This fragment of bone was nearly half an inch long and I heard it 'clink' in the bowl as it shot out of my mouth. It was as if someone had performed a Heimlich manoeuvre on me.

15:15

There were now two doctors hovering above me trying to ascertain precisely where the blood was coming from and they homed in on my gashed eyelid. One of them placed a large bag of crushed ice to slow the blood and then placed a second bag on the right side of my face. The doctors were talking to one another as if I was not there, which was somewhat surreal, but there again the whole situation was surreal. The fact is, I wasn't able to respond to any of their questions but I could hear them clearly as I took quick, shallow breaths.

I think they thought I was unconscious and unable to hear but, oddly, my hearing had become amplified and everything was very clear. Both eyes were swollen shut so listening became my only contact with the outside world.

15:17

Ten long minutes after the incident, I finally felt able to speak: 'I'm okay doc,' I said weakly, which wasn't really true. 'But my head aches,' I added.

One of the doctors decided he should stitch my eyelid there and then to stop the bleeding and then wait until we got to the hospital for a full evaluation. I welcomed this decisiveness.

15:20

The imposing figure of Andy Nelson flung open the doors to the first-aid room. With both eyes firmly shut, I could only hear his voice.

'Can he go back on?' I heard him ask the doctors. One look at me would have given him his answer.

I sensed this question and Andy's rather gruff approach irritated the doctors, one of whom replied with understated sarcasm: 'Not today.'

That was the extent of the exchange. The boss must have turned on his heels and left.

I appreciate that losing a goalkeeper so early in a game is a crisis for a coach and I realised he had some tactical changes to attend to but I still think it would have been nice if Andy had just uttered a few simple words of consolation or encouragement, or even given me a consolatory pat. It would only have taken a second but there was nothing, not a word. I'd always suspected he'd had a heart of stone but this confirmed it for me. He obviously had far more important things to attend to than expressing concern for one of his players who had just received a career-threatening, let alone life-threatening, injury. It made me feel small and an odd thought went through my head. I felt like a slaughtered animal hanging on a meat hook. I was just a commodity to be tossed aside when I was no longer of use. This thought made me angry, which was annoying as it made my head throb even more. I thought of Theo Foley and how he would have reacted. I know for absolute certain that he would have shown considerably more compassion and concern than Andy Nelson did.

Preparations were being made for me to go to hospital but, before I did, I got word from Charlie Hall that none other than Derek 'Killer' Hales was donning my gloves and additional green keeper's jersey and had gone in goal as my replacement. Killer had messed around in training as a goalkeeper on many occasions and knew what he was doing. I liked Derek a lot. We were good friends and I knew that he would do his absolute best between the sticks, although obviously he would have preferred to be at the other end banging them in, as that's what Derek did. But he was without fear. The thought of Derek being in goal took my mind off my own predicament for a vital minute or so. And boy did I need those distractions.

15:25

By now I had been stretchered into the ambulance, which also contained the two doctors who had attended to me. The blaring 'wa-wa wa-wa' siren did not help my headache, dizziness and nausea. It felt as if the siren was wailing to the same rhythm as my thudding head. It continued to feel surreal in the ambulance, lying on my back listening to what the ambulancemen were saying on their radios. I was saying to myself: 'Is this really happening? Is this really happening to me?' I had travelled up with my team expecting to play a regulation game of football, something that happens every single Saturday all over the world. And here I was now, being rushed to hospital. I thought of the match at Roker Park continuing without me.

Even though things were happening super-fast in those tense moments, paradoxically it also felt everything was moving in slow motion, in a dreamlike, hazy state. I was on my back still trying to process what was happening when I heard one of the ambulancemen radio ahead to Sunderland Hospital: 'Hello,' I heard him say. 'We have an emergency head injury, a patient with head trauma in a critical state … we'll be there in less than five minutes.'

'Oh shit,' I thought to myself. 'Apparently I am now in a "critical state".' That was not what I wanted to hear and you'll forgive me for admitting that I was very scared indeed.

My mind was racing. What was wrong with me? Was I dying? I thought of my family and my loved ones back in London. I didn't want to die in a hospital far from home.

I realised I was struggling to breathe and maybe I was showing signs of brain or skull damage. Would I be permanently brain-damaged? I cracked a joke telling my inner self that I already knew I had brain damage by becoming a goalkeeper in the first place. I almost smiled at my own silly sense of humour trying to make myself feel better.

15:35

Once the ambulance arrived, I heard its doors creak open and the paramedics wheeled me straight into the examination room. The two doctors were now joined by the hospital's head trauma specialist. I felt the heat of the overhead spotlight as they checked out my face more closely. I could not fault the care and attention I was receiving. After making a thorough examination of my eye, cheek, nose, head and neck it was agreed that the bleeding and swelling needed to be under total control before they could make any further assessments or move me to the X-ray department.

I knew I wasn't out of the woods completely. I couldn't see out of either eye and could only breathe in a shallow, controlled manner. One of the doctors suggested placing several bags of crushed ice from my neck up to my forehead in an effort to stem the flow of blood and calm things down. This appeared to be a good logical step. There was a small area left open where my mouth could take in some air.

15:45

Then I was wheeled off and, somewhat bizarrely, I found myself in the maternity ward which felt somewhat incongruous. There I was, a bloody mess, still in my kit, in the midst of a ward full of heavily pregnant women. Evidently the hospital had run out of single rooms. I heard some of the women whispering to each other as I was wheeled through the ward. Then I heard the swish of the privacy curtain being drawn to shut me off from the expectant mums.

16:00

Finally, one of the doctors then started talking directly to me. I felt indescribably bad. To this day, I can still recall how the 'conversation' went, although, in reality, it was very much one-way. 'Graham, it's around 4pm on Saturday, 21 February 1976 … you have been severely hurt … but you are okay … you are safe and in a Sunderland hospital … we will diagnose your injuries once we have the swelling under control and it goes down a little … probably in a few hours. So, for now, try to rest but don't sleep. Try to breathe through your mouth only. If you try to breathe through your nose the chances are you will start the haemorrhaging again, so please don't. Just try to relax without going to sleep, okay? It is important you don't go to sleep.'

With that, the doctor prepared to leave but, before he did, said: 'I am appointing Nurse Hilary to look after you and she will not leave your side. You are in good hands with her. Okay Graham?'

I needed all the energy I could muster to give him a weak thumbs-up to acknowledge I understood. The doctor then introduced Nurse Hilary, who kindly asked me if she could get me anything. Her voice immediately made me feel calm and that I was in good hands: 'Blankets please,' was all I could mumble. Because now, I felt like I was freezing to death. What with all the ice and the shock of everything that had happened in the last hour, my body was reacting. I really thought I was going to pass out and never wake up. It was a genuinely frightening and traumatic experience for me. It helped when Nurse Hilary began to cover me from the neck down with some heated blankets. My teeth had started to chatter and my body was trembling.

Nurse Hilary then started to warm my freezing hands and arms which were so cold they were tingling. She started talking quietly and calmly to me, telling me she had been at the match and saw me get injured. She had left the game early to come on duty. She said she would get me anything I needed and that I must rest without sleeping.

When I asked her weakly why I shouldn't sleep she said the doctors did not want me to lapse into a coma.

I liked Nurse Hilary's voice. It was the most soothing voice I had heard in a long time. I realised she was just talking to me to keep me awake. She told me she was a Sunderland season ticket holder and never missed a match. Hilary kept me awake for the next few hours, occasionally gently nudging me if she thought I was drifting off. Every fibre in my body was craving sleep but I knew I couldn't.

Chapter 25

Nurse Hilary

LATER THAT evening I heard the unmistakable *Match of the Day* theme tune from a television set somewhere in the ward. I knew what was coming next. It was the highlights of the Sunderland v Charlton match. Then I heard what I assumed to be one of the mums-to-be saying: 'Look, it's him. The bloke up there. He's being carried off.'

Word quickly spread that I was the goalkeeper who had been kicked in the face and was behind the curtain. I couldn't believe they were talking about the incident within earshot of me. I heard laughter and another woman saying: 'Tell him he's on the telly.'

I asked Nurse Hilary if the TV could be turned down, or preferably off. I didn't want to hear it and I certainly didn't want to relive what had been the worst, most traumatic few hours of my life.

She nodded and within seconds the television had been turned down, though I could still hear some of the women murmuring and whispering to one another.

I felt completely exhausted and it was nearly midnight when Hilary told me they would be transporting me into a quiet, private room. I felt so relieved because my head was still thudding like a bass drum. As I was wheeled out of the ward, some of the expectant mothers wished me well, and a speedy recovery. I was able to give them a feeble thumbs-up which I hoped would convey my thanks and also be seen to be wishing them well. I've often wondered what happened to the babies who those mums gave birth to.

Hilary quickly got me settled in the private room which had a large window in it. It's odd how the mind works but I was immediately transported back 24 hours to when my world had been a very different place. I was back in the hotel room where I could see the moon and I heard that unsettling call to the late-night phone-in. I couldn't articulate it but I felt that had all been eerily prescient. Without thinking, I asked Nurse Hilary if she could see the moon in the night sky and then, more in hope than expectation, if she could get me to the window so I could squint at it through my puffy, bruised eyes.

She told me gently that would not be happening and that it would be a few days before I was on my feet. She said the doctors wanted the swelling to go down first and that they would review the situation in the morning.

I suddenly had a sixth sense that I wasn't being told everything so I came right out with it and asked Hilary if I had lost the use of my right eye. She hesitated for a split second which I found deeply concerning. When she answered, she still sounded very gentle and calm but I noticed a more professional tone to her voice: 'We are not sure yet, Graham. We will know a lot more when the swelling has gone down,' she said.

I felt fear and sadness welling up inside me. I swallowed deeply. Though I was playing professional sport in a man's team, I was still a teenager and I was missing my home and my family.

Hilary could see I was becoming emotional and gently took my hand. At that point I started to crumble and the gravity of the day's events finally hit home. I was scared and started to cry. I tried my absolute best to control my feelings because I did not want to set off any more internal bleeding which would be dangerous.

That fateful night of Saturday, 21 February, going into Sunday, 22 February, Hilary stayed by my side, talking to me until 4am when a doctor examined my state of mind and physical well-being and decided it would be okay for me to sleep. As the doctor quietly exited the room, Hilary continued to warm my cold hands and, within seconds of getting the okay, I fell into a deep, deep sleep.

Chapter 26

Strange Happenings!

IT MUST have been about an hour later when I woke abruptly. My whole body was shaking uncontrollably, I was involuntarily throwing up again and, just like before, I couldn't catch my breath because I couldn't take in any air. When you cannot stop being sick and blood is coming from your nose and mouth, filling your sinuses, believe me it is quite a stressful experience. I felt another small piece of bone shoot out of my mouth into a stainless-steel bowl. Nurse Hilary was still beside me and calmed me down by saying it would pass. I just had to breathe slowly as my body was naturally ridding itself of foreign bodies. I immediately felt better, especially in my stomach area. It seemed that while I had been asleep, blood had started dripping down the back of my throat again and a few stray shards of bone had made their way into my empty stomach.

Hilary, bless her heart, was doing her best to reassure me. She kept saying: 'It's okay Graham, you're going to be fine. You're just getting rid of all that bad stuff in your body.'

Adding more ice bags around my neck, forehead and cheek soon did the trick and once more the bleeding was stopped. Yet I felt dreadful. I was totally exhausted, thinking I was going to pass out and, in reality, I was hoping that may happen. I don't like to admit it but I thought that even if I died, that would be okay. I was ready to throw in the towel but then I remembered my dad's words: 'Never give up, son,' as I drifted off into another deep sleep. I was totally exhausted and I didn't know how much more I could take.

Chapter 27

Sunday Visitors

'MR TUTT? Good, you're with us again,' came an unfamiliar-sounding and slightly officious voice which turned out to belong to Nurse Hilary's replacement. She told me it was 10am and the doctors wanted some X-rays of my face. An hour later, after being prodded around the X-ray table, the doctors finally had some concrete news.

The full prognosis was alarming. The boot had shattered my right cheekbone and the orbit bone that protected and held my right eye in place was broken. About an inch of it had broken off as the boot deflected off it.

Crucially – and something I have always been relieved about – the lower orbit bone deflected Tom's boot away from the vulnerable soft part of my eye.

There was an unsightly gash above my eyelid matching the width of the end of the boot which had followed through to the inner bridge of my nose on the right side. The bridge of my nose was broken and felt out of position. My nose was distorted, bent at the wrong angle and impossible to breathe through. By squinting out of my left eye, I could see a bump protruding where the boot had ricocheted off my face.

The doctor said my right eye would be swollen shut for another day or so, but he thought that by the afternoon my left eye might start to open a little.

There was an elephant in the room, a subject I felt people were tiptoeing around and that was my long-term vision and therefore my future career as a professional goalkeeper. Everyone knew my right eye was badly damaged but to what extent the doctor said he was still not sure. He said we would know a lot more when the muscles working the eye had stopped swelling and started returning to normal.

Another doctor entered the room, introduced himself as an eye specialist and announced that some of my eye muscles could be severely bruised or ruptured. If they were ruptured the eye would be restricted in its overall total movement. Trying to find some good news among the woe, he said in an up-tempo tone that, in his professional opinion, I would not lose my eye.

The specialist confirmed I had likely sustained severe concussion, a broken nose, a shattered right cheekbone and broken orbits surrounding the upper and lower eye casing. He told me he had sewn seven stiches in my upper right eyelid.

There was only one question on my mind: 'Will I be able to play again, doc?' I asked plaintively.

His answer was honest and to the point: 'To be frank, I'm not sure, Graham. It's way too early to tell.'

My mind went back a few years to the autumn of 1972 when the late, great Gordon Banks was involved in a car crash which cost him the sight in his right eye and effectively ended his career when he was still first-choice goalkeeper for both England and Stoke City.

The doctor realised it was a question that warranted a more in-depth answer and continued: 'It depends if the muscles that control your right eye are ruptured or if they have just been severely bruised,' he expounded. 'Hopefully you will be fine but it may take quite some time, months maybe. The eye muscles are very delicate when it comes to trauma like this.'

The word 'months' echoed in my head. That sounded like a very long recovery time indeed.

While I was absorbing this news, there was a tap at the door and I heard Nurse Hilary's voice.

She told me she was not on duty but had decided to come in to see me anyway. I started wondering what she looked like. After all, I was only 19 and still single. Both my eyes were swollen shut but I tried to open them so I could see her.

I told her how much I appreciated her visiting me and asked her to sit down and have a chat as I tried to sit up properly. With some hesitation, Hilary told me there were two people waiting outside to see me but were not sure if I wanted any visitors. One of them was Bob Stokoe, the Sunderland manager, and the other was Tom Finney.

I had little choice but to agree. It certainly would not have been right for me to have spoken to Bob and turn away Tom, although in truth he was probably the last person I wanted to see.

Hilary excused herself and a few seconds later there was a soft tap at the door, followed by a quiet, north-eastern voice, saying: 'Hi Graham, it's Bob Stokoe.'

I beckoned him in and detected genuine sincerity in his voice when he said how sorry he was about the accident. I tried to sit up higher in the bed to get my point across in a direct, honest manner and I told Mr Stokoe that I believed it could have been avoided and that I thought Tom was late when he stretched for the ball. It was my honest response. Bob claimed he did not see the incident due to the cluster of players gathered in the penalty area and that Tom certainly did not mean to hurt me. He was trying his level best to defend his striker.

At the time I was still feeling very raw and bitter and I blamed Tom: 'Well in my opinion, he was very late, sir,' I repeated as I spat some congealed blood into a kidney dish.

Mr Stokoe then changed the subject and asked if I needed anything or if he could do anything for me. He told me he had managed Charlton between 1965 and 1967 and that while the manner of his departure had disappointed him, he loved his time at The Valley, saying what a great club it had always been, with a family atmosphere.

As he was speaking, I remembered my dad saying that Stokoe was one of the best managers in the game and a complete gentleman. His demeanour and the way he conducted himself that day confirmed my dad's opinion. After leaving The Valley, he had managed Rochdale, Carlisle and Blackpool, before, in 1972, landing the top job at Sunderland and becoming a legend by winning the FA Cup at the end of his first season, overcoming the mighty Leeds at Wembley in one of the greatest upsets the competition has ever known.

Only true club legends get a statue erected in their name, but go to Sunderland's new home, the Stadium of Light, and you'll see one of Stokoe. Everyone in the game had the highest respect for him and I was starting to admire him too for the way he was trying his best to protect one of his players. My conclusion was that Bob Stokoe was indeed a total gentleman. He shook my hand again, wished me a speedy recovery and made me promise that if I needed anything at all to contact him. He finished by saying that Tom would really like to talk to me.

To be honest, I was still feeling somewhat bitter about the incident and anticipated an awkward exchange. What I really wanted was for Tom to come in and apologise to me. If he was going to tell me it was an accident then I was not inclined to listen to him because I didn't believe it was. That was how I felt at the time.

Bob said he would talk to Tom, before shaking my hand a third time and wishing me a speedy recovery.

Tom's arrival was similar to Bob's with a couple of light taps on the door before a somewhat hesitant entrance. Immediately he offered me a sincere apology saying he was genuinely sorry about the accident. Perhaps I was a little hasty but I'd suffered so much pain and discomfort and I had literally almost died, so I was in no mood for small talk. I must have appeared very sullen and unforgiving to him.

An awkward few seconds elapsed before he again said how sorry he was.

Maybe I was a bit hard on Tom but, back then, I was convinced that he had, as they say in the game, 'done me'. After another short pause for breath I reiterated that I thought he was late.

As I recall it, Tom tried to hold my arm and apologise again but I was not in the mood. Maybe my mind was not in a good place, maybe I was still suffering from a little concussion but, for some reason, I wasn't going easy on Tom.

He stood quietly by my bed for a few seconds before wishing me a speedy recovery and leaving.

I've often reflected if I was harsh to Tom that day. It cannot have been easy for him to come and see me but you have to understand that I was only 19 and feeling as if my whole career had come crashing down around me. Perhaps I should have been more forgiving but I simply was not ready to be at that point.

After Bob and Tom had gone, Hilary returned to tell me she was back on duty later and asked me if there was anything she could do in the meantime. I asked her if she could ring my mum and dad and tell them I was going to be okay and would be home as soon as possible. I knew they would be worried sick and in some ways it was a relief that they had not been at the game.

She promised she would and took my parents' telephone number before squeezing my hand gently, telling me she would see me in a few hours' time and that everything would be fine. Already I could feel a bond developing between us, something unspoken, but tangible all the same.

At this point the painkillers were kicking in and I simply crashed out for the next few hours.

Next thing I knew, Hilary was waking me gently and telling me I needed to eat or drink something as it had been 24 hours since I'd last consumed anything at all. The only thing I thought I could eat was jelly!

Hilary then said that Rodney Stone, Charlton's executive secretary, was coming to see me and that he was on the phone with my parents at that very moment. I had not realised until then that Rodney had made arrangements to stay overnight in Sunderland. His job was to get me back safely to London when the doctors gave the all-clear.

I hadn't had much to laugh about but the mention of Mr Stone had my face hurting with a grin as I recalled a hilarious story about him.

Rodney was a very cordial, generous man and he and his wife had taken a shine to me and an ex-girlfriend called Sue. One

Sunday they had invited us over to their magnificent home for dinner. As the second dose of painkillers started to work, my mind drifted back to that occasion. I remembered white rabbits hopping around in their spacious back garden. Sue and I sat nervously at the dinner table beginning to eat our hearty Sunday dinner. Lovely people though they were, it was all rather awkward getting the conversation to flow.

I remember Rodney was at the end of a very long dining table, almost like one you'd use for a banquet. Mrs Stone was sat at the opposite end of the table with Sue and I perched opposite each other in the middle. The room was deathly quiet as we served our food and passed the condiments around. It was like being in a library with the occasional whisper of one person to another. In our case it was 'could you pass the salt, please?' or 'would you like some mustard?'

For some reason conversation then completely dried up. I imagine we were all feeling somewhat uneasy with the only noise in the room being the clatter of the cutlery on our plates, the chomping of food and the rhythmic ticking of a huge grandfather clock behind Mr Stone.

Suddenly, I heard a mechanical sound in the clock before it began chiming six times. It wasn't exactly like being in the bell tower of Big Ben but it wasn't far off it.

As the chimes ended, the silence that followed was even more awkward and I felt the need to say something to break the ice. All I could think of was Mr Stone's beautiful grandfather clock and I opened my mouth and uttered one of the most embarrassing things I have ever said in my entire life:

'Mr Stone, that's an absolutely beautiful cock you've got there … clock. I mean clock,' I quickly corrected myself.

There was a couple of tension-filled seconds of utter silence before all four of us burst into uncontrollable laughter. So much so that food shot out of Sue's mouth. Sue grabbed her cloth napkin and covered her mouth as I, red-faced, acted the fool by getting underneath the table and staying there for a good ten seconds, playing on my total embarrassment and hopefully making them laugh even more.

On surfacing from underneath the table, I was relieved to see Mrs Stone with a broad grin on her face. Every time we thought we'd controlled the hilarity someone would start us all off again with a snigger or a guffaw.

At least I had broken the ice and we continued to laugh at my almighty 'cock' up. From that moment there was no awkwardness and the conversation flowed, interspersed with bouts of continued laughter at my classic faux pas.

Since then, whenever I see or hear a grandfather clock, I think back to that dinner with Mr and Mrs Stone and have a quiet chuckle to myself.

Suddenly I was dragged back to reality. What had seemed like a few minutes had in fact been over two hours when I roused from my painkiller-induced slumber. Through the haze, I heard the reassuring tones of Mr Stone's voice. He told me he had spoken to my parents and let them know I would be home in a day or two. He asked – depending on clearance from the Sunderland Hospital doctors – if I felt well enough to travel back down to London on Tuesday lunchtime. He suggested I should see some specialists to take an even closer look at my eye and some facial injury specialists who could assess the damage to my cheek and nose.

I told Mr Stone I needed one more day before I could attempt to travel. The pain in my head was still significant and it took only the slightest movement for the throbbing and dizziness to start over again.

The doctors conferred and agreed Tuesday lunchtime would be the earliest they would be prepared to sign the release papers. I assured Mr Stone that I was in good hands with Nurse Hilary and he should continue to do his club duties from the phone in his hotel room. I couldn't resist a gag as he was making his exit.

'By the way Mr Stone, please say hello to Mrs Stone and tell her I'm moving as slow as a grandfather clock,' I said cheekily.

There hadn't been much to laugh about for anyone in the last 36 hours but Mr Stone did crack a smile before leaving, with a comment which summed everything up: 'I'm just glad you're still ticking, Graham.'

It is no exaggeration to say that at one point I had literally been fighting for my life.

Chapter 28
An Eye-Opener

MY THIRD night in hospital was a real eye-opener. Literally. The ice had done its job and the swelling was at last beginning to subside. It was around midnight and all was quiet. I hadn't looked in the mirror since the incident and curiosity was getting the better of me. There was a small mirror close to the window under a handbasin four steps from the end of my bed.

It was a monumental struggle. Everything seemed so much effort. I reached the edge of the bed successfully and managed to get my feet on the cold tiled floor. With a few shallow breaths I embarked on the few baby steps I needed to reach the mirror.

Then, Nurse Hilary entered the room. I was caught in no man's land. And no goalkeeper ever wants to be caught in no man's land. She had timed it perfectly to catch me red-handed.

'What are you doing, Graham?' she asked. There was a slightly stern tone to her voice and I immediately felt guilty.

'Please Hilary. I just want to see my face. See the damage,' I said to her.

Hilary peered at me dubiously before begrudgingly agreeing to help me shuffle towards the mirror. It was the first time I had seen anything at all since 3.07pm on the Saturday when the incident happened. A large, padded patch remained taped over my right eye, covering that side of my face.

The room was dark. With my left hand I opened the blind, allowing a streetlamp to light up the room. To Hilary's slight irritation, I started to peel off the eye pad. Hilary could tell I wanted to see what damage had been done to my face. I was more than curious. Most importantly I wanted to know if I could see clearly out of my right eye.

I could not see much at all. It was like looking through the slit of a postbox. I felt several stitches across my upper eyelid. I moved my head very slowly up and then down while staring into the mirror and immediately became dizzy. The slightest head movements made me feel unsteady and I realised with alarm that my right eye was barely moving at all.

'It is probably the muscles around the outer edges of the eye. The doctors did say they are severely swollen,' said Hilary, trying to console me.

My nose looked way off-centre. My hair was matted with three-day-old, dried blood and bloodstains were still visible around my cheek. Blood was also still caked in my ear, up my nose and down the side of my neck. I am sorry to be so graphic but it was horrific.

Hilary said the doctors did not want to touch my face, not even to clean or wipe away the blood. They just wanted to get the swelling under control so I could travel back to London to visit my doctors and eye specialist. I agreed that made sense and asked her to wipe some blood from my neck. I was half leaning on her for support as she wiped my neck gently with a warm flannel.

I'm not quite sure what was driving my obsession with the moon but once again I was drawn to it and wanted to know if it was visible.

Hilary drew up the blinds to reveal the moon which was lurking behind drifting clouds but still beautiful. I moved my head slowly up and down again while trying to keep focused on the moon. Alarmingly, I was seeing two moons each time my head moved slightly up or down. It was obvious my right eye was not working as it should.

Hilary sensed my worry and gave me a reassuring hug. I kissed the top of her head. She then guided me back to the edge of the bed and held my hand for several moments without a word being said. Then we embraced. Fear swept over me again and I began to cry. I feared I was losing my sight.

I was relieved that Mr Stone would be escorting me back to London the very next day to visit an eye specialist.

Chapter 29

Back in London, and Surgery

'HE'S COMING round doctor,' I heard my mum's voice exclaim. I was back in London and I had just undergone surgery. The surgeon strode in and told me everything was completely fine while leafing through copious notes he had made as part of his official report.

He told me he had reversed my depressed and partially shattered cheekbone and placed a wad of temporary gauze as packing under it from the top right inside of my mouth. The doctor told me this was to support and restructure my right cheek and that I would be a little sore inside my mouth. He told me I'd feel 'puffy' and a little uncomfortable for a couple of days, after which he'd take the supporting gauze out. He'd also straightened my nose and dealt with some floating bone fragments. He said he'd talk to me more about my eye when the swelling had subsided, which would be a few days.

The eye was what mattered most. I knew everything else could heal given time but the eye is such a delicate organ and I feared the damage might be irreparable. The doctor knew this and could tell I was worried. He took a deep breath, put his hand on my shoulder and said as gently as he could: 'When I drew out some fragments of bone from under your cheekbone, I checked the muscles that move your eye. I'm not sure if the eye muscles are severely bruised or ruptured … only time will tell.' Realising I had no more questions, the doctor turned and left.

All I could do was wait for the swelling to go down and then review the eye movement status.

Mum and Dad were now with me. They had been so brave. It must have been devastating for them to see me in such a way. Their parental instinct kicked in and they told me we would survive the ordeal together and everything would turn out okay. My mum kissed one of my hands and Dad held the other and said we'd all get through it together. Now was the time for us all to be strong. That's what family is for.

I was just relieved to have the operation over and now I could look forward to having a complete rest. The painkilling medication began to dull my mind and I could only groggily tell my parents that I loved them as my body was craving sleep. Before dozing off I prayed internally hoping all would be okay when I woke up.

That spring and early summer of 1976, I laid low at home not venturing out anywhere at all. Though we were heading for a freakish heatwave in the UK, rest was what the doc had ordered and I was only too happy to obey.

Chapter 30

Hello Again, Hilary

DURING THE spring, I had some personal issues that needed to be put to bed. A girl I had been seeing on and off had ditched me shortly after my injury. But, as you might have gathered, Hilary had made quite an impression on me and, during my recuperation, my thoughts would often turn to her.

I finally plucked up the courage to call her, though I was nervous she might have forgotten me.

Before I knew it, I had dialled the number and heard Hilary's lilting Geordie voice saying hello.

'Hello Hilary, it's Cyclops here … how are ya?'

'Fine … but I miss looking after you,' she said in a way which melted my heart.

After I told her I was missing her too she asked me if I wanted to return to Sunderland for a visit which she promised would be better than my last one. I had nearly a month to go before pre-season training started at Charlton and a trip out of London would do me good so I agreed. Hilary had a long weekend coming up so the timing was perfect.

I told her I'd meet her at the train station and would be wearing Elvis-style sunglasses. I was trying to make her laugh but in truth my eye felt a lot more comfortable behind dark shades. That weekend was very special. Hilary took me straight from the station to her local pub where I met her mum, dad, sister, two brothers and a rather large, slightly bovine lady, who played the pub's piano. We had a great time. I enjoyed a few beers, some good pub food, felt totally relaxed and was in a great mood. We even sang a few songs that the piano lady bashed out with suspiciously male-looking hands.

By now you'll have sensed that I love the glow of the moon and so, feeling romantically inclined, I asked Hilary at closing time if we could go to the highest point in the Sunderland area to see the moon. I was thinking like any normal 19-year-old lad would. I wanted to get Hilary in a romantic setting away from prying eyes. We did this and ended the night with a hug and a kiss.

It was a marvellous weekend and Hilary gave me a tour of the area. Then, before I caught the train home, we went to the pub for a farewell Sunday lunch and a few drinks. I was delighted I'd been able to thank Hilary in person because she had been there for me when I desperately needed someone. She was my Florence Nightingale who had held my hand, cared for me and talked me through one of the most stressful periods of my life.

Finally, the 'big-boned' piano player announced that my taxi had arrived to take me to the station. As I was saying my goodbyes to everyone, the formidable piano player started to play a song that very few northerners would ever wish to be caught singing. But sing it they did. To my surprise the whole pub joined in an impromptu rendition of 'Maybe it's Because I'm a Londoner'. That was a very special gesture from them. They had all made me feel so welcome and I truly appreciated it. It was certainly a more pleasant experience than my last trip to the north-east.

Chapter 31

'You're Finished, Tuttie'

I REPORTED to pre-season training a few weeks later, in early July. That summer was a scorcher and every British person of a certain age remembers it. It was hot and sticky, not unlike my right eye in truth. I was using eye drops every few hours because my tear ducts were not providing enough moisture. I tried my best to hide this fact from everyone, even my parents. I figured they had been through enough worry.

I did not want anyone to think there was a problem. The truth is, there was. The double vision was still there. A month earlier the doctor had said he thought the swelling had gone down considerably so I played along with him but my vision wasn't right. The fact my eye had now started to look normal made it easier for me to fool people. I even managed to convince Charlton's doctor during our pre-season check-up. But when I tilted my head just a few degrees the double vision kicked in. I knew I was in trouble but I had to push on and not reveal my secret. My livelihood was at stake.

When I ran at any pace above a jog, my eye felt different. My vision became blurred and hazy, as though I was looking through a frosted window. It was strange.

On the outside I appeared as happy and confident as ever. But inside, I was terrified.

The first two weeks of pre-season training were all about fitness. We would run long distances each morning and do weight training in the afternoon. I could alleviate my double-vision problem when running by half closing my bad eye. But when the footballs were pulled out of storage three weeks in, I knew I was in deep, deep trouble.

I had plenty of excuses at first, like my timing was off a tad because I had not caught a ball for over five months. I told my goalkeeping coach Peter Shearing I was just a bit rusty but Peter was no fool. I had a great deal of respect for the former West Ham and England youth-team goalkeeper and I could tell he knew something was not quite right. The acid test would come in a few days' time when we played our first pre-season friendly at Reading.

I was relieved the game was behind closed doors, away from The Valley with no media or fans present.

I played dreadfully. My depth perception was totally off kilter, a disastrous scenario for any keeper. In the first five minutes I came out to retrieve a long pass and completely missed scooping the ball off the striker's feet. Fortunately, the ball rebounded off my shin and was cleared by one of our defenders. Once again, I knew I was in trouble. Deep trouble. Life-changing trouble. My insides began to knot up and panic started to set in. My confidence was draining away. The penalty area had always been my 'office' and I had always patrolled it with authority. Not anymore. It felt alien and there was nowhere to hide.

Ten minutes later a corner kick came over. The old me could have caught it in my sleep. I would have plucked it out of the air like a cherry picker. It had my name on it so I yelled my normal 'keeper's ball' before running smack bang into Jimmy Giles, knocking him over. We both ended up flat on our backs like a bad circus act, while a Reading striker had the simple task of heading the ball into an empty, unguarded net.

Jimmy simply stared at me and said nothing. He then took a second look at me, this time with a sadder face. He wasn't going to rip into me like most defenders would have done for my screw-up. Perhaps he knew my time was up as he extended his hand to me and, with as much sympathy as he could muster, helped me to my feet.

The final straw and perhaps the death knell on my Charlton career was a long-distance shot from around 25 yards. I thought I had it covered comfortably, just above head height, but it went sailing over my hands and nestled in the back of the net. I must have looked confused but, in reality, I knew what was happening. By this time, everybody did. The absolutely bitter and stark truth was that I had seen two footballs coming towards me and I had chosen the wrong one. A few team-mates tried to console me but reality had hit home in the harshest possible way and my secret was now out for all to know. The two-hour coach journey home went very slowly and quietly. I didn't know where to look.

Next morning Andy Nelson met me before practice. He was waiting for me outside his office as I left the dressing room. He asked me to walk over to the edge of the field for 'a chat'. Whenever the boss did this with a player, bad news invariably followed. He didn't stand on ceremony. He went straight for it.

'I think you're finished, Tuttie. The club will give you a testimonial match and you can keep the gate receipts from the game. That should do you alright.'

At no point did he say he was sorry for what had happened or offer any compassion. He was cold-hearted. Then again, I knew this was the way he rolled and he was doing his job. It was his way of dealing with things.

I could only mumble sadly: 'I understand,' in response.

He shook my hand as I walked slowly back towards the dressing room and past my team-mates who were now congregating on the corner of the pitch ready to start their warm-up, without me. I could not bring myself to say anything to anyone and looked the other way. I felt totally lost. Totally devastated.

I could not say goodbye to any of my team-mates as I continued to walk past a few stragglers into an empty dressing room to change. No doubt they knew exactly what had gone on between the boss and me. There was nothing left to be said.

I was disconsolate as I took off my training gear and, by sheer force of habit, went to the shower area. Everything I ever wanted had been stolen from me. My life's dream was shattered. Everything I had worked for had been ripped away. My future now felt like torture. I dropped to my knees at the far end of the shower area and began to sob, feeling very much alone. I was a cast-off.

With tears in my eyes, I dried off and put my clothes on before anyone came back to the dressing room. I hung up my green goalkeeper's shirt on the #1 peg, folded up my training gear and put my boots under my bench for the last time. My Charlton career and my life's dream were over.

During the 30-minute journey home, while driving across Blackheath and passing the soccer pitches I used to play on as a youngster, I anticipated with dread telling Mum and Dad that my career was finished. This made me even sadder. Mum and Dad had derived so much pleasure from watching me play at The

Valley. It had eased their sadness and lifted their spirits when my elder brother Jim emigrated to South Africa the day after I made my home debut for Charlton.

Dad would soon be celebrating 50 seasons as a Charlton fan. I had been planning to supply more than 20 match tickets for all his close friends and workmates, plus a pre-match tour of the dressing rooms and a party afterwards at The Valley Supporters Club. That wouldn't be happening now.

Dad could tell I was upset as soon as I walked in the door. He knew without me telling him that my career was over, but I had to have closure. I had to get the facts on the table and come clean with my parents that I was seeing double when using my peripheral vision. Dad said his instincts had told him things were not right on the first day of pre-season training just a few weeks earlier. 'You looked worried to death without saying a word, son,' he told me.

Mum's view was different. She was surprised and even said she thought I could play just as well with one good eye as two. But that was just Mum. She was demonstrating her love and undying belief in her youngest boy.

After a few seconds, Dad excused himself and started to sob his heart out as he walked upstairs to his bedroom. I gave him a few minutes to let it all out. I could hear him from our living room, which was located directly underneath his bedroom. His crying was almost uncontrollable. I knocked gently on his door and entered. All he could do was hold me and continue to cry. I knew Dad was crying for both of us.

I'll never forget that day. It felt as bad or possibly worse than the day I got kicked in the face. I knew Dad was utterly heartbroken for me. No more words were necessary as Dad's sobs continued.

Chapter 32

You'll Never Walk Alone

I WENT through several weeks of despondency that culminated in fully fledged depression. Just to get out of the house, I would take my faithful Labrador, Sadie, to One Tree Hill, which was a 30-minute walk from our house. One Tree Hill was a huge forest where you could lose yourself for several hours. At the top of the hill was a magnificent panoramic view of London including Big Ben, Tower Bridge and the city spread out in all its splendour. The view was breathtaking but boy did I feel lost.

I would sit on a bench at the top of the hill, ponder, feel sorry for myself then cry until I was exhausted. Then I would shuffle home with my head down, looking at my shoes as I walked. I did not want to make eye contact with anyone. This went on for quite a few weeks. I was a man in the full throes of depression and it was a dark time in my life. I just did not know what the future held in store for me.

After the sadness came anger. I kept thinking back to the incident at Roker Park, playing it over and over again in my mind. I became bitter about everything and looked around for blame. If only the injury had not happened, who knows how my career would have developed?

But time and again these words would come back to me: 'Never give up. You cannot give up.'

After hitting rock-bottom, I knew I had to get myself back on track somehow by occupying my mind. So, I dragged myself from my trough of despair and threw myself into preparing for my testimonial events and match. It was the best thing that could have happened to me and provided me with a purpose and distracted me from the self-pity and woe which was threatening to consume me.

I went for it with gusto and oversaw more than 50 different player and fan social functions in the pubs and clubs of south London. These fundraisers were huge fun and helped take my mind off my injury. I viewed the money raised as a golden handshake to help set me up for the future.

At many functions I raffled footballs signed not only by Charlton players but those from Millwall, Manchester United, Chelsea, Arsenal and most London clubs. There were also albums signed by superstars like Rod Stewart, Elton John and the four members of Queen.

At one event at The Valley Supporters Club, the raffle prize was a pedigree racing greyhound. I was excited to see what it could do so I went to see it run at the track. The poor thing was so nervous it took ten seconds to leave the starting gate. Five greyhounds bolted when the gates flew open but mine emerged gingerly, only after being coaxed by the trainer. It then peed against the outer railing. Fortunately, the trainer fell in love with the greyhound and ended up adopting it.

Though Charlton and Millwall fans have traditionally been rivals, both sets of fans were absolutely magnificent in showing their support for all the events. The fans from both teams promoted my testimonial match by plastering scores of advertising posters around south London. Most were illegally pasted on train timetables at various stations. It certainly helped get the word out!

One function in particular stood above the rest. It was at The Dun Cow Pub, located on the Old Kent Road, deep in the heart of Millwall territory and known as an area that took no prisoners. It could have been a powder keg but the fans from both Millwall and Charlton were on their best behaviour on an unforgettable night.

About 500 fans showed up at the pub and the place was heaving. As the venue filled, I became alarmed at the sight of so many blue and white scarves mixed with red and white ones. Usually these sworn rivals would have been at each other's throats, especially after a few beers. But to my relief it never happened. The fans of both clubs mixed well and behaved impeccably. They showed respect for each other and, by so doing, they showed respect and support for me.

A dozen or so players from both Charlton and Millwall were also there. It was a never-to-be-forgotten, emotional night capped off with players and fans from both clubs dedicating the last song of the evening to yours truly. In loud unison they sang the ultimate football anthem:

'You'll Never Walk Alone'.

They physically lifted me up and made me stand on the bar. Then all 500 or more began to sing the famous words. Grown men were singing at the top of their voices and had tears rolling down their cheeks. The fans knew I had grown up in a Millwall area, was a Millwall fan as a kid but played for their ultimate rivals Charlton. They also knew my dream of a professional career had been dashed and they were as broken-hearted as I was. We had all grown up together.

It was a fantastic night. I felt very honoured and proud of the fans and all my friends who had helped create a truly special occasion.

My mum and dad were there too and they talked about that evening until their dying days. Each time they recalled it their eyes sparkled with pride before becoming wet with joy. Mum and Dad would always round off their story by singing a few lines of 'You'll Never Walk Alone'. It is such a poignant song which gave me hope for the future. The words mean a lot to me. They echo my 'never give up' mindset.

After 50 or more of these events, I had to face the testimonial game, which was billed as my official 'goodbye'. I had a wonderful band of friends, volunteers and supporters to help me organise the match, in particular Arthur Parsons and a Charlton fan called Bill Gault.

Arthur had seen me grow up. He was a confidant, friend and taxi driver all rolled into one. There was only one problem, which I found amusing, in that Arthur was a staunch Millwall fan! But what a guy. He scheduled his time to drive me from one event to the next. Arthur was great fun to be with and never failed to cheer me up. Being an ardent football fan, he loved rubbing shoulders with all the players that he came into contact with.

Bill, meanwhile, ran an amateur football club called Vanbrugh Park. He and the team were wonderfully supportive in organising various testimonial events including a ten-mile run with hundreds of runners. The finish line was at the Black Prince, a huge pub in Sidcup, that helped refresh over 400 sore-legged, tired and very, very thirsty football fans.

The night of the testimonial match, 14 March 1977, was very special. It was wholly appropriate that newly promoted Sunderland kindly volunteered to come south and play an All-Star Charlton Team. The prolific England and Arsenal striker – 'Supermac' himself – Malcolm Macdonald graciously gave up his time as a guest player for Charlton that night. Supermac notched two goals and was brilliant. Derek Hales, recently transferred to Derby, returned to The Valley, and with Mike Flanagan and Paddy Powell completed a mouth-watering forward line. The score was somewhat irrelevant in comparison to the talent on the field with Charlton winning 3-2.

Before the main Charlton and Sunderland game there was something truly unique which, to my knowledge, has never been duplicated at any other testimonial game. This was an All-Star Goalkeepers XI playing against an All-Star Celebrity XI. The goalkeepers came from all London's top teams and what a line-up they made. There was Spurs and Northern Ireland superstar and top gentleman goalkeeper Pat Jennings, West Ham's brilliant young keeper Mervyn Day, Arsenal's two top keepers Bob Wilson and Jimmy Rimmer, Crystal Palace's long-time favourite John Jackson with back-up keeper Tony Burns. Peter Mellor represented Fulham and Graham Hall came from Luton Town. Charlton's highly respected former keeper John Dunn also turned out as did my friend Jeff Wood, who had replaced me in the Charlton team. The line-up was completed by my goalkeeping coach Peter Shearing, who had played for a number of clubs including West Ham and England Youth.

I felt honoured that the cream of London's goalkeeping world showed me their support. It was truly overwhelming to see so much talent enjoying themselves on my behalf.

The All-Star Celebrity XI was captained by Dennis Waterman, known and loved as DS George Carter in the unmissable *The Sweeney*. Dennis was and still is a highly respected television personality. Also present were some of the country's top football commentators including Brian Moore, John Motson and Tony Gubba and a further array of broadcasting talent with BBC Radio DJs Noel Edmonds, Steve Rider, Dave Dee and Paul Burnett. There was also Bill Oddie of *The Goodies* who was great fun, singer/songwriter Junior Campbell and TV and movie actor Patrick Mower. Additional actors and media reporters Roger Scott, Steve Tongue and George Layton took part. Last but not least was my all-time favourite coach and mentor Theo Foley. I was delighted to witness him lacing up his boots ready to play.

Even the legendary Charlton goalkeeper Sam Bartram, who played 623 matches for the club over 22 years, sought me out in the dressing room before the game. Sam gave me a warm hug, shook my hand and was most complimentary, saying he had tipped me to beat his club appearance record because, at 17, I had had a four-year start on his Charlton career which began when he was 21.

Andy Nelson allowed me to play for 15 minutes in the main Charlton versus Sunderland game. It felt wonderful to be on The Valley pitch one last time.

I will never forget the moment just before kick-off, when, after completing the pre-game coin toss, I ran, for the very last time, from the halfway line back towards the Charlton fans who had gathered behind my goal. It looked as if most of the 10,000 fans had squeezed in there, filling the part of the ground known as the Covered End to the max.

As I ran towards them, the fans began chanting my name faster and faster until it became a deafening roar and then they burst into rapturous applause as I entered the goal area. I stretched my arms wide open, showing my gratitude, love and appreciation. They were loud and magnificent. You never forget something like that.

At the end of the night, after all the fanfare had ended and the floodlights were ready to be switched off, I walked out of the players' entrance. There, waiting for me, were my mum, dad, my uncle Des and my sister Julie. We gathered in a tight circle with our arms around each other. It was painful seeing them all break down and cry at the same time. They were as broken-hearted as I was. My time at this great old London club was officially over. We were all bewildered and confused, with no idea what would happen next.

PART TWO

SOUTH AFRICA

Chapter 33
Thank You, Mr Patel

AT FIRST it was a buzz being recognised when out in public but, after a while, complete strangers coming up and saying they were sorry I got kicked in the head and asking how my eye was began to drag. They meant well but it wasn't what I wanted to hear. Just when I thought I was moving on, a well-meaning person would ask me how I was and it would all come flooding back. I kept seeing the boot. I couldn't get the boot out of my mind.

I was starting to feel I needed to be somewhere no one knew me. I felt incarcerated in a cage of melancholy and sadness. After a few weeks of being approached by well-meaning sympathisers, I did not want to go out or be seen anywhere. One day I was sitting at home when normally I would have been at training and I was feeling sorry for myself. Out of the blue, it dawned on me that nothing was stopping me from doing exactly as I wanted and so, almost on a whim, I decided to visit my brother Jim and his family in South Africa. I had not seen him for three years and I knew my mum needed to get away as much as I did. Dad was happy staying at home looking after our dog, watching football and going ballroom dancing with a new circle of friends he'd found.

I booked the flight that very day and Mum and I left for South Africa shortly after. I was missing football terribly and wondering if I could play again at a slightly lower level. I had heard that several British players had gone to play in South Africa and loved it there. So, I took a few letters of recommendation with me plus some contact numbers.

Back then, travelling to South Africa took forever. It was around a 15-hour flight including refuelling in Nairobi which added another three hours. So, when we touched down at Jan Smuts Airport near Johannesburg, Mum and I were more than ready to see Jim, his wife, Pat, and their three children. From Jo'burg we headed down to the coast, a few hours south of Durban.

Jim and Pat had picked a beautiful spot for our family vacation in a largely unknown seaside paradise called Uvongo. Large colourful parrots were flying everywhere and chattering monkeys swung from tree to tree. We were right on the beach in a huge rented home. Outside our door was a 60-foot waterfall splashing into a bright-blue lagoon. It was capped off with a private sandy beach overlooking the Indian Ocean. It was heaven and just what we needed.

I played on the beach with my nephew James and my nieces Leeann and Kelly. It was wonderful spending time with loved ones, totally away from it all. The eye specialist in London had advised me to get some sun on my face and, if I could, swim in warm salt water, thinking it might help stimulate the muscles around my eye. It was a magnificent place to relax and recuperate.

One afternoon I swam way out – about 1,000 yards – and, noticing a long row of fishing nets, I dived deep to see if any fish had been caught. I discovered later that evening the nets were there to stop sharks coming too close to the beach. No wonder no one else was swimming out there! Evidently at sunset the sharks would come nearer to the beach to feed. I felt a shiver go through my whole body through fear of what might have been.

That night we had dinner at a swanky hotel overlooking the beach. There we heard from our waiter about a single snooker table in the basement. Perhaps on such things, fate is decided. Jim's eyes lit up as he loved snooker so we made our way towards the basement. The hotel was really plush with white marble from floor to ceiling.

A smartly dressed pianist with a bow tie played classical numbers on a grand piano, which added to the sophisticated atmosphere. Of course, I had to put on my best Humphrey Bogart voice and say 'Play it again Sam' as I walked past.

Next to a sweeping staircase was a door with a small sign that read: 'Snooker Table Downstairs'. In the middle of the room sat a dramatically lit full-size snooker table. To the side was a long Hollywood-style bar with a couple of dozen framed photos of famous movie stars along the top.

Jim and I thought we were the only people in the room and gave each other a gleeful smile before a person popped up from the other side of the bar. He was wearing a turban and introduced himself as Mr Patel. After we ordered our Lion Lager (they say if you drink more than five, you'll start roaring) Mr Patel asked if we would like some background music. We gave him the double nod and he started to tinker with an antique-looking radio at the back of the bar.

As Mr Patel scanned the airwaves, various snatches of African music faded in and out, before I heard the name Arcadia Shepherds among some foreign football commentary. I asked Mr

Patel to go back to the station that sounded like it was covering the match.

It was a million-to-one chance that I'd heard the name Arcadia Shepherds in that random fashion. In fact, it was pure fate. About six months earlier I had heard that a former top Charlton player called Roy Matthews, who had moved to South Africa in 1967, was now assistant coach at Arcadia Shepherds. I remember at the time thinking how odd it was for a pro club to bear the name Shepherds. I imagined the coach standing on the sidelines with a long shepherds' crook, using it to hook off a player when deciding to make a substitution.

Mr Patel then asked me if I liked football and, after I nodded, he told me excitedly that Arcadia Shepherds was his team. He told me they were based in Pretoria, about a seven-hour drive away and that he knew of Roy Matthews. He then told me they were good but were struggling because their excellent keeper, Trevor Gething, had retired. This news was obviously of great interest to me.

I could sense Jim looking at me for an extra-long time before he said: 'You miss the game don't you, Buster?'

'I certainly do, Jim,' I answered.

It was a brief, emotional exchange but Jim quickly said: 'Okay, let's call Roy Matthews in the morning. Sounds like they need a good goalkeeper and that's you my brother.'

Chapter 34

Good Shepherds

THE NEXT morning, I called Roy Matthews and he was everything I hoped for and more. He had a strong Scottish accent and a brilliant sense of humour to match. No doubt our Charlton connection helped because we talked about the club for the first ten minutes, which helped us bond.

Roy suggested I got to Pretoria as soon as possible. He confirmed he was the assistant coach, and the head coach was Kai (pronounced 'Kye') Johansen, a 37-year-old Dane who had played for Glasgow Rangers in the 1960s and won 20 caps for Denmark. He also confirmed Mr Patel's words that the team needed a goalkeeper. Straight after breakfast, I set off.

On the way, I stopped in Durban to buy some boots, a goalkeeper shirt and shorts, long socks and a pair of gloves and, about seven hours later, I was walking through the players' tunnel at the Caledonian Ground, where the Shepherds played. The first-team were nearly finishing practice. Roy and I recognised each other straight away. Kai Johansen was on the pitch practising set plays.

'Have you got your gear with ya laddie?' Roy asked as he jogged towards me.

'Yes mate,' I answered.

'Okay good, get your gear on, Tuttie, and join in the last 20 minutes or so,' directed Roy in his strong Scottish brogue. 'And don't forget to put your gloves on the right hands.' We both smiled at the joke and seemed to have built an instant rapport.

He then said more seriously: 'Good luck son, show Kai how good you really are,' which made me think of my dad back in England.

I trotted over to Kai who welcomed me and said: 'I'm letting the lads go now because I drilled them quite a bit today. We lost last night against AmaZulu and we should have won. Do you fancy trying to stop a few shots from an old timer like me?' Kai was grinning like a Cheshire cat.

Straight away I could tell he was no slouch. For sure, he had put on a few pounds since his playing days but he still looked pretty fit. He was built like a refrigerator. His dark hair was receding and matched his trimmed moustache and brown eyes, which I thought was unusual for someone from Denmark.

Kai warmed my hands by continually and accurately striking the ball firmly towards my upper body before warning me that fiercer shots were coming my way. He told me he had scored the winning goal for Glasgow Rangers in the Scottish FA Cup Final against their bitter rivals, Glasgow Celtic. It was from a free kick 25 yards from goal. 'So, I want to give you the heads up on my brilliant shooting abilities,' he chuckled, laughing at his own immodesty.

In reply, I told him I didn't think Danes could hit a ball very hard and that no Scandinavian had ever scored against me. He laughed at that. I was pleased Kai still had plenty of fun left in him. I could also tell he was not kidding about his ability to strike a ball. He could hit one firmly and with pinpoint accuracy.

This was where it was starting to get serious and I had a choice to make. I could close one eye to try to focus or simply keep both eyes open and follow the ball by moving my head, a bit like looking through a submarine's periscope. I decided to follow the ball by moving my head rather like spectators watching tennis at Wimbledon.

Kai came up close – about six yards away – and finished the warm-up by knocking the ball at me consistently from knee to chest height. It felt good to catch a ball again. He then moved back towards the penalty spot and began hitting some firmer shots straight at me to see if I could catch a ball at a greater speed.

I was feeling comfortable with my new 'Wimbledon' technique, which meant I wasn't relying on my peripheral vision. It was working because I was catching the ball cleanly.

'Okay Graham, I am going to bang some long-distance shots in. Are you ready to pull the ball out of the net son?' Kai laughed.

Obviously, Kai knew about my eye injury and wanted to know if I could see the ball clearly and follow its trajectory from such a long distance. I knew this was the real acid test and I prepared to fly. It had been 16 months since I had dived at full length and hung in the air. Now was the time to find out if I could make such saves again. Kai hit some beauties with both feet but I felt my new technique could cope. There were one or two that got away from me but Kai reminded me that Pretoria was over 4,300 feet above sea level, meaning the air was thinner, which made the ball move more quickly through the air.

That sounds encouraging, I thought.

At last I was growing in confidence. It was starting to feel like Theo and I at the shooting box at Charlton. Kai could certainly whack a ball just like Theo and could bend it in similar fashion too. I was starting to read the flight of the ball and my handling was getting cleaner. Kai sensed it too … me being me I started with some Alex Stepney-style banter.

'Come on Kai, no namby-pamby rubbish. Give me your best shot like the one you scored for Rangers against Celtic in that FA Cup Final a century ago.'

It was a bit of a cocky move on my part but it felt right. I immediately had to raise my game if I was going to live up to my bravado. Then the fireworks started:

'Okay Mr Cockney, game on. Pick this fucker out,' said Kai as he smacked the ball with all his might from 25 yards. With no time to think I launched myself towards my top left-hand corner. Being five foot off the ground and having some hang time felt brilliant again. I was flying at full stretch with my right hand slightly stretching above my left as the ball neared the top-left corner of the goal. With an extra five-inch stretch in me I just managed to get my fingertips on the ball and deflect it over the bar. Kai screamed: 'Brilliant save, you cockney shit head.' With a compliment like that, I knew I had a contract coming my way.

I wondered if I was fully recovered or had I just got lucky? After I showered, we went out for a lobster dinner at a fine restaurant called Bacardi's '73 and Kai insisted we celebrated with a few Lion lagers. Over dinner he said he would like to see me play for the reserves in a practice match against the first-team. I said that was fine as long as we could decide on my future directly afterwards because I felt obliged to get back to my family down on the south coast. I wanted to seal the deal quickly.

I slept like a baby that night. Kai kept me out until 2am but it was worth it. I liked Kai, who reminded me a lot of Theo.

The next day dragged because I was anticipating the inter-squad practice match. I spoke to Jim and Mum and they were all for me playing in South Africa. At that time, I did not understand the politics of apartheid so it's not something that I really considered. I was naïve – as green as the grass – I just wanted to play at a decent level again.

Kai picked me up early from the hotel. I knew he wanted me to do well because he took me on a tour of Pretoria. I certainly liked what I had seen of South Africa so far, although occasionally I would get flashbacks to England and the boot.

The next few hours flew by and now it was time to get down to business. The game kicked off at 7pm and by 7.30pm it was a done deal due to the bad weather and my solid performance. In fact, I had very little to do except for one crucial moment when I had to make a brave dive at someone's feet to retrieve a one-on-one 50/50 ball. It felt good to get that particular save out of the way and I knew I had shown courage diving head first for the ball. As soon as I came up with the ball I looked towards Kai and Roy. They smiled and I smiled back. I had passed the all-important test of my nerve by diving at someone's feet for the ball.

Then the heavens opened. I had never seen rain like it. It almost hurt as it fell fast in heavy drops. It was like a monsoon with lightning bolts electrifying the sky. Being one of the tallest players, I was ready to exit the field and bolt, excuse the pun, towards the dressing rooms.

Once all the players got settled in the dressing room Kai introduced me to the lads, which was another positive sign of approval. I was delighted to see some familiar faces. Arcadia's big-name striker was the Scotsman Gerry Queen who had played for St Mirren, Kilmarnock, Crystal Palace and Leyton Orient. I knew

Gerry from his Palace days. Then there was Maurice Hepworth, a full-back who had played a sprinkling of games for Sunderland and Darlington and looked a decent player, as did another defender, the Yorkshireman Steve Ingle. He was as hard as nails and had enjoyed a good career, mainly with Bradford City and Wrexham. Steve loved to moan, but he was funny with it. Defensively he was brilliant, the type that would have no qualms crunch-tackling his granny if it meant denying her a goalscoring opportunity.

Then I met a skilful midfielder called Alex Morrison who had come through the Glasgow Rangers youth ranks. The other players who had looked more than useful were Spoedie Bronkhorst, Robbie de Graaf, Vincent Julius, Plankie Naude, Dave Herholdt and Nathan Sacks, who I liked a lot. Nathan was all left foot and had the ability to get away with it. His father, Saul Sacks, was the owner of the club and president of Pepsi-Cola for South Africa.

Kai asked me to wait in his office next to the dressing room where I could just about hear him asking the team how they felt about me joining. Fortunately, it was all very positive.

In his broad Yorkshire accent, Steve Ingle said something that made me laugh out loud: 'Tooty's fookin' better than t' keeper wi got. Even if 'e has one dodgy eye, a parrot on't shoulder and a wooden leg like Long John Silver, we should still tekk him.' All the lads laughed out loud.

After that endorsement, Kai dismissed the lads and came to his office as I scrambled to sit down, pretending I hadn't been listening through the wall.

'So, you like it here Graham?' he said, crossing both feet on the edge of his desk and lighting a curved, Sherlock Holmes-type of pipe.

I'd been expecting the question and had rehearsed my spiel: 'Yes I do Kai,' I said. 'Especially if you pay me well, give me a decent long-term contract and look after me. I will not let you down.'

That's a good-enough answer, I thought to myself, still trying not to smile as I thought of myself in goal dressed as Long John Silver.

Kai then said he would offer me a two-year guaranteed contract, a penthouse apartment overlooking the city of Pretoria, a free vehicle, a decent signing-on fee and a worthwhile salary with bonus incentives. The contract would take effect in January, in four months' time.

'You did not mention numbers Kai, and why four months from now?' I asked.

Kai said he had to check some figures with the owner first and, as the season was three-quarters complete, he would sooner get me settled in after Christmas and begin in the New Year, ready for pre-season. Kai said he would know about the numbers the next day and that we'd have a chat over breakfast.

'I'll give you a decent contract, Tuttie, so don't worry about that,' he said with a smile.

We had another night at Bacardi's and, by the end of the evening, were both confident the numbers would work.

Next morning Kai called at 7.30am to tell me he had a contract ready for me to sign. Just 30 minutes later, with Kai ordering us eggs benedict, I read over the agreement. The deal was generous and more than I expected. I could have cried with happiness and did well not to. This was my second chance of a football career and I had to take it. I felt more than grateful. Now I could really enjoy the rest of our vacation.

The seven-hour drive back through some stunning scenery gave me plenty of time to reflect. At first, I kept on looking back and wishing I was still plying my trade in England and, whenever I did that, I saw the boot flying through the air towards my head. But then reality kicked in and I remembered I had a two-year, no-cut contract, a penthouse apartment, a brand-new vehicle and a signing-on bonus and decent salary with incentives. It had been a great vacation and it wasn't over yet. I decided that night I was going to treat my mum, Jim and his family to a lobster dinner and neck a few Lion lagers.

We planned to leave Uvongo in a few days and drive up to see my uncle Bill, Mum's brother, in Benoni for a few nights before leaving for England. I was looking forward to seeing Uncle Bill as he was always a fun character to be around. He had played with us as kids and now made us laugh as adults.

I remembered when I was 11 – Uncle Bill, and his wife, Aunt Maria with their three sons saying their final goodbyes at our house in Brockley before leaving England for South Africa. I remembered Uncle Bill giving me the longest goodbye hug and telling me he loved me very much. I remembered thinking there and then that if ever I had a son, I would call him Bill or Billy in recognition of my uncle Bill. That's how much I loved him.

As I would now be spending some time in South Africa, I felt I needed to educate myself on the country. I had more than a few concerns about the apartheid situation and I wanted to understand it. I remember reading a report in a Pretoria newspaper about Steve Biko, an anti-apartheid activist, dying in unexplained circumstances during an interrogation by police. It was not entirely clear how he died but a number of things didn't stack up. I further read he was reportedly the 21st black person to die in police custody over the last 12 months.

Because my understanding of the situation was limited, I was also scared there might be a revolution in South Africa which would be frightening. Kai had mentioned Arcadia Shepherds' league was going multi-racial the next season. Previously there had been separate leagues for black and white teams. Kai added that Arcadia would be one of the first white teams to sign three black players and then play in Soweto, a township just a few hours away, where over a million black people lived, many in squalid conditions. Kai emphasised that playing in Soweto was going to be a historical and probably nervy experience. That would be an understatement.

The next few days flew by and, before we knew it, Mum and I were back in London. It had been a brilliant trip. I had secured a contract and would be ready to play in four months. It was a vacation that carved out a new chapter in my life following a chance meeting in a hotel. I felt alive again. Thank you, wherever you are, Mr Patel. You did me proud, sir.

Chapter 35

Playing (and Drinking) with Faversham

I HAD 16 weeks before I was due to return to South Africa and felt the need to get match fit. I needed to stay sharp and prove my display at the trial wasn't a flash in the pan. I also wanted to keep busy. I had learned that periods of inactivity were not good for me as I would start to mull over past events and that was unhealthy.

I could not play in the English Football League anymore because there had been two insurance payouts; one received by Charlton that was rumoured to be £50,000 for my injury and the other a one-off cheque for £750 for me from the Football League, which I felt was derisory considering my lost earnings.

I then heard through the footballing grapevine that a semi-professional club called Faversham Town were looking for a goalkeeper. Faversham is a lovely quaint town in Kent and famous as the home of Britain's oldest brewery, Shepherd Neame.

The Faversham coach was Tommy Coulter, a big-time Charlton supporter. We liked each other straight away so for the next three months I practised three times a week and played on average two matches per week. Getting match fit was the goal.

I quickly realised it was much tougher being a semi-pro footballer than a full-time pro. Most semi-pro lads work all day before arriving half exhausted to practise. Some would work on a Saturday morning and then play in the afternoon. For this reason, I have a tremendous amount of respect for the serious semi-professional player.

I mentioned that Faversham was a town well known for its brewing and early on I thought that the players were doing their best to drink the brewery dry. The majority would meet in a pub called The Ship opposite Faversham Town's ground at noon. They were not shy about guzzling several pints of beer and then thinking they were ready to play a few hours of football. It was crazy stuff.

I did it a few times before my conscience got the better of me and I stopped before it became a habit. Also, the fact most of us were puffing away on cigarettes did not help our cause. We had a lot of fun but I felt awkward about drinking and smoking while the whole point was to get fit for my contract with Arcadia Shepherds. After a few weeks I came to the obvious conclusion you can't function 100 per cent when you are burning the candle at both ends and stopped the boozing and smoking.

I think a lot of this boozing had to do with the players' own frustrations at being good footballers but not quite good enough to play at a higher level. A lot of the lads were simply drinking their careers away and not progressing like they could have. I tried to understand why they would sabotage themselves like that. It was bewildering.

Nevertheless, I was thankful for my Faversham experience and pleased that, eventually, I was able to maintain a decent level of fitness. I was ready for my move to South Africa just after Christmas in 1977. I knew 1978 was going to be a crucial year in my effort to get back on top.

Saying goodbye to my family was especially difficult. I was still only 21 but going to South Africa felt the right thing for me to do. I knew I had to get out of England. If I had not left London I would have been forever living in the past and endlessly reminiscing on the glory days of being a Charlton goalkeeper. I didn't want that. I could have ended up very bitter indeed.

Meanwhile, for all you romantics out there, any serious friendship with Nurse Hilary had fizzled out. The distance between Sunderland and London proved too far and we were both focused on our careers. We kept in touch and she became good friends with our family. To this day, once a year, Hilary travels from Sunderland to Kent and stays with my sister Julie and her brilliant husband Kevin in Sittingbourne.

Hilary was, and still is, my Florence Nightingale. After being a staff nurse, she moved into occupational therapy and then became a Macmillan nurse working in the Sunderland community looking after the elderly with cancer, giving medication and injections. We have remained friends and I feel so grateful that she was there when I needed her and helped me through such a difficult period in my life.

Chapter 36

A Nightmare In Windhoek

WE HAD three weeks of intense training before our first – and nearly my last pre-season game. It was truly an unbelievable experience. We were playing a friendly in Windhoek (pronounced, 'Vind-hook') in Namibia, south-west Africa. To get there we had to fly over the Kalahari Desert for nearly three hours. It was a total nightmare from start to finish.

The club had an arrangement with a local private airline. The plane was not impressive. The four-propeller engine looked like it came out of World War II and had the appearance of a big hairdryer with a couple of wings bolted on. It looked like it should have retired to a museum for old planes years ago. The seats were not arranged conventionally. Instead, there were two 30-foot-long wooden benches, with only thin padding, facing each other, running down the length of both sides of the fuselage. For back support we had to lean against the curved shell of the fuselage. There were no windows. You would have thought we were about to parachute over Germany at the end of World War II. That may actually have been preferable to what followed.

I asked Gerry Queen whether this was our normal mode of transport to matches or were we preparing for a parachute jump.

Gerry half laughed and told me Kai organised these so-called 'goodwill matches' to promote our club and the game in South Africa. He said the opposition guaranteed a sum of money for us to simply show up and play their local pro team. Kai fancied himself as a pioneer for the game and our club which meant we played in some odd places, explained Gerry, before adding with a grimace: 'And we've played in some very odd places indeed.'

Even the everyday task of boarding the plane was bizarre. We had to ascend a six-foot painter's-style ladder to a single door opening. On clambering in, I asked our sweaty, rather overweight pilot when the plane had been built. His answer did not inspire me with confidence. 'About 1943,' he answered blankly.

The pilot then added, mischievously: 'It still has four propellers. At least it did the last time I checked.' He then giggled like a schoolgirl while checking some of the overhead switches. I was pleased he had a sense of humour but was not relishing the journey one bit.

After a wobbly and somewhat uncertain take-off in our winged hairdryer we left Johannesburg behind to fly over the Kalahari Desert. And that's when we began to suffer some serious turbulence. And when I say serious, I mean turbulence like you've never known. We were told by our captain, who was now drenched in even more sweat but still giggling, that our plane's violent 'ups and downs' were created by the intense heat coming from the differing heights of the vast sand dunes of the Kalahari Desert. The plane was like a yo-yo, violently jerking up and down. I noticed a few of the players had gone very quiet and were starting to look distinctly greyish and queasy.

Within ten minutes we were, to a man, all throwing up. The only receptacles we had to be sick into and prevent an utter mess were some thin brown grocery store bags. In fact, nearly all of us were vomiting for the majority of the three-hour flight. There was no steward/stewardess, no food and no drinks served. Nothing offered at all – just plenty of grocery store bags for each of us. Infuriatingly, I could still hear the pilot giggling over the noise of the engine and our retching. I'm so pleased he found it funny.

To say this was a budget airline was the understatement of the year. Between bouts of throwing up, Kai was getting verbal stick from all of us. We honestly felt so nauseous that we thought we were going to die – that's if the plane didn't crash and kill us first, which felt a distinct possibility.

Eventually, we landed on a sandy runway located on the edge of the desert. The sand was yellow, our faces were green which reminded me of Norwich City's kit. No one felt like playing football. We had empty stomachs and felt totally dehydrated. When the side door panel was forced open, we were assaulted by a temperature of 102 degrees Fahrenheit. The sweating, giggling airman who had piloted this excuse for a plane began scrabbling around for the stepladder for us to disembark. But we couldn't wait and we all jumped five feet out of the door to the ground. We all wanted off asap.

We agreed that there was no way we were going back on the same plane and pleaded with Kai to organise another. But first we had a football match to play and we were all feeling half dead. The next problem was getting to the stadium and I prayed that, magically, Charlton's luxury team bus would emerge from the desert haze and take us to our destination. But it didn't.

It was almost funny when a misfiring, multi-coloured hand-painted school bus chugged up alongside the plane accompanied by a battered-looking dusty police car ready to escort us to the stadium. The 15-minute non-air-conditioned ride in searing heat went very slowly indeed. None of us spoke at all except Kai, who was manfully trying to assure us that things would get better.

When we entered the stadium, we all appeared totally bemused and I heard someone mutter under his breath 'what the fuck?' The stadium seating structure was made entirely out of cheap, wooden scaffolding, enough to seat up to 10,000 people. It was a most peculiar sight. It looked more like a shipyard than a football stadium.

The all-black crowd was chanting their team's name while vigorously bouncing up and down on the scaffolding. The plank seating extended the whole length of the field and about 30 rows up on both sides of the poor-quality pitch. The structure looked like a precarious house of cards. The carpentry and workmanship were not good. Cross-beam planks had been hammered into each other for support. It looked like a disaster waiting to happen.

There was no grass at all on the pitch. I didn't really know what it was. It was a mixture of dirt and sand that had been raked, mixed together and then rolled flat. The crossbar was tilted at one end because one goalpost was a foot higher than the other. My technical drawing master at Roger Manwood School would not have been impressed! The goalposts were painted red and white like a stick of candy. The goal nets looked handmade. The pitch markings were hand-sprayed in red. If we hadn't felt so sick, we would have been laughing our heads off.

Our senior player, Steve Ingle, screamed in his strong Yorkshire accent: 'Let's get this fookin' game over with.' I couldn't have put it better myself. We all wanted to get the hell out of there as soon as possible. There were no changing facilities so we used our bus, which looked like it had been painted by a hippy that had been taking too many hallucinogenic drugs. Then it got even weirder.

The opposing team was on the field ready to kick-off. I began doing some stretching in the goal area when to my utter horror a witch doctor jumped out from behind my goal. To say I was shocked would not even begin to describe my reaction. He was dressed in full witch-doctor garb with rattling bones around his neck and an animal skull for his headdress. Staring intently at me, the witch doctor produced something from behind his back and held it high and triumphantly above him. It was a dead chicken. I knew it was dead because it was minus its head!

I was startled to realise that the witch doctor seemed to be fascinated by me and proceeded to do a most peculiar dance in my penalty area. Then to my horror he began sprinkling red liquid in my goal area. As he once again held aloft the chicken, I realised with some alarm it was the poor bird's blood.

It was utterly surreal and so far out of my sphere of understanding that all I could do was stand there with my mouth wide open as he chanted and sprang around me in the goal area. Because I didn't understand the cultural significance of the dance, I didn't know whether the witch doctor was being aggressive or not. But I then made the mistake of trying to kick some dirt over the chicken blood in the goalmouth area. This angered the witch doctor who, in truth, hadn't looked particularly happy at any point during his routine. He wagged his finger from right to left at me and shouted something in my direction in his native tongue. I had displeased him so I sheepishly backed off with an apologetic and submissive two-hand gesture.

The witch doctor continued to eye me warily as he exited stage left and I wondered if I was going to end up on the post-game menu, and that in a week's time, he'd be wearing my bones around his neck. I half expected him to pull on a number nine shirt and appear in the match. As the witch doctor departed the scene, I couldn't help but wonder if I'd imagined what I'd just witnessed.

Fortunately, before things could get any crazier, we kicked off with an overwhelming aural backdrop of ear-splitting, high-pitched whistling. Within 20 minutes we were 3-0 down and were being roughed up badly. The pitch soon churned up and became uneven, making it impossible to pass or dribble.

After their third goal, Gerry Queen faked an injury so we could regroup and talk about what we could do to stop us from being beaten up so badly. The opposition, from the off, had been kicking the crap out of us with lethal tackles. It was almost like playing on the bombsite again when I was a young lad.

Kai apologised to us in our team huddle but that didn't mean anything to anyone by then. We all wanted to run off but were cautious not to upset the home fans who, by this time, seemed to number close to 20,000 and were hanging off every possible part of the stadium. It was chaotic.

Gerry devised a plan for us to spread out as far as possible and kick the ball long and wide. Total football it wasn't but it was necessary to prevent getting caught with the ball at our feet by our opposing hit men! We agreed not to run with the ball but to stay in our designated areas. We discovered that trying to dribble the ball down the field was near suicide. Our legs became heavy very quickly and gave our friendly opponents ample opportunities to take us down from behind. Within ten minutes Gerry's strategy proved successful. We managed to pull two goals back before half-time making it 3-2 in their favour.

The half-time activities were also an experience. We were used to a cup of tea or a slice of orange. Now another interesting character emerged. He was the local chief dressed in all his splendour. He had bones through his nose and ears and was wearing a most interesting cloak for protection from the sun. On closer inspection we realised it was a full-length lion skin which I certainly had never seen on the streets of Brockley. You have to realise that these were different times and we were less aware of different cultures and traditions than we are today and, because of that, maybe less respectful. But the chief was a friendly sort. He moved towards us with his lion skin swaying and offered us a huge plate of various fruits and some cooked meat of unknown origin. A 1970s joke alert! As the chief offered the plate, Steve Ingle, wryly quipped in his Bradford brogue, 'The meat's probably the chief's moother-in-law.'

The fruit was welcome and I scoffed a few bananas to get something in my stomach and gulped what conceivably could have been goat's milk. I felt too thirsty to ask too many questions and I did not trust the grey-looking water offered from an old metal bucket.

A marching band had now assembled on the crooked halfway line. It was ten African warriors bashing their drums in unison. It sounded quite impressive. A running joke was that we were going to be sacrificed for dinner. It was our way of easing the tension and was not meant to insult our hosts. Kai said: 'Don't worry lads it's not their tribal pre-dinner song.' He was trying his best to make us laugh, but no one did.

We confirmed our tactics for the second half, which were to stay as far away from each other as possible and kick long. No short passes or dribbling. We would stretch them as wide as we could and shoot on sight from anywhere because the ball would make some unpredictable bounces in front of the goalkeeper, which we'd follow up.

As we prepared to start the second half, Kai told us to avoid any tackling or fouling as we didn't want to rile our hosts.

Sure enough, our plan worked. Within ten minutes we had made it 3-3. Then a few minutes later their huge defender, wearing a painted number five on front of his shirt, and looking more like a basketball player than a footballer, chopped down Gerry from behind in the box. The referee instantly blew for a penalty kick. Then another amazing incident occurred.

The big number five walked over to the referee and punched him on the side of his head. The poor ref went down like a sack of potatoes and was out like a light.

For a second the world stood still. Gerry was first on the scene and gestured to our trainer Tony Caron to come over and attend to the spread-eagled official.

After a few minutes the referee started to come around. The offender started yelling at him in his native tongue and then gave the ref his whistle back, which he had dropped. We all waited for the ref to send the big man off. Astonishingly, he didn't.

Instead, the groggy, bamboozled ref blew his whistle and pointed to the corner. He had been persuaded to change his mind and was awarding our team a corner kick instead of a penalty. The fans were starting to get very excited, bouncing around on the precarious wooden scaffolding which did not look structurally safe.

The referee, obviously terrified by the man mountain, collapsed like the proverbial blancmange. He had now lost control completely. The two linesmen were no use and cowered meekly more than 20 yards away, clearly not wanting to be involved. Obviously, these officials lived locally, and feared the worst for themselves or their families if they argued with the big feller. It turned out the number five ruled the roost. He was the only local policeman and it was him and his beaten-up police car who had escorted us from the dirt runway to the stadium where he parked in front of our team bus.

The atmosphere was now starting to become a little scarier. The crowd was getting restless that their side had thrown away a 3-0 lead. From the corner kick Vincent Julius, who could bend a ball like few others, curled the ball straight in the goal. The ref had no choice but to give the goal. We were now 4-3 up. Our opposition were in shock and so were the fans as an eerie silence descended.

We had now taken control of the game. We had that professional edge our opponents lacked. Gerry's plan of stretching them across the width and length of the field was working perfectly and we banged in two more goals in the last 15 minutes.

We were now 6-3 up and the crowd was getting even more restless. It was starting to feel dangerous, with some bottles being thrown on to the pitch.

Kai had moved to the far end of the players' bench, closer to my goal, and then went down on both knees, cupped his hands around his mouth and shouted towards me in a panic three times: 'Tuttie, let them score.'

I was totally taken aback and shook my head defiantly. No way was I going to throw any goals in. My pride would not let me do it. Looking back maybe this was a foolish move.

By this time, Kai, our trainer, and the scared subs were ready to make a run for the bus. Kai was imploring the referee to end the game but he was ignored.

To me the safest place was on the field so we continued to play with a cautious eye on the angry crowd and the other on the bus for a quick getaway. The big question was whether we would try to hold on for five more minutes until the end of the game. Our minds were quickly made up when we heard the driver starting the bus at Kai's demand. Finally, the referee also realised it would be best to end the game. No doubt he was also concerned for his own safety.

I abandoned my spare pair of gloves and cap in my goal and sprinted like Usain Bolt towards the 'explosion in a paint factory' bus, knowing I would be the last on board because I was simply the furthest player away. Like Bolt I had my arms and legs pumping like pistons and a petrified look on my face. It was the fastest time for 60 yards I've ever recorded. The bus was starting to move as I lunged through the closing doors screaming, 'I'm in. Go driver, go. Thank you, thank you, let's fucking go.'

Almost instantly rocks started to rain down, smashing against the side of the bus. A few side windows gave way followed by another rock coming through the back window.

'Oh God, please let us out get of here safely,' was my one and only prayer.

Apart from our courageous driver, we were all crouched under the seats fearing the worst. I was under the front seat and facing one of our new black players who was starting to panic as more rocks began hitting the bus and the terrifying sound of breaking windows made us even more afraid. My black team-mate began to scream, 'They're going to kill us.' I locked hands and eyes with him and urged him to calm down and not panic like the rest of us! He then started to pray in his native tongue and I joined him.

The heroic driver pressed his foot down heavily on the gas pedal. We were on our way to the airport and didn't even wait for our crooked police chief to escort us in his beaten-up vehicle. It was the longest 15-minute drive of my life. When we arrived at the dirt runway, around a dozen soldiers, presumably waiting for their own military plane to arrive, escorted us straight on to our old flying crate. We never thought we would be so happy to get back on that rickety old plane. Fortunately, the pilot had refuelled and was ready to roll. Never have I been so scared and so pleased to be taking off in such a deathtrap of a plane.

'That was fun,' shouted Kai as the plane took off. He was met with total silence. We just looked at each other in disbelief at what had just happened. 'Anyone missing?' was Kai's next line. With great relief we realised we had all made it. We were alive! That was the last of our out-of-town promotional games. No more pioneering matches for us, we all chimed. Even Kai agreed, mumbling, 'I think we'll play in the bigger cities from now on lads.'

Chapter 37
Apartheid

WHEN I first arrived in South Africa, I knew very little about apartheid. I vaguely knew it involved segregation but I quickly learned how fundamental it was to South African society and also how controversial it was, to say the least. I knew it was deeply frowned upon by most parts of the world so I realised I needed to educate myself. I discovered it had been established in 1948 and was based on white supremacy, which meant that South Africa was dominated politically, socially and economically by the minority white population. It also involved a caste system where whites had the highest status followed by Asians, and black South Africans occupying the bottom rung of society.

I fundamentally disagreed with this system. In my youthful naïveté and to rationalise the enormity of it, I compared it to a playground bully but on a horrific scale. During my time I personally witnessed some things which were simply unacceptable to me.

I lived in an apartment complex where a young black lad was employed as what was termed a 'garden boy'. He was nicknamed 'Flash' because of his quick and efficient work ethic. Flash was also a huge Arcadia Shepherds fan. He was a fantastic lad who would wash my car without being asked and then politely refuse my offers to pay him. Flash loved to talk about Arcadia Shepherds especially when he heard I was their new goalkeeper. To show my appreciation I happily gave him a couple of tickets here and there to some of our games.

For one game, I offered to take Flash to the match myself, along with two other team-mates I used to pick up for home games. Flash was in heaven rubbing shoulders with the Arcadia players and chatting excitedly about our season. After the game, he waited outside the players' entrance to thank me for taking him and giving him a ticket. He was such a lovely fellow. I offered to drop Flash off at the bus station to catch the bus that would take him to his 'location'. Each tribe, whether Bantu, Zulu, Xhosa or Indian (Pakistani Indian), lived in designated townships or 'locations'. Incredibly they were told where they could and could not live and were barred from residing in cities like Pretoria or Johannesburg, which were dominated by the white Afrikaners.

Flash gladly accepted a ride and, as we were all peckish, I offered to pick up a takeaway from a hamburger joint. I could tell he liked that idea as he clapped his hands gleefully. I went into the burger restaurant without Flash because that was unfortunately the accepted protocol. About 15 minutes later, I came out with our meal to discover three white Afrikaner policemen brutally laying into him. They had dragged him from the back seat of my car and were beating him across the head and back with their long sticks known to us as truncheons. They were about to toss him into their van when I intervened.

I told them Flash was with me and asked one of the policemen why they had beaten him up. Speaking in a heavy Afrikaans accent he replied that the 'kaffir' did not have a pass to be in the city of Pretoria after 7pm and that he would spend the night in jail.

I was horrified that such harsh, violent action would be meted out over a simple pass. I pleaded with the police officer to see sense, explaining that I had invited Flash to the game, and that he was a good person, who worked at my apartments. I offered to take Flash to the bus station or even back to his home because he was so badly beaten. The officer gave me short shrift, threatened me with 'obstruction of justice' and said I would be joining Flash in a cell if I intervened any further. At that point I backed off in genuine fear of being their next punch bag.

I felt so angry about the incident that I called the Pretoria Police Department when I got home to complain. When the operator heard why I was calling he kept me on hold until I gave up waiting for someone to pick up. So, this was apartheid in action! To my eyes it was nothing short of state-controlled suppression sustained by fear and violence.

Another example of the dreadful apartheid system was brought home to me when we played a pre-season exhibition game in Port Elizabeth. Kai had recently signed three very talented black players – Selby Busang, 'Gumshoes' Lewis and Vincent 'Tanti' Julius. We were traditionally an all-white club so this was breaking new ground and it was very controversial. All three were great players, good guys who spoke excellent English and blended seamlessly into our system of play.

The night before the game, Kai was checking us in to our hotel, when the hotel clerk stopped dead in his tracks as he realised that Selby, Lewis and Vincent were with our party. The clerk nervously called the hotel manager who was in his back office. They spoke softly for a few seconds and then the manager marched out of his lair and announced that the white members of the team could stay in the hotel but the three black players would have to stay somewhere else because blacks were prohibited from staying in the hotel.

Kai and the rest of us were up in arms. Kai threatened that our squad, a party of about 25 people, would leave for another hotel and they would lose our business. The hotel manager simply walked over to the automatic sliding doors at the main entrance, and pointed towards the parking lot as if to say 'fine, you can all leave now'. This we did, with some well-chosen insults thrown at the manager as we left.

Kai found another hotel not too far away. This time we wised up. We checked in while our black friends hid on the bus. Then we smuggled them through the back entrance up a fire escape and into their rooms. The next day, as we were leaving for the game, Kai was thanking the manager for his hospitality. At that very moment, to the horror of the manager, Selby, Lewis and Vincent sauntered slowly with the rest of us out of the hotel's front entrance. Being a bit of a wag, Selby remarked loudly how wonderful and soft his bed had been. Then the three of them held up their hands as if they had just scored a goal. We cheered them all the way to the bus. It was the first time they had stayed the night in an all-white hotel. We were delighted for them. It may only have been a small victory in the grand scheme of things but it pleased us to think we were subverting a rotten system.

Mixed marriages were strictly forbidden in South Africa with serious jail time for both parties if this law was broken. On our team we had a white guy who I'm going to call 'Sniffer' who had come from England to play for us. Within a few months he fell in love with a black girl who worked in a downtown restaurant during the day. Because she could not stay overnight in Pretoria, Sniffer moved to her township location to be with her. Sniffer was protected by a tight-lipped community which kept it quiet for the sake of his girlfriend and her family who would have suffered the consequences. The community grew to love Sniffer because he went undercover as a taxi driver and gave free rides, when going back and forth to Pretoria with his girl, to her friends and family members who needed to hitch a ride to downtown. Sniffer ended up marrying the girl in England and then moved back to South Africa to live in her township. If Sniffer and his girl had been discovered they would have both been beaten, given jail time and Sniffer permanently ejected from the country. Not one person in the township ever squealed on Sniffer. He risked a lot for love and triumphed in the end.

Every three months I had to go to the South African Embassy to get my visa renewed. It was a real pain in the neck and each time I went, I got grief. I had to book an appointment with this little Afrikaner who always wore a powder-blue polyester safari suit and had his comb tucked in the top of his knee-high matching powder-blue socks. It was not a look I would choose myself. I would try and sweet-talk him by offering tickets to one of our games but it never worked, simply because he preferred rugby. He also openly begrudged signing my visa, claiming I was taking a job away from another South African. It was only because our owner was well known as the president of Pepsi-Cola, and hired hundreds of Afrikaners for his plant, that Safari Suit man was willing to approve my visa. He wanted me to know he was doing me a huge favour each time he signed my papers. I soon came to the conclusion that Afrikaners only liked other Afrikaners. Even though I had a contract with a decent pro sports team it didn't cut much ice with this power-hungry little man.

Another example of Afrikaner bias came after we had signed the three black lads I mentioned before. Our stadium, the Caledonian Ground, was owned by the city of Pretoria and therefore fell under Afrikaner rule. When the city authorities learned that Kai had signed some black players, they threatened to cancel our lease and eject us from our stadium. Their petition to evict us nearly went through and it was only our owner coming to the rescue with his various political connections that saved us. It goes without saying that our owner was also an Afrikaner.

A few afternoons a week I coached soccer and cricket at a local high school. It was fun, kept me busy and reflected well on our club in the community. One afternoon, I was coaching soccer when I heard a short screech of brakes followed by the awful crunching sound of two cars hitting each other. It sounded like a head-on collision. I sprinted to the nearest phone to call the emergency services and after more than ten rings the operator picked up and I asked for an ambulance and gave our location. Then the operator asked if the people injured were white or black. I was confused at first. What a stupid question to ask and why did it matter was my immediate thought. The operator then explained with alarming straightforwardness that there were two types of emergency services – one for white people and one for black people. I told the operator I did not know because all I heard was a horrible crash. The operator said she would hold while I found out what colour the injured people were. I pretended to shout to somebody to ask and then just made it up that there was one white person and one black person injured. I thought I could not go wrong with that answer.

The ambulance for the so-called white person turned up within ten minutes while the ambulance for the black person took nearly 30 minutes. Fortunately, no one was killed or seriously hurt and it turned out to be two black drivers involved. Astonishingly – and to my utter disgust – the ambulance intended for the white victim left the scene empty when they found out there was no white person involved. I was beside myself. Did it really matter that much that the injured drivers were both black? Clearly in this mixed-up nation, it did. That was an experience I'll never ever forget. As a symbol of South Africa's perverse racial politics, it was a striking example.

Towards the end of my second season with Arcadia Shepherds I felt that South Africa, and Pretoria especially, was a racial cauldron ready to boil over with bloodshed and violence. I know if I were black I would have felt utter animosity towards the white population.

A girl called Betty came to my apartment three times a week to clean and do my washing for only 80 rand a week, which was next to nothing. One day I asked her if she thought there would eventually be bloodshed between the whites and blacks. Without hesitation she nodded. Betty went on to explain that she liked me very much because I treated her with respect and was kind but her brother who did not know me would have no problem in killing me. That was a sobering admission when statistically the black population outnumbered the whites by seven to one.

The Afrikaners and, to my sadness, many Europeans who moved to South Africa adopted the apartheid ways quickly and openly. I was sickened when I saw some of the European men and women bossing around their cleaning girl or gardener who were being paid a pittance. I witnessed some of my brother's workmates, who were British, saying and doing derogatory things to their black workers. These are things I'm sure they would not have dreamed of saying back in the UK. Often it was the men but the wives were just as guilty. All of a sudden, they realised they could lord it over black people with great power and importance. Their arrogance made me sick. Some wives would boast about slapping 'their girl' if they stepped out of line or did something wrong. It was cruel, pitiful and disgusting. And it happened way too frequently for my liking.

Before I arrived, South African soccer had been segregated with separate white and black leagues. White fans would attend but that all changed when the leagues amalgamated. In my first season, teams were either all black or all white but, during my second season, players of both colours were now being transferred meaning black and white players became team-mates, which you would have thought was excellent for the sport and racial harmony. However, the Afrikaners and most Europeans turned their backs on South African soccer and focused on rugby instead. The majority of the black population loved soccer but it seemed that many ignorant white people decided they were too good to sit in a stadium alongside black fans. As our season progressed the white fan base dropped off and no white fan would ever consider going to watch a game in a black township. It was such an education for me.

Ironically, going multi-racial with our league did not help politically at first. FIFA had expelled South Africa from soccer in 1976, the year before I arrived. The expulsion was triggered by the Soweto uprising and it was not until 1992 that South Africa was readmitted to FIFA after apartheid was abolished.

While I was there the situation was quite volatile. The supporters in the townships were extremely passionate and crowds of 40,000 to 50,000 were not infrequent. They desperately wanted to see their home team beat teams that were historically white. It represented a microcosm of their struggle and a desire to see the underdog triumph. It was a chance to release some pent-up emotion when their team beat a white team on their home turf. And when this happened all hell would break loose. It was simply a reflection of the racial temperature of the whole country and it took me some time to understand it.

Another interesting event was an exhibition game against the famous Kaiser Chiefs – the best team in South Africa – where we got hammered 5-0. Any incentive to perform was removed when each of us was guaranteed a decent payout to play whether we won or lost. The second reason for not performing to the standard we would usually set ourselves was that the majority of us broke curfew and sneaked out to a disco to party until the small hours the night before. We felt we deserved to let off some steam because we had just finished three weeks of pre-season training where we had worked our socks off. We were totally unprepared emotionally and physically with most of us nursing a huge hangover. We did not realise it but we were entering a lion's den of 25,000 or more hyped-up fans ready to witness their team demolish a bunch of out-of-towners.

We were 4-0 down at half-time and no one wanted to come out for the second half. It was blazing hot and we just wanted to get the match over and done with as soon as possible.

The opposite must be said of the Kaiser Chiefs. They were magnificent and put on a true exhibition with tricks and flicks that would not have been out of place in a circus. The fans were bouncing with excitement when their star striker executed a perfect bicycle kick leaving me rooted to the ground watching the ball clip the underside of the crossbar to enter the top right-hand corner of the goal.

We all learned a lesson that day and to rub salt into our wounds we had to wait over three hours in the dressing room until the crowds had finished celebrating and dispersed. It taught us never to go out partying before a game again and we realised you had to prepare professionally and properly for every single match, whether an exhibition game or a regular league match.

I like to think my two-season stay in South Africa from early 1978 to late 1979 happened during crucial years for the game. Pro soccer could have easily folded. The Afrikaners, and the government, had turned their backs on soccer like the majority of white Europeans and the game was surviving through the enthusiasm of supporters in the townships and some very brave team owners who were also wise businessmen. They loved the game and rode out the apartheid storm until 1992 when FIFA reopened its doors to South African soccer. But those first few multi-racial seasons in the late 70s, while I was playing there, were an unforgettable experience. Yes, they could be scary at times, but we felt right on the cusp of change and it was a tremendously exciting historical time.

Chapter 38
Clever Trevor

WHEN I arrived in South Africa I was not quite as fit as I thought and most certainly not in the right frame of mind for professional sport. I was burning the candle at both ends, chasing girls, drinking beer, smoking cigarettes and struggling mentally to get myself back. My match-day confidence was suffering because I knew I was doing all the wrong things off the field. Quite simply, I found I just didn't care as much as I did when I was at Charlton. Maybe my drive had gone? Possibly I was still subconsciously worrying about my eye and my vision.

Kai sensed this and hired a highly respected goalkeeping coach called Roy Bailey to work with me. Roy had enjoyed a great career with Crystal Palace and Ipswich Town, where he won the First Division Championship under Alf Ramsey before emigrating to South Africa in 1964. There was no doubt Roy knew his stuff and had the nous to get me firing on all cylinders again.

Another big plus for Roy was the credibility he gained from coaching his son Gary who had stayed at my mum and dad's house in London the night before he went to Manchester United for a trial. Gary was a fine young goalkeeper who spent several seasons as United's first choice. He earned a great reputation at the same time I felt I should have been rising to prominence in the game. Maybe I felt it could have been me in his shoes if it had not been for my eye injury. Maybe the regret I was carrying had become too heavy and I just did not know it.

Roy knew his stuff but, as a coach, I found him a little too technical. He wanted to change my style so much that I felt I was losing my goalkeeping instinct and mojo. I became confused about my positioning and my stance for take-off dives. When I began thinking too much, I started to trip myself up emotionally and my game started to suffer. It was mostly a problem in my head.

The other problem was that my contract was guaranteed for two years so maybe I was getting complacent and simply treading water. Frankly, my work ethic and attitude were not good enough. Towards the end of my first season in South Africa I was so worried about my overall play I went to see an eye specialist thinking he could advise me in some way. The truth was I was still seeing double. It was not as bad as it had been but it certainly wasn't right.

The specialist came to the conclusion that half the lower muscles in my right eye were ruptured and not functioning at all and that no operation could fix it. He suggested reprogramming myself to move my head instead of my eyes, the 'Wimbledon' technique which I'd stopped doing to some degree. The specialist also suggested that racquetball and table tennis would be good activities for me to consciously move my head instead of my eyes. It was a good suggestion. I saw this specialist without the club's knowledge as I feared they could cancel my contract on medical grounds.

Soon the penny dropped, as they say. I had muddled through the first season by closing my bad right eye slightly, then closing it fully sometimes, sometimes not closing it at all and then trying to do the 'Wimbledon' method. I had bamboozled myself. With Roy trying to change my goalkeeping technique it was becoming even more confusing.

So, for two months in the off-season I played a lot of racquetball, tennis and ping pong for several hours each day hoping to retrain my brain to move my head and not rely on my peripheral vision. It was like learning a completely new life skill – like writing with your non-writing hand – and was very difficult at first.

I also helped myself by talking through every movement as it was happening. I told myself during a game to keep my head steady and level, to move my head not my eyes and, most importantly of all, not to rely on my peripheral vision. By then Roy had left the club to be a television colour commentator for one of South Africa's networks.

Gradually, I felt my timing getting better. Another big positive came when the club hired former Arcadia Shepherds and Springbok goalkeeping legend Trevor Gething to work with me at the start of my second season. Trevor was an unbelievable goalkeeper in his prime, quite possibly the greatest goalkeeper South Africa has ever produced. He quickly became an incredible influence on me.

Trevor would work with me for only 90 minutes four days a week but he would work me so hard that the games became a piece of cake. My fitness over the next three months became even better than in my Charlton days. I felt like Superman again and I owe so much to Trevor. He saved my career, which was going south quickly before he came on the scene.

Here is an example of how Trevor would start our session. He would have me lying face down in the middle of the goal, my head towards him. Trevor would have a dozen soccer balls about ten yards out, close at hand so there was no let-up. Each command he gave had to be executed swiftly and immediately. This is how it went:

Trevor: 'Ready to die, Graham … and where would you like to be buried son? Here we go.

'Up and touch your right post.'

From lying flat on my chest, I'd get up and run as fast as I could go to touch the post, then …

'Forward roll' then 'backward roll' (a quick backward roll throws your balance off) … then

'360 spin' then 'Shot' … at this point Trevor would throw the ball three to four yards from my reach so I had to dive. He would then throw a second ball to dive for immediately after the first dive …

Then: 'Touch the crossbar' … then a 'forward roll', a 'backward roll', 'turn 360', then more quick-fire bullet shots. Then he would try and trick me by inviting a high-five which would draw me off my goal line and he would throw a high looping ball over my head forcing me to sprint back towards the goal and launch myself backwards like a high jumper reaching four to five feet off the ground in an almighty effort to tip the ball over the bar.

This entire drill was repeated four times, very quickly. I would rest for 30 seconds and then repeat the drills three more times, which equated to 12 minutes of full-on pressure training. It was incredibly hard at first. And this was just the start of our 90-minute session.

Trevor worked me non-stop from start to finish. He would never talk about technique. Just stop the ball from going in was his deal: 'It doesn't matter if you stop the ball with your cock as long as you stop it,' he would often say, which would make me laugh.

He would drop kick a succession of crosses into the box from both sides of the pitch. My job was to call 'keeper', venture to the penalty spot or beyond and claim the crossed ball at its highest point. No punching the ball was allowed. After executing over 100 crosses I got into a confident rhythm. I later discovered coming off my line for five or six crosses in a match was easy in comparison.

Trevor would make me dive continuously, like a sideways diving frog, catching the ball and instantly throwing it back to his hands after I landed while moving forward five yards each time from one end of the field to the other and then the same going back, totalling 200 yards of diving sideways.

Next were rapid-fire 'bullet-shots' from the penalty spot. Trevor would strike the next ball as I was clambering to my feet from the previous dive. Pure reflex saves were demanded. Most of the time I didn't know how I stopped the ball because they happened so quickly and some simply flashed past me into the net.

It was incredibly difficult, at first, but possible if I stood my ground and focused intensely on the ball. Sometimes I would surprise us both by diving and catching a ball that I had no right to save. Trevor would yell with delight when that happened, which also pleased us both immensely.

It wasn't over then either. Next came five sets of 30 sit-ups using a ball. Lying flat on my back I would stretch the ball over my straightened legs and then swing back my hands, without the ball, to touch the ground at full stretch behind my head and then swing forward picking up the ball and placing it at full stretch behind my head. With just a 30-second break between sessions I continued until five sets were completed, totalling 150 pressurised sit-ups.

To finish, the whole squad – about 25 players each with a ball – would face me 15 yards out, in a large semi-circle and shoot alternately from one side of the semi-circle to the other. This particular drill made me skip right then left so quickly that I didn't have time to look back at the posts to check my angles. It was hard work but great fun.

Trevor was a fantastic goalkeeper coach, the best I'd say. I felt 200 per cent fitter and sharper within a few weeks. I was leaping higher, saving shots I had no right to save and performing even better than at my Charlton peak, which was great considering my eye was still not working properly.

To let you know how good Trevor was in his prime, he had a serious offer to join Tottenham Hotspur (Spurs) in London during the early 60s when Spurs were undoubtedly the best team in England, if not Europe. He turned them down because his mother was physically and mentally handicapped. He looked after his mother daily and felt it would have killed her if he had left South Africa. She was struggling to get through most days and needed his assistance 24/7. I genuinely believe he could have been one of the world's greatest-ever goalkeepers. He was in my view, but not being able to leave South Africa probably prevented him from sealing that prized reputation.

I was extremely lucky to be coached by the best. Any knowledgeable South African football fan will tell you Trevor was special. He was also one of the most modest guys you could ever meet. He had so much energy and passion for the game. It was contagious. I would do anything for him.

I remember one important league game in Soweto against Kaiser Chiefs. Trevor came in the dressing room a few minutes before the game, like he always did, to wish me luck. He always held up his hands and showed them trembling and sweating to show he was nervous. It was like he was playing but he was transmitting his goalkeeping genius to me. He told me there were two of us on the pitch and that he was with me and that the opposing team would have to beat both of us to score. That was such good motivation.

He would then shake my hand vigorously and give me a big bear hug. I just loved the guy.

Sometimes during a match, I'd catch his eye and we would give each other a smile, nod and thumbs-up. We both knew he had turned my game around and were proud of what we were achieving together. I was playing better as each week passed. We worked together for the whole season and I loved and respected him like a member of my own family.

Sadly, there is no happy ending to this story. In fact, what subsequently happened was a tragedy which affects me to this day. Trevor committed suicide in the mid-1980s at the age of just 49. I was absolutely devastated. I had heard he never got over the death of his mother and also lost his daughter who also had some serious physical and emotional challenges. It was too much for Trevor to take. In the end he suffered from a deep depression that he wasn't able to conquer and led to him taking his own life. I still miss Trevor and, every so often, I'll look upwards, wave to him and give him a double thumbs-up. This happens especially if I have been working with a young keeper on the same drills Trevor taught me.

I think every player needs a coach who he or she respects and would go to the end of the earth for. In my experience, there are very few coaches of the quality of Trevor Gething. He cared so much and gave everything he had to offer. I do wish I could have helped him the way he helped me. I'll see him one day and give him the biggest bear-hug ever. I'll never forget Trevor and I'll be forever grateful for his coaching, guidance and friendship.

Chapter 39

Dancing to the Beat

HALFWAY THROUGH the season we had an inconvenient ten-day break without a match. Because Kai wanted us to stay sharp, he scheduled an exhibition game in an all-black township called Rustenburg, 70 miles from Pretoria. From the moment we heard the words 'exhibition game' we all looked at each other and thought 'uh-oh, Windhoek'. Kai knew what we were thinking and hastily put our minds at rest by telling us the area we were playing in was safe and that our opponents were keen to join our league the following season, meaning everyone would be on their best behaviour. With Kai's words of reassurance ringing in our ears, we boarded the team bus.

We were playing at a decent new stadium with a capacity of nearly 20,000 and an excellent playing surface. The game itself was embarrassingly one-sided. We took an early lead and went on to crush our opponents 9-0. We didn't want to rub it in or be disrespectful to our hosts so we took our foot off the gas in the second half. I don't particularly enjoy games like that because you are just an observer and barely in the game at all. Thankfully, the fans remained in good spirits and some of them had installed a huge sound system that The Who rock band at their peak would have been proud of. It was constructed directly behind my goal and was blaring throughout the game. It was just about tolerable.

Starved of any action, I decided to have a bit of fun and soon started tapping my feet and clapping my hands in time to the heavy drumbeat. Anyone familiar with the brilliant South African musical *Ipi Tombi* will know how the infectious rhythmic drumming can get you singing and dancing. Before I knew it, I began a little dance routine I had seen a Zulu warrior performing a few weeks earlier when we had played AmaZulu FC in Durban. This involved slapping the outside of my thighs and my right and left ankles while moving in a stomping mode. I wasn't sure how the crowd was going to react. I hoped they wouldn't think I was mocking them in any way, as I certainly wasn't. I was showing them how much I was enjoying their music. Thankfully, I could hear the crowd laughing and cheering so I knew they were entering in the fun. So, I decided to have some more fun.

I turned and spied a lovely, large black lady losing herself in the beat and dancing enthusiastically behind my goal. She was beaming with happiness and dancing up a storm. With play at the other end of the field, I danced my way back behind my goal and asked the smiling security guard to open the gate in the surrounding fence so that I could beckon the dancing lady onto the pitch. She was delighted to be asked and shimmied her way over, moving in time to the beat. She came right into the centre of my goal just a few feet off the goal line, continuing to boogie away. I took my cue from her and, to the delight of the crowd, copied her every movement as she twisted and twirled and jumped up and down. I was just hoping she didn't start doing somersaults as that might have been beyond me! By now the crowd was clapping, cheering and crying with laughter.

Everyone was happy. It was a more than memorable moment. It was perhaps a symbolic moment too. A white man dancing with a black woman in South Africa, in an area like this, was a less than common occurrence. But we were just people having fun and I'm convinced events like that provided a tonic in a country that at times felt on a knife-edge.

We were having such a good time that I briefly forgot that I was in the middle of a football match and, when our opponents had a rare breakaway, I had to reluctantly stop jiving and shoo my dance partner behind the goal, where she went, still smiling broadly. After saving a routine long-range effort, I kicked the ball back up field and completed my dance at the side of the goal with my new friend before chivalrously escorting her back through the gate to her place on the terraces. That experience was certainly a first, I can tell you.

Chapter 40

Making History in Soweto

WE WERE preparing to be one of the first predominantly white teams to play in Soweto. Kai said this was a historic game for the club, not to mention an important league match, and so we should have a pre-match breakfast about two hours outside Soweto.

Soweto (short for South Western Townships) is South Africa's largest township and home to more than a million mainly black people trying to survive in homes that are no bigger than a typical garden shed. The kick-off was at noon, the hottest part of the day, when it would easily reach over 100 degrees. Our opposition, the Orlando Pirates, insisted on a noon kick-off, because they presumably figured they could handle the temperature a lot better than we white-skinned players.

After our terrifying experience in Windhoek, our team's security had been tightened up.

We were escorted by four police wagons, two in front, two behind. Each carried six policemen with automatic weapons. It was intimidating at first but we soon got used to it. In fact, we were all comforted to have such efficient-looking security.

The Afrikaner police were fearsome. They had a reputation for shooting first and asking questions later. I asked an officer as we boarded our team bus if he thought there would be any trouble: 'Maybe, but not for long,' he replied, stroking his automatic rifle.

It was a stunning sight when we arrived on the outskirts of Soweto. As we crested over a long ridge the township stretched out in front of us. We saw thousands upon thousands of aluminium sheds, little more than shacks in truth, which were family homes. In the middle of this vista, we saw an enormous 40,000 bench-style seater stadium.

I gulped, knowing the temperature would easily exceed 100 degrees during the match. Our team bus had eased past two security stop gates. Several of the stadium security officers had Alsatian dogs and handguns ready in open holsters. The last security gate looked like the entrance to a POW camp with what seemed to be an excessive quantity of barbed wire.

Our police escort stayed close. Even though we were in a so-called restricted area, over 1,000 people milling around our team bus was a little unnerving. We darted off the bus and pushed open a heavy steel door that had 'away team' hand-painted on it and entered a concrete structure with two long benches. A solitary light bulb made for an eerie, shadowy atmosphere. We had an hour to kick-off so Kai suggested we got changed and examined the pitch.

The crowd was starting to chant and jump up and down. We could feel the vibrations. I told myself to stay calm and enjoy the atmosphere.

Our access to the pitch reminded me of how a lion might enter a circus ring from a cage. The entrance had high, three-sided mesh fencing that went out towards the field about 30 feet. Then we crossed a 20-foot-long bridge, over a deep excavated trench that encircled the outer perimeter of the field: basically a moat with no water. The playing field was like an island all by itself.

The stadium was starting to fill with nearly 30,000 fans. I did not spot a white face in the crowd. There was another 40 minutes to go before kick-off and the fans were pouring in. I felt butterflies in my stomach. I just knew the atmosphere was going to be exceptional.

I trotted towards the goal, eyeing its dimensions and getting a feel for my penalty area. I then checked the pitch markings. Both goalmouths were pretty rough with a mixture of small pebbles and dirt mixed with sand. I was relieved there was no witch doctor present. One witch doctor in a career seems like plenty to me.

I managed to borrow one of the match balls from a linesman. It looked one size bigger than a regular size five. I was bewildered: 'Bloody heck, this is the first size six ball I have ever seen.'

I shouted to Gerry Queen. It felt as if it had a rubber casing, making it look bigger. The ball felt strange and I thought it might do unpredictable things. My instincts were right.

With further permission from the linesman, Gerry began warming me up with the oversized ball and we agreed it felt odd. He took a crack from a long way out of the box. The ball moved at a golf ball speed towards me and seemed to increase in velocity during mid-flight. It was like one of those rubber 'super' or 'wonder' balls we used to play with as kids.

I asked Gerry to move back so I could take a long-distance drop kick. To our surprise the ball sailed at least 15 feet over Gerry's head. This ball was going to take some getting used to.

Back in the dressing room Kai told us not to worry too much about the ball but to adjust to it as we went. He was more concerned about a highly rated left-winger who was fast, skilful and nicknamed 'CX3' after a South African engine oil: 'He's so quick and slick he can slide uphill,' said Kai, telling Steve Ingle he would be marking him. I didn't envy CX3 because when Steve marked you, he really marked you for life.

'Come on lads, let's kick some arse,' roared Kai, as we headed for the 'lion's' tunnel.

The stadium was now packed to the rafters. At least two dozen fans had scaled each of the four floodlights to get a better view. The stadium officially held 40,000 but there must have been at least an extra 15,000 squeezed in somehow.

The atmosphere was like nothing I'd experienced. We were only halfway down the tunnel when both my knees buckled for a split second due to palpable tension. I recovered quickly by grabbing a handrail. Outside the tunnel the high-pitched whistling of the fans was reaching a crescendo. It was at fever pitch. It was time to stand up and be counted.

It was time for Kai to show some leadership and he didn't disappoint. Standing in front of the last closed door before entering the stadium he delivered the most rousing pre-match speech I have ever heard. Here is the gist of it: 'Lads. This is brilliant … this is what the game is all about … you will never forget this game as long as you live.' Pause. 'Don't get too wrapped up in the emotions off the field … focus only on your own job … be first class … but don't do what you can't do … keep things simple … pull each other through … play as a unit … play as an army that never gives up on defending or attacking.' He paused again to observe our reactions.

'When you get tired, start playing for someone you really admire or love,' he continued. 'Someone like your wife, your mum, dad, best friend, girlfriend, your brother, your sister.'

He paused again and watched us puff our chests out. I looked straight at him. His eyes were blazing and focused. 'Now let's do the business. Good luck lads.'

Kai had done his bit and we all clapped our hands, clenched our fists and roared: 'Come on lads, we've got this.'

We were pumped up and ready to do battle with the Pirates. Kai opened the doors and led us through the lion's cage entrance with both arms raised in the air. He looked like a gladiator already claiming victory. The noise was deafening as the electrifying atmosphere took hold.

My mind turned back to my dad and the advice he gave me all those years earlier about enjoying myself, never giving up and showing everyone how good I was.

As I crossed the line and sprinted on to the pitch, I screamed out loud: 'This game is for you, Dad.' I smiled, knowing psychologically Dad was out there with me. I felt confident and equipped to do battle.

The noise was so intense I did not even hear the referee's whistle to start the game. Our tactics for the first five minutes were to take the sting out of the crowd, settle our nerves and pass the ball between us to get used to it. The crowd didn't like our early play and thought it was negative, but we didn't care. It was a necessary part of our game plan.

The temperature was over 100 degrees and climbing by the minute. I could see the crossbar and goalposts at the far end of the field shimmering in the heat.

We could only keep possession for so long and eventually an Orlando Pirates player intercepted a pass. The crowd were demanding that CX3 be given the ball. A tricky midfielder who had gained possession zipped past two of our lads and pinged a pass out wide to CX3. The volume rose perceptibly when the star man finally got the ball at his feet. He controlled it perfectly with a cushioned one touch and drew Steve Ingle towards him like a matador enticing a bull. Then, in a flash, CX3 threw Steve off balance with a double fake step-over and cut inside. It was a fantastic piece of footballing artistry and it left Steve for dead.

It now sounded like most of the stadium were shrieking with emotion as CX3 barrelled towards me. His brilliance had caught us square and there was no one between him and me.

CX3 was now 25 yards out and closing in fast at an acute angle from the edge of my box. Then things seemed to go into slow motion. I could see him deciding what to do next. I stood my ground waiting for this mercurial player's next move. He looked brilliantly threatening in his silky all-black kit with the front of his shirt adorned with a menacing bright white skull-and-crossbones – like an oversized and intimidating Orlando Pirates badge coming at me.

CX3 was now in the box. I saw him pull his left foot back ready to shoot. My instincts told me he was going to fake a shot with his left foot before cutting the ball inside to finish with his right. Fortunately, I was spot on. I threw myself into a full-length dive towards CX3, anticipating that my hands would block his shot.

There was an almighty collision of my hands, the ball and his right foot. I had judged it perfectly. I jammed his shot and Steve, who had now recovered after being skinned by CX3, came in with a lunging slide tackle to toe the ball out for a corner. It was still 0-0 and their first attack had been thwarted. The crowd was going bonkers and chanting CX3's name. This fellow could play.

CX3 was up in a flash, dusted himself down and raced over to take the corner. Trying to read where a corner kick will be placed can sometimes be difficult for a goalkeeper but, on this occasion, there could be little doubt. The Pirates' centre-forward was massive, a few inches taller than me, so about 6ft 7in. He had a 'lion claw' scratched tattoo on each cheek, which made him look even more intimidating.

He looked me in the eye and got inside my six-yard box heading towards my goal line. The man mountain was jumping up and down in front of me, trying to unsight me as CX3 prepared to whip the ball in from the corner. All I had to do was get in front of this giant and catch or punch it away.

I anticipated well, or I got lucky, and caught the corner at full stretch with the 6ft 7in striker doing his best to crane his neck to the ball. It must have been ten foot up and inches from the big man's forehead. I attributed catching the ball to all the hard work Trevor Gething had done with me.

As I looked around, wasting a few extra seconds for the goal area to clear out, Steve Ingle delivered another one of his dry, Yorkshire one-liners: 'That bloody CX3 feller is so fookin' quick, I can't kick t' bastard.'

Later in the half, the unusual ball worked to my advantage. I was known for my long drop kicks but one I hit after half an hour was remarkable, even if I do say so myself. As I kicked it, it felt so sweet. It travelled like a missile and just kept travelling before glancing off their keeper's desperately outstretched hand and over the top of the bar for a corner. I had been inches away from scoring from my own area.

I stood there in shock at what I had just seen. My sweeper, a lanky solid Afrikaner called Plankie Naude, shouted, 'Tuttie, get some more power on it if you are going to shoot at goal.' Plankie was laughing his head off and so was I. But it made me even more wary of the ball and what I could expect from the Pirates.

We kept them at bay for 45 minutes and congratulated each other as we jogged towards the dressing room. We also knew they were going to throw the proverbial kitchen sink at us in the second half.

Kai was waiting just inside the dressing-room doors and was pumped up, screaming, 'Brilliant lads … Well done, well done, well done. Now, how do ya wanna play the second half?'

I thought this was an unusual question for a coach to ask his team. Then again Kai was such a brilliant psychologist he wanted us to arrive at the decision ourselves.

'Don't change anything,' Plankie said.

'Kill them on the counter-attack,' Gerry Queen suggested.

'How about knocking the ball into the channels, just behind their defence?' chipped in our speedy attacking midfielder Robbie de Graaf.

'Let's kick t' shit out of t' bastards,' chimed in Steve Ingle.

Kai had now gone into pensive mood, calling to mind a lawyer pondering a complex case.

'All are excellent suggestions … except yours Steve,' he said, smiling. 'But let's think like them for a second.' Not being the tallest chap in the world, Kai then decided his words would carry more weight if he stood on a chair. He reminded me of a preacher at Speakers' Corner in London.

He took a quick breath before delivering his analysis: 'I would feel under immense pressure if I was in their shoes,' he proclaimed, as if speaking from a pulpit. 'If we can hold them at bay for the first 15 minutes, they will become very anxious and so will the crowd.'

He looked even more like a pastor or a minister when he launched both arms aloft and pointed upwards: 'We then pray to God and hang on for the next 15 minutes by knocking it long down our right and left attacking channels. It's okay to knock it to no one if you have to. Just don't get caught giving the ball away in our half of the field. Then we'll get them even more frustrated by giving nothing away.'

Kai was now on a roll, as he became even more animated. His eyes were yet again burning into us, but in a good way as he continued to race on with, 'And then in the final 15 minutes, we have a chance to steal the game. They will be going crazy on and off the field and pushing so far forward that our two strikers, Gerry and Vincent, might get a breakaway. So, knock the ball extra-long – and I mean extra-long – over the back four for Gerry or Vincent to chase down … and pray they will have timed their run to beat the offside rule.' We were all nodding in agreement. Kai was ready to round off his Churchillian speech with: 'Lads, we can do this … Can you do it? … I think we can … I know we can. Now believe we can. Remember this … We Never Give Up.'

Then he said: 'When the final whistle blows, sprint off the field and stay in here and we'll wait patiently for the crowd to disperse. We then go home victorious and I'll buy you all the best lobster dinner in town.'

As if written in the stars, the game went almost as Kai had predicted. We battled to keep our head above water for the first 15 minutes and were under intense pressure but stood firm. Their frustration began to show in the second 15 minutes of the half.

We were solid at the back and showed tremendous will, stamina and defiance to not be breached.

Kai was on the sidelines jumping up and down, kicking and heading every ball. And just as he'd predicted, the Pirates' tempers began to fray. The crowd had started to turn against their own team for not scoring. We had barely had a sniff of their goal for 20 minutes.

As we entered the last 15 minutes of the game we started to run out of steam and began to simply bash the ball out of our danger area and well into their half. It gave us just a few extra seconds to catch our breath, have a break and prepare for another one of their relentless attacks. It wasn't a pretty way to play but it was effective.

Then, with about eight minutes to go, I came for yet another corner and caught the ball cleanly, nice and high, just past the penalty spot. Instead of stalling and wasting time, which I'm sure the Pirates expected, I remembered Kai's theory about them pushing too far forward and so I acted as fast as I could with a laser bulleted drop kick sustaining a low ten-foot height, rocketing diagonally across the field.

It caught their last two defenders square, flat-footed and totally surprised as it fell between an on-rushing Gerry Queen and their goalkeeper, who was caught in two minds whether to come out or stay on his line. Suddenly the goalkeeper was in no man's land. Gerry, being a wise, experienced striker, knew just exactly what was required and with one touch he lobbed the ball gently over the keeper's head. One of the defenders chased back and desperately tried to keep the ball out but to no avail. The defender ended up meeting the ball in the back of the net. Our supreme goal poacher Gerry Queen had nicked the only goal of the game … so far!

It was a classic sucker punch and we were ecstatic. Gerry sprinted towards Kai to celebrate. The rest of us met Gerry and Kai on the halfway line. We also knew we hadn't quite done the job yet because there were just under eight minutes left on the clock.

The Pirates desperately wanted to kick-off as quickly as they could. We sobered quickly, knowing all hell was about to break loose. It was no secret who they wanted to get the ball to and another long direct pass went out on the left wing to CX3. Steve had wised up by now and intercepted the ball, heading it over the moat and the barbed wire fence to waste a few more precious seconds. The crowd instantly threw the ball back to CX3.

Steve tried to slow down the play even more by standing on CX3's toes while he was taking the throw-in. Fortunately, the ref and linesman had their eyes elsewhere and missed it. However, the crowd didn't and went berserk. Steve had physically slowed CX3 down for the next few minutes as the star player hobbled around until the pain had almost gone.

No sooner had CX3 recovered then Steve, never one to stand on ceremony, hacked him from behind, making the star Pirates player bounce twice before disappearing into the moat. It was not a discreet challenge by any means but it was quite funny seeing CX3 vanishing from view into the moat. The ref had no choice but to send Steve off. As he took his leave, he turned around and gave the finger to the crowd, which did nothing whatsoever to endear us to the locals.

With less than four minutes left on the clock, we, as they say, parked the bus in front of our goal with Gerry dropping to Steve Ingle's right-back position and our other front runner Vincent 'Tanti' Julius coming back to help our exhausted back four. We were now playing with no strikers! We all remained extremely focused, determined not to concede and to cover our missing sent-off player. It was going to be pure guts that would see us through the next four minutes and injury time.

The Pirates had three more chances and fluffed them all. The last cannoned off the crossbar after a reflex touch-save that I didn't know much about. When stuff like that happens, you know it just might be your day.

We now had to battle through four minutes of injury time during which we had a goalmouth scramble that had to be seen to be believed. It must have looked like a slapstick comedy routine but it happened.

First, their huge number nine produced a sizzling, dipping shot from 20 yards. The best I could do was take two quick steps back towards my goal and then throw myself somewhat blindly backwards, knowing if I didn't get a touch it was going in just under the bar. It was a carbon copy of my hardest Trevor Gething drill. I took one more step back towards the goal and launched myself, not knowing exactly where the ball was but hoping to connect somehow. I threw up my right hand, which was just enough to deflect the ball on to the bar. It amazingly rebounded back, high towards the penalty spot.

Plankie and Spoedie Bronkhorst both went for the ball at the same time to try and head it away and out of danger. In their desperation they collided in mid-air, both missed the ball and collapsed like a couple of circus clowns. The ball bounced once before their speedy midfielder smacked it towards goal again. It hit the foot of the post and rebounded to another striker, seven yards out. All he had to do was to side-foot it home, but I took an educated guess – once again drawing from Trevor's training – and threw myself fully committed to the opposite side of the goal. His shot hit me straight where it hurts the most and the ball lodged between my legs for a split second. As I landed, it bounced out of my control. Suddenly the Pirates forwards were like a herd of buffaloes bearing down on the loose ball that was begging to be kicked in the goal from two yards out.

Three of their guys lunged in, trying to stab the ball home. With my left hand I barely managed to scoop the ball towards the side of the six-yard box as my right hand broke my fall. Robbie de Graaf, our smallest player, somehow got in front of another stampeder and knocked it wide for a corner.

I instantly started to laugh through the pain of the ball hitting me square between my legs and remembered Trevor Gething's comment in training: 'Stop it with your cock if you have to, just stop it.' Anatomically, it was actually just below and in a more painful area, but this wasn't time to split hairs.

With seconds left on the clock, all the Pirates players flooded my six-yard box for the corner kick. Even their goalkeeper came up and was jumping up and down excitedly on my goal line. The ball was obviously going to be aimed at their huge number nine. Leaping as high as I could, I managed to get a slight touch to guide the ball towards the other corner flag.

We were so exhausted that no one rushed out to challenge their greyhound of a right-winger as he chased down the ball to keep it in play. Then something happened that I've never seen before or since. All nine of our outfield players ran back to be on the goal line leaving myself as the only person off the line, six yards out.

By this time the right-winger had retrieved the ball and was on his way back to goal with only me going towards him. The rest of the lads were spread out across the goal line, looking like the Great Wall of China. This really was 'parking the bus' in front of the goal.

I knew the winger was going to shoot as soon as the angle was right. And dribbling frantically towards me from the corner flag was not the best of angles for him. He had to do something magic to improve his angle. As he drew even closer towards me, I realised he was going to try and go around me and then shoot. The winger did a quick step-over, dropped his right shoulder and went to his left. I bought his fake as he blew by me to shoot, aiming for the far top-left corner of the goal.

The winger's rocket shot hit Gerry Queen smack on the upper forehead. Now the ball was spiralling up 30 feet into the air. This gave me just enough time to sprint three more steps towards my goal and to dive towards the top left-hand corner with a blind backhand knuckle punch at the ball that connected and pushed it over the crossbar for a corner. It was a miracle save that came from within without me really realising it. I landed or should I say collapsed on Gerry and a couple more team-mates.

We were all completely spent. The referee then blew the whistle for the final time. We had won 1-0 in an extraordinary game.

We could barely find the strength to celebrate and dog-piled on top of Gerry for heading the ball off the line. The Pirates team then did something amazing. They picked us off the ground one by one, congratulating us on our never-give-up attitude. They obviously respected our determination and will to fight right to the end.

What an incredible last ten minutes. We had no need to sprint to the dressing rooms. The profound sportsmanship shown by the Pirates team genuinely moved us. To our surprise, the crowd, which at one time had looked like it was going to boil over, stopped whistling and was now standing to applaud us. We had won them over. All the players from both teams shook hands and congratulated each other. We all knew we had played in a special match.

The game could not have been a better advertisement for our new multi-racial league. Both teams showed mutual respect and, as professional sportsmen, we felt a warm glow inside each one of us. We celebrated for over two hours before we headed back to the bus. We had made history and survived to tell the story. Kai was right. We would remember this game for the rest of our lives.

Chapter 41
On the Road Again

AFTER OUR victory in Soweto, Kai attracted some more talented players and secured a major corporate sponsorship deal for the team, which meant we changed our team name from Arcadia Shepherds to Arcadia Pepsi. The fact our owner was the president of Pepsi South Africa may have had something to do with this. Another bonus was the majority of our games were now being televised. To cap it all, we kept winning, and television loves winners, so we were drawing bigger crowds, home and away.

With the acclaim came a nice surprise towards the end of my second season. Three of us were selected for a South Africa All-Star Team to play against an American All-Star touring team. The game was billed as a goodwill exhibition match. Unfortunately, all three of us had to decline because it clashed with our last game of the season against Hellenic in Cape Town. If we beat Hellenic by more than two goals, we had a chance of edging out Kaiser Chiefs on goal difference to be champions. Club loyalty trumped the chance of being noticed by the American All-Star team coaches and players. The news media got hold of the story and praised our decision – so much so that this would help me in the long run.

I had been doing a lot of thinking and had several good reasons for wanting to leave South Africa for a professional soccer contract in America. The main thing was that I had been feeling increasingly concerned for my safety. I had many friends in the country from all parts of the community but it was just too volatile.

I'd had an alarming episode playing against Kaiser Chiefs when a screwdriver was thrown at me from behind my goal. Luckily, it missed my back and stuck in the ground near my right foot but it could have done me a serious injury.

My second scare came in another league game; when I was running up the players' tunnel towards our dressing room, a sharpened bamboo stick, about 6ft long, was jabbed at me. Fortunately, it missed my shoulder by only a few inches and avoided a nasty stabbing, but it was enough to shake me up and make me start to think about leaving South Africa to play in the US.

The final straw came when a two-litre glass bottle was thrown at me from the first tier of a stadium. Fortunately it missed me, but it struck a cameraman on the side of his head, knocking him out cold. It seemed the fans were getting crazier, more unpredictable and we found certain security arrangements at more than one ground to be substandard. I loved my team-mates and the beauty of the country, but it felt like a powder keg ready to be lit. I made up my mind, for my own safety, that I wanted to play in North America.

PART THREE

AMERICA

Chapter 42

A Sprinkle of Magic

THE LATE Tony Waiters, who died in November 2020, was a highly respected former goalkeeper who made his name at Blackpool, making 257 appearances for the men in tangerine between 1959 and 1967. He was a brilliant keeper who also won five England caps as an early back-up to Gordon Banks. When he hung up his gloves, he managed Plymouth Argyle before moving to Vancouver Whitecaps. I had played against Tony's Plymouth team a few times and hopefully played well enough for him to remember me. So speculatively, I called him to seek a trial for the Whitecaps.

It was perfect timing. Vancouver had won the NASL Soccer Bowl the season before and were having some goalkeeping problems. Their previous goalkeeper, Bruce Grobbelaar, had left for Crewe Alexandra on loan before getting a dream move to Liverpool. The other keeper was former Wolves man Phil Parkes, not to be confused with his namesake at QPR and West Ham. Parkes was a regular during the Whitecaps' title-winning season but had not yet agreed terms on a new contract. So, it looked like there might be an opening at a first-class club.

Yet, when I arrived in Vancouver, everything felt wrong. They played on a synthetic pitch with little or no padding underneath, which was horrible for a goalkeeper. Then I broke my finger on the second day. There was a thin layer of ice on the field and a striker who was also on trial accidentally kicked my hand as he slipped. It was just a freak accident but enough to sour the deal for both of us.

They say when one door closes another opens and, on my return to England, I got a call from Paul Taylor, head coach of Columbus Magic, in the American Soccer League, based in Ohio. Keith Peacock, my former Charlton captain, had been his assistant coach the year before and had kindly recommended me to Paul when he heard I was looking to move to the States. We ended up being a perfect match.

Columbus Magic was a great introduction to the American soccer scene, plus I liked Paul Taylor and the city itself. Paul was raised in Sheffield and had played professionally for several British clubs before transferring to the Los Angeles Skyhawks and then on to Columbus Magic, where he graduated to head coach. He had a tremendous passion for the game and recognised the importance of player visibility in the community.

Similarly, I quickly understood that a community-minded approach would bring spin-off benefits too. Kids started coming to games wearing my # 00 TUTT shirt. The fans were kind and invited many of us to dinner or speaking engagements at their kids' schools, where we always finished off with a soccer clinic or demonstration.

Each player averaged two to three community appearances a week in the area's schools and youth clubs. It was an excellent learning experience and certainly helped to draw thousands of new fans to our games.

I liked Columbus even though we played on synthetic turf at the Franklin County Stadium which we shared with the Columbus Clippers baseball team. We had some great British players in the squad including the talented Mike Barry who'd played for a number of clubs, including Carlisle and Bristol Rovers, and a very skilled tall striker called Ronnie Wigg, who became a good friend and had played for Watford, Ipswich and Rotherham, among others.

We also had an excellent winger in the shape of the Lancastrian George Dewsnip who had played for Southport but then made his name in America with the LA Aztecs, Fort Lauderdale Strikers and the Atlanta Chiefs.

Alongside George was 'Storming Norman' Piper, a fantastic addition. He'd made his name when selected for the England under-23 team and had successful spells at clubs like Plymouth and Portsmouth. We'd played against each other several times and became good mates. Not many could stop Storming Norman when he was on the attack with his pace and dribbling ability.

Another solidly consistent British defender, Neil Hague, had played for several clubs including Rotherham, Bournemouth and Darlington before arriving in the States. You could count on Neil making brave tackles inside and outside our six-yard box.

But for me the player who took the biscuit was a huge Argentinian called Daniel Mammana, a 6ft 5in sweeper built like a tank. We became great pals and would room together on away trips. The guy was crazy on and off the field but was an excellent defender with it.

I have a whole bundle of stories about Daniel and a few have to be told. First up there was his large safety-pin trick. Daniel would secrete the largest safety pin he could get away with in his shorts before a game. When a corner kick was being taken, at either end, he would surreptitiously remove the pin and jab whoever he was marking or whoever was marking him in the arm, back, backside or somewhere where it hurt. They would jump in pain thinking it was a wasp or bee sting which would give him enough time to head in a goal or head the ball away if defending. It was a brutal trick that worked on more than one occasion. He had it down to a T. It was amazing a referee or an opponent never caught him performing his crafty jabs.

Another popular Daniel trick was even more unpleasant. After bringing down an opponent, usually from behind, Daniel would extend his hand to pick the guy up in a goodwill gesture of sportsmanship. However, as he pulled the guy to his feet with one hand, he would poke the player in the eye with his thumb on the other hand. I didn't approve of this tactic at all and after witnessing Daniel doing it a few times, I politely asked him to stop, telling him of my eye-injury experience. He didn't stop but, from then on, he would always come and apologise to me after he had done it to an opponent, saying, 'Sorry Graham, that's how we play in Argentina.'

Daniel had such disarming charm that he would rarely get booked. In fact, it was quite the opposite and frequently other players would get sent off after tangling with him. He was very sly. For instance, while he was running on the blind side of the referee, Daniel would slap his own hand against his thigh very loudly and crash to the ground clutching his face, writhing in agony. He had it down to a fine art and the referee was nearly always conned. The innocent player would be gobsmacked as the referee sent him off while Daniel would continue rolling around with his hands covering his face, faking pain while trying not to laugh. He pulled this little trick off perfectly several times. It was cheating, nothing more, nothing less, but nothing seemed to be able to stop him from doing it.

So, with a combination of good players and Daniel's con-artistry we did very well and reached the play-offs. But there were problems behind the scenes with some suspect ownership dealings which led to money troubles. The full extent of Columbus Magic's financial downfall was brought home when I had a knock on my apartment door early one morning. It was the apartment manager, a policeman and another official-looking type. The apartment manager said the rent had not been paid for two months and I had two days to move out. The other official was there to pick up my car because the car rental payment from the club's new owners had not gone through. The so-called new owners had simply done a runner. About 20 players received eviction notices and had rental cars confiscated all in one day.

Perhaps the new owners had bitten off more than they could chew. I could understand why, because the teams in our league were scattered all over the USA. We would sometimes go on a ten-day road trip to play three teams in California, which would cost a fortune. Then after two or three home games we would go on another long road trip to play against the Cleveland Cobras in Ohio, the Pennsylvania Stoners, New York United and the Miami Americans. It was ludicrously expensive for every club. Even so, playing at venues like the famous Shea Stadium, where the Beatles performed in 1965, was a brilliant experience.

I discovered the New York crowds were as aggressive as anything I had faced in England, with some of them throwing coins and hurling insults in my direction. I made them even angrier when I looked their way, cupped my hand to my ear and laughed every time we scored in our 3-0 victory in New York.

I felt sorry for our coach Paul Taylor when the owners packed up and left us high and dry – especially after Paul had worked so hard to establish the club. The rug was pulled from under all of us, because we were producing on and off the field. We had reached the ASL Final the previous season and we were on our way to completing the feat again when the money started to dry up. In fact, Columbus Magic's new investors disappeared overnight.

Paul recommended I call a guy called Bill Williams who was moving to the Atlanta Chiefs in the NASL as an assistant coach. Bill and I had met before when our Columbus team faced his Sacramento Gold in an away game in California. Fortunately, I had been on song that night and we had stolen a decent victory against the run of play. Bill had a good team and was undoubtedly an excellent coach. I respected him immensely. When I called Bill, he said he would recommend me to his new boss, the head coach of the Atlanta Chiefs, David Chadwick, who was building a new team. Within two days I was heading south to Atlanta, Georgia. Little did I know then how important Atlanta would become in my future.

Chapter 43

Georgia On My Mind

THERE WERE one or two flashbacks to 'the boot' and the events at Roker Park during the flight to Atlanta. Nothing major, just a slight niggle but, at moments of change, it seemed my mind always wanted to take me back there. I was never able to satisfactorily explain 'the boot' to myself in detail. I also never really knew where Atlanta was until the plane touched down there in late October of 1980.

George Dewsnip, my team-mate in Columbus, had played for the Atlanta Chiefs the year before and raved about southern hospitality. George added that Atlanta was growing fast and would soon become a major city in the south. George was spot on with his prediction.

Eleanor Minshew, the Atlanta Chiefs' executive secretary, picked me up from the airport.

She epitomised the southern hospitality George had told me about. Eleanor went on to tell me about our team owner Ted Turner who sounded like an interesting character with his fingers in plenty of pies, including television on a massive scale.

I gathered that Turner owned four Atlanta professional sports franchises, including the Atlanta Chiefs, the Atlanta Braves, a

Major League baseball franchise, the Atlanta Flames ice hockey team and the Atlanta Hawks basketball team. Eleanor told me that every one of our Chiefs games – home and away – was to be aired across the USA on cable television.

Turner's first national cable television network was called Super Station Channel 17. Turner was savvy because his four teams attracted massive ratings and the advertisers followed. He was also launching CNN, which became a major 24-hour national and international cable news network.

After showing me around the impressive, 55,000 all-seater Atlanta Fulton County Stadium, Eleanor took me to the club's offices to meet my new head coach, Dave Chadwick.

I had done my homework and knew that Dave 'Chaddy' Chadwick had enjoyed an excellent professional playing career in England and the USA spanning over 25 seasons. He'd started at Southampton and then played for a number of other decent clubs including Middlesbrough and Gillingham. I'd played against him at The Valley when he played for Gillingham. Most importantly I had had a good game where Charlton had won 2-1, which I hoped he would remember. I knew straight away that Chaddy wanted to sign me when he introduced me to the club's PR officer, Michael Oglesby, saying: 'Graham's going to be our new goalkeeper.' He told me he had a heavy afternoon securing several players' contracts before their deadlines and would I mind if we got back together in a few hours, later that afternoon? Of course, I agreed, and then he generously gave me the keys to his car and suggested I go and explore the Atlanta area while he buttoned up the contracts.

Directly across the road from the Chiefs office I pulled into a gas station to get some tourist information. I asked the woman at the till where I should visit in the area.

Because it typified southern hospitality, her answer and our subsequent exchange has stayed with me: 'Go to Stone Mountain, my honey child,' she said, lovingly.

I also remembered her giving me directions. 'Go straight for five miles and you will see the mountain straight in front of you. It's the entrance to heaven's front gate, my honey child. God will bless you for going to the mountain,' said my new-found friend, before closing with, 'Y'all come back now.'

So, I remember turning around and walking back towards her and just standing there and wondering why she called me back. She said, 'What did you forget, my honey child?'

'You said you wanted me to come back,' I answered her, half laughing.

Then she tapped her forehead and with a giggle said: 'Y'all come back now means I hope to see you again – some other time.'

I thought to myself, how friendly was that!

Ten minutes later my breath was taken away. In front of me was an enormous mountain of huge granite. I drove up to the entrance gate and a cheerful attendant advised me to take a cable car to the top of the mountain. It took about 15 minutes to reach the very top. Being a weekday in late October there were very few people around. It was coming into the fall, which made the view from the mountain one that can only be termed as spectacular. Before me lay a quilt of multi-coloured trees in iridescent, autumnal colours that went on as far as the eye could see. It was an incredible view and a privilege to witness. At that moment I felt I could stay on top of the mountain forever.

The cable car attendant had told me I would be able to see for between 50 and 60 miles and he was not wrong.

I sat up there taking in the views for the best part of two hours. It was wonderfully therapeutic and valuable thinking time. I witnessed a small aircraft circling the mountain and amazingly it was 100 feet lower than where I was sitting. That was extraordinary in itself.

When you start wishing your mum and dad and members of your family could share what you are witnessing, it makes you miss them even more. I had a burst of homesickness and the panicky realisation that Mum and Dad were not getting any younger. I began to realise how much I missed them. I resolved to get them over for a visit as soon as I could.

I also knew I loved what I had seen so far and that if Atlanta was to be my new home, I could live with that. Chaddy had delivered the perfect sales pitch without saying a word. By telling me to discover Atlanta I had stumbled upon nirvana. I was now hungrier than ever to get our deal done.

Chaddy and I quickly came to an agreement and I happily signed a four-year contract with a two-year 'no cut' clause and a two-year option for both of us. The base salary was decent with a signing-on bonus, and a free apartment was the icing on the cake. It was autumn 1980 and I was feeling like a new, reinvigorated me.

Chaddy's pre-season training was very different to any other I'd experienced. The schedule included running twice around Stone Mountain, on Monday, Wednesday and Friday, for the first two weeks, which was more than 80 miles of running. Undoubtedly, we would be one of the fittest teams in the NASL. We were preparing for our NASL indoor soccer season which ran from late November to early spring. Only in America could they turn an indoor soccer game into an event. The set-up was six players per side with unlimited substitutions. It was intense, with 20 players per roster being kept busy by substituting for someone every two to four minutes. The matches were four quarters of 15 minutes. If the game ended in a draw or tie, we would play sudden death, where the first-team to score won.

We played in a professional NHL ice hockey arena, with capacity seating for 16,000, called the Omni. It was also home for Atlanta's basketball and ice hockey teams, and big-name music stars like Elvis, Elton John and Bruce Springsteen had previously performed there.

The flooring was synthetic turf. A 4ft wall encircled the arena and shatterproof plexi-glass 6ft high was attached to the wall. A 7ft by 14ft goal was inserted at each end. The game was fast and furious with players using the wall to their advantage whether by skilfully rebounding the ball off it or, using rather less finesse, by smacking an opponent into it.

Most fans loved to see a punch-up, and they were not infrequent. It seemed appropriate that our colour commentator, aptly named Bernie 'Boom Boom' Geoffrion, was a professional ice hockey player, a former head coach and National Hockey League Hall of Famer. Boom Boom had a rapport with thousands of ice hockey fans which enticed many of them to come and watch our indoor soccer games.

One morning before practice, Chaddy explained that the New York-born-and-raised Lou 'Rocky' Cioffi would be the first-choice goalkeeper for the indoor season and I would don the gloves for all the outdoor games, which made sense. Chaddy said he didn't want me injured and needed me fully fit when the outdoor season began in April. Nevertheless, I still played seven indoor games.

Being an indoor keeper can cause all sorts of injuries, like broken fingers, wrists, twisted knees and dislocated shoulders, so I was relieved not to play a full indoor soccer season.

Indoor soccer can also produce some bad habits for an outdoor goalkeeper. I tended to drop on one knee in anticipation when there was a snapshot. That's what happens when you're trying to cover a small goal. It was fun to play and watch but mostly a vehicle to keep our team name in the public eye during the outdoor off-season. However, it served me well with getting tuned up for the outdoor games.

One of my seven indoor games was at the Silver Dome in Detroit, Michigan and was an epic event. It was against the Detroit Express, coached by Ken Furphy, the former Watford, Sheffield United and New York Cosmos manager. Can you imagine that there was a massive curtain that split the 60,000 all-seater stadium into two halves? One half of the stadium had the Detroit Pistons NBA basketball team playing against the LA Lakers and the other side of the 100-yard curtain had our indoor soccer match. It meant fans could witness two different pro sports at the same time. It produced a superb atmosphere.

Being an Elvis Presley fan, I was thrilled to know that 'The King' had performed a New Year's Eve concert there some six years earlier, smashing the attendance record for an indoor concert with 62,500 fans. We attracted half that, which wasn't so bad.

I heard after the game there were more people watching the soccer than the basketball, which was a great sign of professional indoor soccer growing fast.

The NASL teams, then in 24 cities across the US and some in Canada, looked at indoor soccer to sustain and continue fan interest in the club when they were not playing an outdoor season.

However, I believe the indoor game got short-changed by some ego-driven owners who viewed it as a nuisance and did not give it the required financial backing. Looking back, I believe NASL owners dropped the ball regarding indoor soccer. Undoubtedly it could have equalled or bettered the outdoor game in support and popularity.

It was a perfect product for the North American market, delivering, on average, between 12 and 18 goals per game and just as many saves. With no need to understand the offside rule or the intricacies or tactics of the outdoor game, it was a perfect sport for all age groups. We had many unattractive midweek games scheduled that were inconvenient to families because they fell on school nights. However, our four weekend games were most successful, drawing two crowds of more than 11,000 and two of over 13,000 fans. We were outdrawing the Atlanta Hawks NBA team, the Atlanta Braves Major League Baseball and the Atlanta Flames NHL Ice Hockey. So, the full potential was there but not recognised.

Chaddy did well and steered our indoor team to a Division Championship, beating Tampa Bay Rowdies, New England Tea Men and Fort Lauderdale Strikers.

Nevertheless, I was pleased when the indoor season finished so I could get on with our outdoor campaign. The pundits were tipping the New York Cosmos to win it all. The team was owned by Warner Communications, which made massive funds available. They were definitely the team to beat. They had attracted some huge big-name players over the years like the one and only Pelé, and Franz Beckenbauer. Now it was the turn of a brilliant Italian striker called Giorgio Chinaglia. He would become the NASL's All Time Top Scorer. Another Cosmos star I admired, playing at the other end of the pitch, was their goalkeeper, a talented German called Hubert Birkenmeier. There was also a certain Brazilian called Carlos Alberto who was poetry in motion. He could hit a ball so hard it would move in a corkscrew motion that was near impossible for any keeper to catch.

Overall, the NASL was attracting some world-class names, like George Best, Johan Cruyff, Bobby Moore and my goalkeeping idol Alex Stepney to name a few. Money appeared to be no object for a lot of clubs and it made sense for a number of top players to extend their careers in the United States, making far more money than they could elsewhere.

Our Southeastern Conference league consisted of Tampa Bay Rowdies, Fort Lauderdale Strikers, the Jacksonville Tea Men (moved from New England) and ourselves, the Atlanta Chiefs.

The Rowdies included Rodney Marsh in their ranks and were coached by Gordon Jago who had played for Charlton and managed QPR and Millwall. The Rowdies were tipped to sweep the board.

The Fort Lauderdale Strikers had an array of internationals including West German goalscoring machine and legend Gerd Muller. He had a tremendous touch and could hit a ball on the turn like no one else. Meanwhile the Tea Men had an assortment of quality players from all over the world including Mike Flanagan, my former team-mate at Charlton. Mike did very well for the Tea Men, scoring on a regular basis.

Then there was us – the Atlanta Chiefs. Our star player was Brian Kidd, the former Manchester United and Manchester City star who was then at Bolton Wanderers and on loan to us for the summer. Brian was undoubtedly the best striker I ever played with. He had it all and had proved himself a top-class player from the moment he announced his arrival on the scene by scoring for Manchester United on his 19th birthday in the European Cup Final against Benfica back in 1968. The thing I loved about Brian was that he not only made things look easy, he was also the most modest guy I had ever met. He never spouted off like some lesser players and was always friendly and down to earth. My mum thought the world of him, especially when, after one of our games, Brian invited her to sit on his lap in the players' lounge because there were no seats available. It was all in good fun. Brian was top drawer both as a footballer and as a man.

Alongside Brian was the Brummie Paul Child, who ended up the third highest all-time league goalscorer in the NASL and had been a star for the San Jose Earthquakes. Brian and Paul forged a superb partnership. Paul especially made the best move of his life by coming to play in the US while still a teenager. When I purchased a house, just around the corner from Paul, he and his wife spent several hours helping me settle in – even down to the vacuuming and dusting. Paul was another class act and totally modest with it.

Another quality player was our midfield-striker Keith Furphy, son of Ken. His speed, cleverly disguised step-over and powerful shot were wonderful attributes. He could surprise goalkeepers by scoring from the most acute angle. We nicknamed Keith 'poser' because he would turn to the crowd and put his hands on his hips and smile at the fans in an arrogant pose. The opposing fans hated him, while our home fans loved him. Against Tampa Bay Rowdies, their fans set fire to a full-size effigy of Keith in an Atlanta Chiefs team kit, which was something to behold. Keith could walk the walk and was a decent striker.

Our captain was Branko Radovic, a former Red Star Belgrade defender. Branko was a very steady defender with immaculate tackling and distribution skills.

One of my favourite players was Tony Whelan, who played sweeper-cum-defender. He came through Manchester United's youth ranks and spent three seasons at Rochdale before coming to the States. 'Wheels' was a tremendous defender who could win the ball off anybody and pass effortlessly. He became the assistant academy director at Manchester United in his later years.

You can't get on with everyone and someone I didn't see eye-to-eye with was David Byrne. David's dad was Johnny 'Budgie' Byrne, who had starred for West Ham in the 1960s and won 11 England caps as a striker. Like his dad, David was a striker and a consistent scorer. I can't sugar-coat the fact that David and I simply did not get on very well and I found him highly irritating: so irritating in fact that I struck him with four solid punches to his head on a flight to the west coast. Chaddy fined me $400 telling me it was $100 a punch. He then laughed when I said if I had known that it was only $100 a punch, I would have invested $800.

It was one of those things that seems silly in retrospect but at the time was hugely annoying. We were halfway through a flight to California for a five-game road trip. David was sitting directly behind me and for some bizarre reason started shaking the back of my seat. He did it constantly for several minutes. I warned him three or four times to stop otherwise he would pay the price. It became beyond irritating. He simply refused to stop, which I found most odd. Eventually I ran out of patience, spun around and, with both knees firmly planted in my seat, caught him with two straight right-hand punches, a left hook followed by another straight right that caused a black eye, a split lip and a bloody nose. It was totally out of character for me to act this way but, for whatever reason and only he knew, he had pushed me to my limit.

The unfortunate thing about the incident was that it happened in front of our own television crew, commentators and some newspaper media guys from Atlanta. Fortunately, they chose not to leak it to the public and, having seen what happened, apparently felt I was justified. In fact, they all praised me afterwards and endorsed my actions.

Brian Alderson was one of our dynamic midfield players who could tackle strongly and score goals from long distances. There were times he hit the ball so hard it would wobble as it torpedoed through the air. Brian came from Scotland via long stints with Coventry and Leicester City and we lived next door to each other in Conyers, an Atlanta suburb. Tragically, Brian got killed several years later in 1997, when taking a long metal pole out of his truck that touched an overhead electrical cable connected to his house and electrocuted him.

Big Don Droege from St Louis was my centre-back and also my party mate when disco was all the rage. Don was undoubtedly one of the best central-defenders in the league and made eight appearances for the USA team. He loved the physical side of the game and didn't care for reputations. When he came up against the famous Johan Cruyff, Don whacked him so hard in a 50/50 tackle that Cruyff didn't emerge for the second half. He could play a bit too.

Mark MacKain, Carl Strong and Bruce Savage were our other young American defenders who all proved they had what it took. So, all in all we had a competitive and honest hard-working team.

Chaddy wisely set up a pre-season game against his former club Dallas Tornadoes who, to my delight, had my idol, Alex Stepney, playing in goal for them. I genuinely felt so privileged to be on the same field as my childhood hero. Afterwards, I shook Alex's hand and reminded him of the advice he had given me when I was ten: 'Practise every day, do your very, very best. Never give up and you'll be a pro someday too.' What an incredible influence he was in my early years and what a pleasure it was to have met him on equal terms and played against him. I still feel honoured.

Our first home game was coming up and what was in store would give me national and international attention in a way I definitely would not have chosen.

Chapter 44

It Was the Sprinkler Head, Boss!

LITTLE DID I know that my first home game for Atlanta Chiefs would go down in the record books following an almighty 'oops' by yours truly. To say it was embarrassing would be an understatement.

Our opponents were the highly rated Washington Diplomats. Just before kick-off, I always made a point of studying the wind conditions and on this particular day the wind direction was totally baffling, with the stadium flags flapping this way and that. It appeared that our circular open stadium roof was creating an unpredictable tornado-like swirl. That's my first excuse anyway!

My second excuse for my boo-boo was that our playing field was only 100 yards long and barely 65 yards wide. Compared to most pitches, it was like playing on a postage stamp.

Now I'm going to give you one final excuse. Don Droege, our centre-back, had just executed a brilliant slide tackle on Johan Cruyff, which had created a 3ft-long, deep scar on the wet turf about five yards beyond my 18-yard box. This would be the straw that broke the camel's back.

The Washington Diplomats goalkeeper, Jim Brown, struck a punt up field and the swirling wind carried the ball an extra

15 to 20 yards. The ball landed directly on the scar on the turf caused by Don's tackle on Cruyff. So, the ball skidded off the divot, changed direction and rocketed into the top-left corner of my goal. To make matters look worse, I slipped backwards in surprise and landed flat on my arse.

Don stared at me in disbelief before calmly asking: 'Tuttie, what happened?'

I was speechless and cradled my head in my hands, sitting on my backside, bemused by what had just happened. I couldn't believe I had been scored against … by the opposing goalkeeper!

'You'll never live this one down, Tuttie. That was a good fuck-up,' were Don's next words. I could tell Don was trying his best not to laugh because we were live on national television. But he did and so did I. We then both shook our heads in shock.

What made it worse was the fact it was an equaliser for them, making it 2-2, right on the stroke of half-time. As everyone knows, it's the worst possible time to concede a goal. I was still in something of a daze when Chaddy opened his half-time team talk by asking me how it was possible for a ball from nearly 100 yards away to sail over the head of a 6ft 4in-plus goalkeeper? I panicked and fumbled for a new excuse and came back with the remarkably lame-sounding: 'It must have bounced off a sprinkler head.'

Chaddy snapped back: 'We don't have a sprinkler system on our field.' All the lads burst out laughing. I knew it was something I would have to take loads of stick about. I half smiled at Chaddy and said: 'Well that's my story and I'm sticking with it.'

'A bloody invisible sprinkler head,' Chaddy said. He was now seeing the funny side of it. Thankfully Chaddy moved on to his next coaching point.

Back in London, *The Sun* newspaper picked up the story with the inevitable headline 'Tutt Tutt'. The report was accompanied by an unflattering photo of me sitting on my arse with the ball in the back of the net. My mum sent me the newspaper cutting and had written next to it: 'Good article on you son. I suppose this means you will not be coming home for a few years. That may be wise.' Mum had a great way of dealing with life's mishaps. She would always 'sprinkle' some humour on a situation when things went awry. We were brought up to think that what's done is done and therefore don't wallow in it. Which I immediately tried not to do!

Mum came out to visit me towards the end of the season. She was shocked at how hot it was in late August: 'To play in heat of around 100 degrees you must all be bloody nuts,' was her considered, down-to-earth verdict.

She also had something to say when the legendary George Best received what can best be described as a very muted reception when his name was announced before one of our home games when he was playing for the San Jose Earthquakes. Mum suggested the lack of soccer knowledge among the American fans was evident.

Mum was right – most Atlanta fans had no idea how many quality players were on show, who were well recognised as world-class players in their native lands and in Europe.

In terms of George Best, you could see there was still a wealth of talent left in him. We had comfortably beaten the Earthquakes at home the previous month but it was the away game in San Jose, California that I will always remember. We were coming to the end of a long three-week road trip with the Chiefs and this was our last game.

Throughout the first half George was simply tearing us apart down our left flank. He still had the skill, confidence and speed to do almost anything he wanted. Then I had a chance to make history. George was making another weaving run from just inside our half, ten minutes before the break. He beat two players with sheer speed and a third with a crowd-pleasing nutmeg. He was entering the penalty box and gearing up for a shot when a vicious scissor slide tackle from behind by Branko Radovic took his legs away. The referee, a well-known English ref called Gordon Hill, immediately awarded a penalty kick. George grabbed the ball from the supposedly regular penalty-taker saying to him that he wanted to take it.

Trevor Gething and I had discussed some goalkeeping psychology around penalties and therefore I went into my repertoire and asked referee Hill who would be taking the penalty kick.

Hill pointed and said: 'George Best,' to which I replied, 'Oh that's good, I know where George puts it,' and smiled confidently at Hill then George.

I then continued my rehearsed repertoire as I stood in the middle of my goal, one yard off the goal line to slow things down. I knew the linesman would intervene and make me stand back on the goal line. After getting back on my line I then skipped to my left goalpost and kicked it gently to get any excess mud off my right boot and then side-skipped to the other post and kicked it gently to get the excess mud off my left boot. By this time, I was pushing my luck on trying to break George's concentration so I smiled at Hill, then at George Best, and settled on my line with one large step to the right, just to unbalance the visual landscape. Hill blew his whistle as the crowd anticipated screaming 'goal!'

George wasn't above a few mind games himself. He had already placed the ball on the spot and walked slowly towards it and then took five paces back. For me it was decision time. Should I guess and commit myself or should I stand my ground? I figured that against a world-class player like George, guessing was my best option. Bestie ran up and placed the ball firmly towards my bottom left-hand corner. Fortunately, I had launched myself in the correct direction. It was then all about adjusting in mid-flight. With an extra stretch of my left arm, I got a slight touch that was good enough to guide the ball around the post.

I had saved a penalty kick from George Best! I was rejoicing, when the ref, Gordon Hill, blew his whistle and ordered a re-take saying I had moved before the ball was kicked. Hill was now smiling at both of us. 'Hey, come on ref,' I begged him.

Hill walked over to me and said quietly with an even bigger grin: 'Sorry son, but it is George Best and you know he's going to score sooner or later.'

Of course, the second time, Bestie sent me the wrong way but, in my mind, I had stopped a penalty by a footballing genius. It's just a pity the record books would not show it!

Penalty kicks were my speciality that year. Out of seven penalties, I saved three, one was missed and three scored. And one of those scored was by George Best, so I could live with that statistic.

Another memorable game came in Anaheim against the California Surf. It was a very busy night for me with many saves to make and included another last-gasp penalty save that assured us of a 3-2 win. A reporter compared yours truly to the famous television evangelist Billy Graham, who was also in town for a

Christian Rival Crusade. The reporter wrote: 'Atlanta Chiefs goalkeeper, Graham Tutt, made more saves last night at the Anaheim Stadium than Evangelist Billy Graham who was across the road at the Anaheim Convention Center.' I liked that.

We finished our season as the Southeastern Division Champions by beating Tampa Bay Rowdies 5-4 in Atlanta. Fort Lauderdale Strikers came in second, Jacksonville Tea Men third and surprisingly the Tampa Bay Rowdies finished fourth. We surprised the pundits!

It was a very tight league. We won our division because we were harder workers who never gave up. Even so, we did well against some great players and outstanding teams to win it. Unfortunately, we then took a nosedive when it came to the play-offs. Our star player, Brian Kidd, had returned to Bolton Wanderers and our team was carrying far too many injuries. Consequently, we lost our winning rhythm. After losing to Jacksonville at home in overtime in the first round of the play-offs we lost to them again in Jacksonville with a half-baked squad. Our season was over and finished. Shortly afterwards we were hearing rumours that our owner, Ted Turner, was about to pull the plug on the whole shebang.

Turner was apparently fully focused on developing CNN and CNN International and losing interest in his sports franchises. Proof of this came when he sold his financial interests in the Atlanta Flames NHL ice hockey franchise and they moved to Calgary to become the Calgary Flames. Turner kept some financial involvement in the Atlanta Braves and Atlanta Hawks basketball teams but showed little interest in keeping us going, so the Chiefs franchise folded even though we had had a relatively successful winning season.

I had bought a house just six months earlier thinking I had three more seasons to run on my contract, which suddenly became invalid. I was now in a quandary. I had fallen in love with Atlanta and did not want to move to another club in the States. The question was, what was I going to do next?

Chapter 45

Should I Stay or Should I Go?

I FELT angry and betrayed by our owner about what had happened and, like many others, considered it a poor business decision given that support for both indoor and outdoor operations was growing fast and showing great promise.

I was at a crossroads and decided to return to England for a few weeks to be with my family. My sister Julie needed my support after her husband left her for another woman. I couldn't believe that he left Julie with four children, aged nine, six and two-year-old twins. I felt devastated for my lovely sister. She certainly did not deserve that treatment.

Her husband had also left her with no car, so she had to walk with her two boys to their school and then drop off the twins at day care before she went to work. Then she had to pick them up again at the end of the day. It was obviously a tougher time for Julie than it was for me. I knew I had to be with her helping out, as did my parents.

Her husband had been my best mate, but not anymore. Julie was such a true, loyal person, a loving wife, a great mother, a brilliant sister and best friend to all she met. He just announced one Friday morning as he was heading for work that he was leaving her for his secretary. How he could do such a thing was something I couldn't answer.

I was pleased to be back home. It felt an important time to be with Julie. We decided it was time for a mini family vacation. So, my mum, dad, Julie, her four children and I went to our old childhood holiday spot called Dymchurch on the Kent coast. It was something of a disappointment. The small funfair we used to visit as kids had been abandoned. A small handwritten note was attached to a padlocked gate. It read starkly: 'Permanently Closed. Run out of money'. The entrance was starting to fall apart with rotten wood and peeling paint. It seemed like a suitable metaphor for our plight and did not improve our mood. I looked at the sad faces of the children and my heart bled for them. They were confused with what was happening.

We then all walked along the shingle beach and played with the kids. We bought cockles and winkles – a traditional English seafood – and sat on the sea wall overlooking the empty beach and cold, grey English Channel. Mum and Dad were now tending to the twins and Julie's two young boys were busy skipping stones along the seashore. It was a perfect time for a heart-to-heart with my sister.

'So, what are you going to do now, Buster?' Julie began.

'I was going to ask you the same question, Julie,' I replied, in truth not knowing my next step.

'I know exactly what I'm going to do,' Julie said assertively. 'I'm going to sit tight and tread water until things settle down and then decide on my next step when I'm ready. I'm strong enough to survive this. How about you, Buster?'

I found myself gazing out to sea. I told Julie I wasn't sure. I'd have to get my house sold or rented if I didn't return to Atlanta.

Julie then gave me a big sisterly smile and said to me confidently: 'You'll figure it out, Buster. The right decision will come to you, especially if you think about it long enough. It always does. You know that.'

We were helping each other with our unflagging love, belief and loyalty towards one another.

And Julie was right. The answer to my issues came a few days later when my mum's phone rang at six in the morning. It was Chaddy calling from Atlanta. He got straight to the point: 'How would you like to come back to Atlanta and play for the Georgia Generals in the ASL outdoor league?' he asked.

'I would love to, Chaddy.' And then I immediately asked, 'What's the deal?' He told me it was a couple of grand a month plus incentives, possibly a car, but could not confirm that yet. He told me he was building a team from scratch and that I was his first call, which made me feel valued.

I had missed Chaddy and Atlanta. I had been back in England for nearly three weeks, but my inner voice was telling me to start playing again pronto. The clock was ticking and my fitness level was starting to dip. I knew I had to go and I told Chaddy I was two feet in.

It was a bittersweet feeling. Leaving my family had never been more difficult. Saying emotional farewells has never been my strength and my goodbyes were especially hard because they were always for such a long time. But I knew I had to go. Less than one week later I was back in Atlanta, Georgia.

Chapter 46

The Georgia Generals

CHADDY WAS pumped up as I walked into his new office. He got straight to the point and asked me if I wanted to earn an extra couple of hundred dollars a week working in the front office selling season tickets during pre-season.

The next three weeks were both exhausting and exciting. After intensive training at Stone Mountain, which usually finished around 5pm, I would go to the office to call a list of soccer fans, trying to sell season or group-ticket packages. It taught me a lot about selling on the phone by simply being thrown in at the deep end.

Our Georgia Generals team was fully formed by the end of the second week. Chaddy had recruited talent from all over the world, including star players like striker Jose Netto from Brazil who had a silky touch and could score with either foot. Then there was Peter Carr who had played almost 350 league games for Darlington and Carlisle United. He was a hard-nosed defender who rarely missed the ball or the man! He teamed up well with Mike Balson, a former Atlanta Chief who had played nearly 300 times for Exeter City. Mike and Peter were wise heads between them and captained the side. They kept our back four tight as a drum.

I was pleased to see that Mark MacKain, a former Atlanta Chief team-mate and highly skilled midfielder and defender, was also joining us. Mark could control the midfield and could play just as well at the back. I always liked to jest with Mark, especially if we were making a community public appearance together. I used to tell people in our opening introductions, especially at our soccer clinics together, that if it weren't for Mark MacKain I would be the best-looking player on the team. Mark could have been a male model with his blond curly hair, blue eyes and all-year tan. He looked like a Greek God and the girls loved him.

Then there were some very talented local Atlanta players like Kevin Fouser. Kevin was a skilful and very quick natural goalscorer. I loved reaching Kevin on fast breakaways by giving him a bullet-driven drop kick to chase. He read those breakaways very well and notched several goals during the season.

Another great local Atlanta addition was Griff Sims who was outstanding on either wing. Griff could play the game very well and score goals, giving us even more punch up front. The third local Atlanta star was a hard-tackling midfielder-cum-defender, Gary Levengood. Gary would put his body on the line whenever needed, was a great tackler and had some skill too.

Our American players proved their worth many times over. We carried no passengers. It was not an Atlanta Chiefs rerun with big international names and a big budget but I was happy to be back in Atlanta with a group of talented, hungry go-getters. They revitalised me with their own enthusiasm and talent.

The travel budget was small compared to the Chiefs, but we soldiered on with some long bus rides and did fine. One particular away trip involved another aviation-related incident. We were ready to take off from a small local airport called, rather comically, the Charlie Brown Airport. We nicknamed our jet 'The Brown Pencil' as it was an 18-seat passenger plane with turbo propeller jet engines and it really did look like an H2 pencil.

We were scheduled to play in Oklahoma City against the Oklahoma City Slickers, so-called because of the number of refineries and oil wells dotted throughout the state. Just before take-off there was a loud clanking noise. Peering out, it was obvious a propeller was slightly off-centre and vibrating loudly. It sounded very serious and the captain immediately turned off both engines. We were worried that the blades would come loose or shatter and cut the plane in two. Before the captain could say anything, Peter Carr tried to open the plane's door to jump out. He had made it very clear earlier that he was terrified of flying and was now demonstrating it. The plane's power was now totally cut and there was no inside light or air conditioning. We decided Peter was right and we all forced open the door and leaped down to the tarmac like lemmings.

The captain tried to assure us everything was going to be fine and to stay close to the plane. With us all nervously shuffling about on the runway, the captain stepped out of the plane with a large piece of wood that resembled a baseball bat and proceeded to bash the problematic propeller five or six times. We all stood there with our mouths wide open in disbelief as the captain carried out what looked like a less than sophisticated repair job. As he struck the propeller one last time, he shouted: 'I've fixed it. It just jumped out of sync. It won't happen again. Let's go.'

It took 20 minutes for us all to gingerly get back on board. It was only when the propeller had run for ten minutes without any issue that we felt confident enough to fly. With the air conditioning still not working, we flew near naked with just our underpants on because of the 95 degree-plus temperature.

Towards the end of the season, we had so many injuries that I had to play up front with Griff Sims as a dual striker, which was a first for me. I actually should have scored in the first five minutes but tripped over a seam in the artificial turf six yards out. There again it might have been a sprinkler head, even though sprinklers are not used on an artificial field!

In practice, I had often fancied my chances as a striker. I could win the majority of high balls and had a decent touch for a tall player. The funny thing about playing up front was my Georgia Generals game shirt.

In the rush to have my outfield shirt numbered 00, it came back in a medium size and I take an extra-large. The shirt was not only ultra-skintight, it also exposed my midriff and bellybutton. My double zero number on the back looked like two frog eyes. The players said I should enter a wet T-shirt contest like they do in Fort Lauderdale.

Anyway, we had a decent season finishing with a winning record. Then we heard rumblings that a second season was in doubt due to the travel expenses and stability of the league. What did not help was that the economy was hurting and petrol prices were going through the roof. Money yet again became tight across America.

I certainly did not fancy playing anywhere else because I had quickly grown to love Atlanta. I had made some wonderful friends, was enamoured with the North Georgia Mountains and felt comfortable in my surroundings. I was ready to make a go of it and get what most people would consider to be a normal nine-to-five job. I did not realise how difficult that would be.

Chapter 47

The Love of My Life

I WANTED to make my home in the Marietta area, a 20-minute drive north of Atlanta. A Lincoln Mercury car dealership owner and friend offered me a job as a PR guy and sales rep. At the time, I did not know what else to do so I accepted. It was a tough gig. Trying to sell Lincolns in autumn 1982 when there was a fuel crisis going on was not easy. It seemed everyone was buying Japanese cars and people did not want a big gas-guzzling Lincoln. Pretty quickly, I realised I had to get out of the car business and return to soccer in some capacity.

After six weeks of minimal car sales and frustration I decided to contact a small up-and-coming local college called Kennesaw with the idea of running summer soccer camps for children aged six to 17. The college responded favourably with a decent percentage deal. It was a saviour and I thanked God I had something to do in soccer again. For the next three months, through late winter to early spring, I scheduled a tremendous amount of soccer clinics at more than 55 elementary and middle schools. I was advertising my first series of summer soccer camps for beginner, intermediate and advanced players.

At each school I would demonstrate a skill such as juggling, then select three boys and three girls to teach them the basics like kicking and catching, and challenge them to see how many they could do in a minute. I made sure I included those children who looked least sporty to show that soccer was a game that could be enjoyed by everyone and that you did not have to be the perfect athlete.

It was a gruelling schedule but great fun. Sometimes I made as many as three school soccer clinic appearances in one day. At the end of each session, I handed out dozens of sponsored summer soccer camp T-shirts with my camp brochure to all the kids in the hope they would sign up.

The headmasters and PE staff loved it because it gave them a break and I was free of charge. The results were amazing. Over 750 kids registered for three one-week sessions.

While completing my final week of summer camp at Kennesaw College, a parent called Chuck Wolf approached me and asked if I wanted to consider developing an old roller-skating rink into an indoor soccer facility. Chuck had three young lads attending my camp and was an airline captain and entrepreneur. We quickly formed a business relationship and as soon as I saw the roller rink, I loved the thought of creating an indoor soccer facility for kids and adults.

So, Chuck bought the unused roller rink and I rented it from him at a reasonable price. Between us we designed and constructed the indoor soccer facility with goals, surrounding walls and a tight net encircling the whole playing area. We even installed two long rows of movie theatre seats that were perched on a platform three feet off the ground running the full length of the arena. The parents had a great view and were more than comfortable eating their popcorn, drinking a Coke and cheering on their kids. The atmosphere was absolutely perfect.

I then began calling local youth-team coaches offering them a free hour to see if they liked it. I then asked each coach who their greatest rivals were and, with their permission, called their rival team's coach to set up a game at our new indoor arena for free. The coaches jumped at the opportunity to play indoor soccer against their arch enemy. It also produced some great games, packed the arena's seating and encouraged them to sign up for a season of ten games.

After two months of giving free playing time to over 50 teams, more than 70 boys' and girls' youth teams, aged from six to 17, registered for season one. By season three we were maxed out at 144 teams. Running from late October to mid-March we were full seven days a week. When the youth outdoor season started the adult indoor leagues would also begin. To my delight, the adult leagues became a smash hit, especially the so-called Wreck Co-ed League, where three men and three women would play on the same team. I had to expand the Wreck League to three divisions offering beginner, intermediate and advanced levels. The fun part was watching the kids cheering their parents on. It was incredible that I was just as busy with the adult leagues as I was with the youth leagues. I was starting to feel that I needed more help.

Then fate lent a hand. An old team-mate from Arcadia Pepsi, top goal scorer, Ian Gillies, wanted to move from South Africa to the USA so I offered him a business partnership splitting the profits 50/50. We ran the indoor soccer business successfully for over four years before Chuck sold the facility to the Veterans of Foreign War (VFW) Association which developed a fully blown bingo social club. Our 'phase two' plan was to open an outdoor soccer complex with an indoor soccer facility on the premises. More about that later but for the time being Ian and I ran the indoor soccer business in the North Atlanta area.

It was hard work and we needed some downtime so, some nights, we would go to a disco in Buckhead, Atlanta. We had such a laugh doing our John Travolta disco thing. We didn't have a care in the world. Ian and I were both 27 years old, making money, both as fit as a fiddle and in our prime. The girls loved us. At least that's what we thought! However, we ended up giving the parents a good laugh on one occasion. We tried as they say 'to burn the candle at both ends' one particular night and boy did we get burned.

It was a Friday night, and Ian and I went out on an all-nighter. The partying never stopped as we hooked up with a group of women soccer players who were also in a party mood. We danced and drank ourselves to the limit. Before we knew it, we had to be at our indoor soccer facility because our first game kicked off at 8am. Ian and I still had our disco clothes on when we opened the doors just before 8am. We were well late! The opening two teams and parents were patiently waiting and stamping their feet because of the cold weather as we unlocked the entrance doors. No doubt we also stank of beer but I'm positive we looked the business in our tight white disco shirts, black flared pants and wooden platform shoes. We looked straight off the cover of the *Saturday Night Fever* album. Yes, I'm absolutely positive we looked great!

Fortunately, I won a coin toss and Ian had to referee the first game. My job in the meantime was to get the concession stand going and make the coffee and popcorn. Yes, some parents would

Dad and me … summer 1958 (two years old).

My first soccer ball, shirt and shorts – Christmas 1961 (five years old).

A 'flying bomb' just before it hit a London row house. It's identical to what happened across from my parents' house causing the bomb site where we played football!

Reminiscent of the bomb site opposite our house … before clean-up!

11 years old – London Cup Final – wearing Slazenger 'steel-toe-capped' boots.

Charlton Colts Team 1974: Back row: Coach Peter Shreeves, Harold Powell, Danny Jennings, Graham Tutt, Les Berry, Alan Pacey, Ben Odeje. Front row: Mark Wright, Mark Penfold, Peter Mills, Alan Hart, M Bailey.

Charlton Athletic 1975/76 Season: Back row: Les Berry, Jimmy Giles, Graham Tutt, Colin Powell, Bobby Goldthorpe. Middle row: Arthur Horsfield, Bobby Curtis, George Hope, Mark Penfold, Harry Cripps, Richie Bowman, Mike Flanagan, Ray Tumbridge. Front row: Phil Warman, Peter Hunt, David Young, Derek Hales, Keith Peacock.

Making a save at the Valley against Sunderland in November 1975. Big crowds back at the Valley to see the 'New' Charlton.

SUN Sport

CUP WEEK CONFESSIONS!

TUTT, TUTT, PALACE!

QUOTE

MALCOLM ALLISON (Palace manager): "We'll still finish above Charlton — no problem. I thought they flooded the pitch and we just couldn't get used to the conditions."

ANDY NELSON (Charlton manager): "We should have been three up by half-time and then could have lost it in the last minutes. Promotion is still a long way away. Talking about it just puts pressure on the players."

ROONEY STONE (Charlton general manager and secretary) said of the bottle incident: "It was one nut in a 25,000 crowd. He got a bit excited. It is a police matter."

By BRIAN WOOLNOUGH: Charlton 1, C Palace 0

CHARLTON forced Crystal Palace manager Malcolm Allison to eat his words last night as they moved into second place in the Third Division after a full-blooded London derby in front of a 25,535 crowd.

Six weeks ago, Allison criticised and taunted Charlton, even betting manager Andy Nelson £100 that Palace would go up before his South London rivals.

Allison watched in horror as Palace were torn apart in the first half and then squandered late chances.

GRAHAM TUTT

Charlton keeper stuns Mal

TOP OF DIV. 3

Collecting the life

Revenge on Malcolm Allison, the Crystal Palace manager. He told me 18 months earlier while playing for Crystal Palace Colts team, and in earshot of other players 'Gotta let you go … you are not good enough.' I had the last laugh. Thanks Mal … it made me even more determined to make the grade and go pro at 17 years old.

With the 'New Boss'
Andy Nelson.

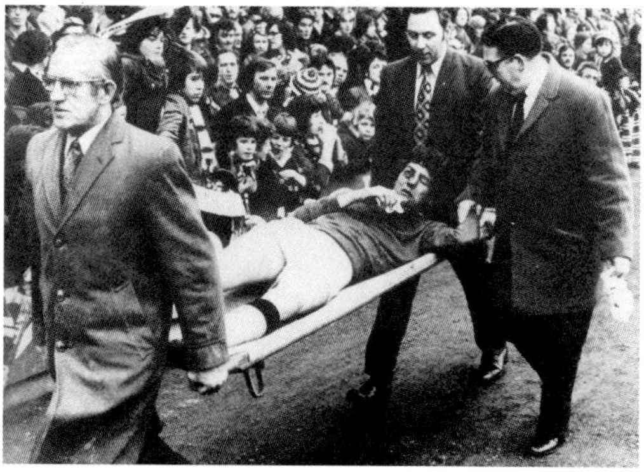

Saturday, 21 February 1976
Sunderland versus Charlton at Roker Park.

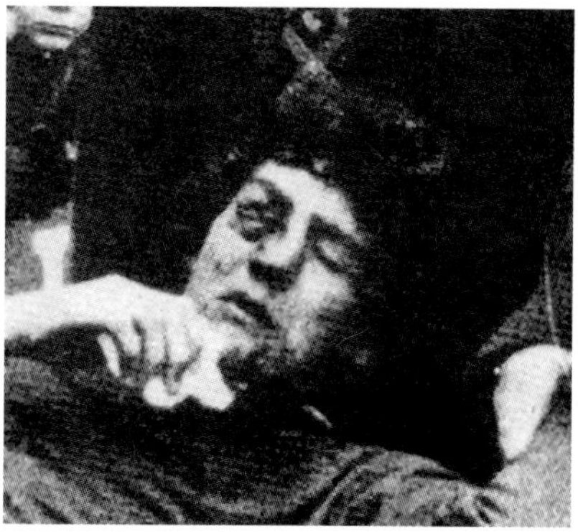

Broken nose, eyelid lacerations, fractured cheek and orbit resulting in permanent double vision.

Testimonial match poster: Malcolm Macdonald, England and Newcastle striker playing up front with the incomparable Derek Hales as guest players. Charlton won 3-2. Plus a unique All Star Goalkeepers XI versus Television and Radio All Star team preceded the main Charlton versus Sunderland game.

Thanking the pre-game All Star Goalkeepers XI and TV/Radio All Star team on my testimonial night.

The unique All Star Goalkeepers XI … Goalkeepers from far left: Pat Jennings, Spurs and Northern Ireland. Third person, Peter Shearing, West Ham and former England youth and my goalkeeper and assistant coach at Charlton. Fourth person, Peter Mellor, Fulham. Fifth, John Dunn, Charlton and former Aston Villa. Sixth, John Jackson, Crystal Palace. Seventh, Bob Wilson, Arsenal and BBC TV commentator. Eighth, Mervyn Day, West Ham and England U-21. Ninth, Graham Horn, Luton Town. Eleventh, Tony Burns, Crystal Palace. The Goalkeepers XI won 3-2 against Dennis Waterman and Theo Foley's Television and Radio All Stars. Top football commentators Brian Moore, John Motson and Tony Gubba were also in attendance.

PROFILE ON GRAHAM TUTT
by Colin Cameron

When Graham Tutt's career came to its tragic end on February 21, 1976 he was still six months short of his 20th birthday yet had already played in 71 league and cup matches for Charlton plus another four league outings while on loan at Workington.

Seventy five matches in all by the age of 19½! A remarkable number of games when you consider Charlton's record holder, Sam Bartram who played in 623 league and cup matches was two months short of his 23rd birthday when he reached 75 matches.

Six of the players still at The Valley, Bob Curtis, Peter Hunt, Colin Powell, Keith Peacock, Mick Flanagan and Phil Warman played in Graham's debut match at Shrewsbury on March 19, 1974 — the result that day was 3—3 and the attendance a meagre 1,232 and followed the 850 gate at Rochdale, were the two lowest crowds to watch Charlton since the war.

In contrast Graham's final three matches were watched by 74,553, including 30,000 plus gates at Molyneux and Roker Park. All but Mick Flanagan of the players who appeared in Graham's first match were also in the side in his final game.

Our genial giant was considered too tiny when he went for a trial with Millwall Colts but he later had a spell with Crystal Palace Colts and in fact played for them against a Charlton Colts team.

Young Graham was persistent in his quest for league fame for apart from helping local teams Heathfield Celtic and Plumstead Working Men's Club he spent a week on trial with West Bromwich Albion before Theo Foley signed him for Charlton on October 22, 1973.

Testimonial Game Programme

Arcadia Shepherds, South Africa, 1978. Note height of the security fence. Back row: Head coach Kai Johansen, Peter Frelich, Nathan Sacks, Gerry Queen, Graham Tutt, Dave Herholt, Maurice Hepworth, Steve Ingle, Plonkie Naude, assistant coach Roy Matthews. Front row: Starting third from left; Spoedie Bronkhorst, Alex Morrison, Robbie De Graff, Vincent 'Tanti' Julius, Johnny Ferrera.

Playing for Columbus Magic against New York United at Shea Stadium, NY.

Coming for a cross, in my first Atlanta Chiefs game at Lockhart Stadium, home of the Fort Lauderdale Strikers. 'If he can't see the ball he can't score.' I had punched it away with my right fist. We lost 1-0 in five 5-second 'one on one' shoot-outs from 35 yards. Much more exciting than penalty kicks. There were no draws or ties.

'Just a touch' – A left-handed save was good enough to guide the ball away for a 2-1 win in five 5-second shoot-outs against Fort Lauderdale Strikers in 1981 at Dekalb Memorial Stadium, located near Stone Mountain. It was the last kick of the match. The win captured the Southeast Division Championship over the Fort Lauderdale Strikers, Jacksonville Tea Men and the Tampa Bay Rowdies. The Dekalb Memorial location proved to be a better venue than the 55,000 all-seated Atlanta Fulton County Stadium. There were over 14,500 in attendance, our largest home game attendance of the season.

Celebrating the shoot-out save and victory with Brian Kidd, David Byrne and Hayden Knight. Brian Kidd was an incredible striker. He went back to play for Manchester United and was later assistant coach under Alex Ferguson for many years. Brian continues his career as an assistant coach at Manchester City. He's the best example of how a pro player should be on and off the field.

Player community appearances were frequent. We did some pioneering, that's for sure. This player appearance was at the Stone Mountain Spring Festival in 1981.

Georgia Generals 1982.

The Georgia Generals 1982: Top row: Guilio Bernardi, Jose Netto, Danny Nevin, Griff Sims, Charlie Greene, Mark MaKain. Centre row: Danny Payne, Mark Turner, Robbie Olsen. Front row: Head coach David 'Chaddy' Chadwick, Kevin Fouser, Craig Scarpelli, Greg Willin, Aiden McKenzie, Peter Carr, Mike Balson, John Bapst, Graham Tutt, Sonny Askew, physio Mike Sabatelle. Standing on the General Steam Train at Stone Mountain.

Playing goalkeeper and as a striker. Left: At the Silver Dome in Detroit with my Georgia Generals captain Mike Balson. Right: Silver Dome again but two weeks later – playing as a striker in the play-offs. We had so many injured players Chaddy had not much choice but to play me up front. My capable back-up keeper Craig Scarpelli went in goal. We lost in overtime 1-0 to the Detroit Express. It was my last professional game, 1982.

'The Ambulance'. This was my promotional vehicle in 1983. It was a 1970 ambulance from Dobbins Air Force Base in Marietta, GA. It could transport over 300 inflated soccer balls and four sets of portable goals for my weekly soccer camps. Note: The Ambulance had a spotlight and a siren that worked! Great for getting home early in heavy traffic!

Life University team photo. Note the time on the clock at 5:44pm. The team photo was scheduled for 2pm. I eventually went looking for Dr Sid (front and centre) and drove him from his home back for the photo. Not bad for Dr Sid being only three hours and 44 minutes late. If the photo was taken without Dr Sid I would have been likely fired!

Coaching at Life University (probably giving the referee some stick). In the background from left to right: Mark Tonner, from South Africa, then Tony Annan from Newcastle, England and Adrian Biundo from Australia. Tony Annan went on to be the youth development director for Atlanta United MLS team.

First soccer camp at Life University with over 100 campers.Keith Ingram, far right, was my brilliant camp director for ten years.

With the world's greatest and most popular player, Pele. Taken at a Zoo Atlanta fundraiser. We did a soccer clinic earlier in the day. Pele was a total pleasure to work with. No wonder they call him the King.

Lizzie, the love of my life. Taken just before we went up in the hot air balloon where I proposed to her a few thousand feet in the air. We were married six months later.

'Saint' Jerry Wilson at the Gwinnet Arena Exhibition Game on my 50th birthday.

The media used my Atlanta Chiefs diving save to promote the announcement of the Atlanta United MLS team in 2016.

Theo Foley, my mentor, on his 70th birthday at Charlton's 100-year anniversary celebration in 2005. Theo encouraged me to be the best that I could possibly be. I still love him! Sadly Theo died in 2020.

Being honoured as a former Atlanta Chief and pioneer for soccer in 2018. Taken before an Atlanta United MLS game in the new Mercedes Benz Stadium. It was a nice surprise showing appreciation for 38 years of promoting and developing soccer in Georgia. Liz and I were both escorted on to the field before the game where they made the announcement. It was an emotional moment for Liz and I. We had gone full circle in our soccer careers, culminating in over 70 years of Liz and I coaching and promoting soccer in the Atlanta area.

Taken during the pre-game recognition – game attendances range from 50,000 to 70,000. At last after nearly 40 years of helping promote the game Pro Soccer had arrived!

eat popcorn at 8am and wash it down with a Coca-Cola. Only in America!

I soon noticed Ian was barely moving down at the far end of the arena while refereeing. He said later he didn't want to blow the whistle because his head was hurting so badly. We were both nursing monumental hangovers. Then it happened. Ian threw up through the protective net at the corner of the arena. As luck would have it the ball was at the opposite end of the pitch so the parents were not really focused on Ian, but I was.

Witnessing Ian's predicament – his head at this point was almost through the protective netting – I burst out laughing to the point where I also began to feel queasy and rushed to the kitchen area finding the sink just in time to emulate Ian's performance. That was the last time we partied hard on an indoor soccer work weekend. We learned our lesson not to do that again.

Things were going well so we decided to search for some land to build an indoor soccer arena and have additional space for some outdoor fields. It would then give us a year-round business. After two years of searching, Chuck and I settled on a beautiful 26-acre horse farm. By then Ian Gillies had met his future wife, Tanya, and left to focus on developing soccer in the north-eastern part of Atlanta while Chuck and I concentrated on the north-west.

To develop a 26-acre soccer complex from scratch was a huge challenge. On the upside, being a former horse farm, the site had a decent base of manure which made the grass grow very well. There was also a four-bedroom house on the property that we converted into offices.

By the time of our grand opening in May 1988 over 650 boys and girls were registered. By season two we had grown to nearly

900 registered players. I was then able to hire an assistant and a groundsman.

Even though we were growing fast, the facility running costs were quite high and I was feeling mentally and physically burned out. So, I figured the best thing to do was make it a non-profit organisation and hand it over to the parents to run on a voluntary basis. This drew more parents to come forward and volunteer their time and effort. I had some other plans that had been with me for a while. The facility continues to thrive to this day with nearly a couple of thousand players on several fields every weekend. It was critical that volunteers-cum-coaches, like Tim Bradigan, John and Judy Scheve, Jim Archer, Jose Camara, Wayne Arnold, Carl Krauth, Bruce Stewart and my assistant, Carol Havens, all gave many hours of their time, for which I will be forever grateful. These types of good people were now covering North America and growing the game at a rapid rate. In the mid to late 80s we were in the pioneering stages of developing soccer facilities, recruiting coaches, volunteers and upgrading the game throughout America.

My summer soccer camps had now blossomed to four colleges – three in Georgia and one in Alabama – plus five youth soccer facilities spread across the Atlanta area and North Georgia. Just over 3,000 kids and 35 coaches were participating in my summer soccer camps. It had become a business.

I then started contacting high-school soccer coaches to register their teams for my overnight summer camps. One such coach became very important to my campaign. Her name was Liz Potts, from Pace Academy in Atlanta. Liz had a thriving high-school soccer programme that could possibly participate in my summer camps at Auburn University in Alabama. After chatting with Liz on the phone for a few minutes I knew I had to go and meet her. She sounded so friendly, positive and had developed a successful girls soccer programme almost from scratch.

I decided to take the plunge and made an appointment to visit Liz and hopefully recruit her as a coach and bring one or two teams to my new camp. Liz told me in the first minute of our conversation that she normally took her teams to another Atlanta summer soccer camp, but was not happy with the arrangement. I was then a bit cheeky and asked her how much they paid her. She told me and I immediately doubled it with incentives for bringing in more players. I'm pleased to say it worked. In August of 1988 at Auburn University I fell in love with the greatest woman I could ever meet.

Liz coached her team with a love and care that you could only admire. She gave clear coaching directions that produced excellent teams and quality players but, more importantly, ensured that everyone had fun at the same time. It was no wonder her team had recently won a state championship. I thought she was wonderful in every way. I had gone totally 'Goo-goo gaa-gaa'!

Sadly, for me, the feeling was not immediately mutual. Liz had just exited a relationship and was wary about getting involved. I instinctively knew that if I was going to win her over, I would have to be patient and that meant from my side going 'Gently Bentley' – no rush!

So, at the end of the Auburn camp, I invited Liz to celebrate my 32nd birthday with me, some camp coaches plus a few friends. I was thrilled when she accepted. Back then I had a very relaxed attitude towards timekeeping – I didn't even care to own a watch – and made a bit of a blunder on the day which nearly derailed our relationship before it had even begun. I had agreed to meet some of my soccer mates for a few drinks earlier in the evening. I didn't want Liz to feel it was just she and I celebrating my birthday. Time with my mates flew by and, before I knew it, I realised I was going to be an hour late for my own birthday party, meeting up with Liz and the camp staff members.

I bolted from one side of town to the other hoping she would still be at the upscale bistro where I had reserved a small area for about 20 people. As I opened the front door, Liz was walking out. She obviously thought I was standing her up and politely, with a lot of class and tact, told me I was an hour late and that she was leaving.

I apologised profusely, slowed her down, made her smile a little and gently coaxed her back to a quiet corner table where the rest of our coaches were still having a laugh and a good time.

At first, we sat at different ends of a long table. I would glance in her direction looking for a glimpse of forgiveness in her eyes and then, after a beer or two, I got bold and moved to sit next to her when another coach admirer went to the restroom. I had a feeling she thought he was a pain so I played the rescuer. By now, I had cracked a few jokes and blamed my team-mates for not being on time. I was edging out of the doghouse.

Liz and I talked effortlessly. I tried hard not to go too overboard with her but I was falling fast.

The evening closed at a respectable time with a hug and a birthday peck on my cheek. I hoped I had made enough of an impression to warrant her seeing me again. I was trying my best to play it cool because I didn't want to scare her away.

The next morning, I was standing on top of a ten-foot stepladder painting the crossbar of a goal at the outdoor soccer facility we were developing in Kennesaw … Suddenly I realised that I could be talking to Liz. I was smitten. I dropped my paintbrush in the can and ran as quickly as I could past three soccer fields and towards my office to call her. I really wanted to hear her voice and see her. The thought of not seeing her again hurt. I was at the point of no return.

Chapter 48
Up, Up and Away

BY THIS time, I felt ready for a new career challenge. The non-profit status on the 26-acre soccer facility had gone through and was accepted by the parents. My new goal was to develop and run a professional indoor soccer franchise in Atlanta.

I had given a presentation to an Atlanta businessman called Ron Terwilliger who was a potential investor for a pro indoor soccer team. Ron was keen to proceed and wanted to launch in the upcoming season, which was only three months away. So, from late July 1989, I began recruiting and hiring staff. First, I hired a quality coach and front-office people to devise a coherent marketing plan. Hiring Keith Tozer as head coach was a masterstroke as he selected quality players, was active in the community and became the best indoor soccer coach in the business. He later became head coach of the USA Men's Indoor Soccer National Team which won global tournaments. Keith did his job while I operated the front office with John Durham, an experienced indoor soccer promoter. We called our team Atlanta Attack. I was given the title executive vice president/operations. It sounded impressive but in truth it involved wearing various hats at different times and juggling marketing, sales, promotions, public relations, camp director and attending community appearances. There was plenty to do.

Incredibly, we played our first game in front of 11,000-plus fans at the Omni just 12 weeks after the team's announcement. I had been putting in 12-hour days, six days a week for three months. We got off to a great start, winning our first home game against Indiana Kicks 23-11. Back then it was three points for a goal, two points for a penalty and one if you scored on a Power Play, meaning the opposition had a man short for two minutes due to an infringement.

The overall season was successful for a new franchise and we won 23 and lost 17, averaging around 6,700 fans. Our highest attendance was 13,858 against the Memphis Rogues and that was only because E. Presley played up front. I jest of course but it was great to be in Elvis country when we went to play in Memphis at the Mid-South Coliseum, a 10,000-plus facility where Elvis had sung to many packed audiences.

The indoor game was showing great promise with decent attendances but again the running costs were high. Three-quarters of the way through the season the owner started making noises about wanting to sell the franchise. Even so we ended the season on a positive note with two 11,000 and two 13,000 home attendances.

We had an unfortunate start to the second season with the USA announcing war with Iraq on the same night as our opening home game. It was a tense time in America with everyone at home watching the news. I counted 75 fans in our 16,000 all-seat arena, which was disheartening to say the least.

Then it turned into a nightmare. The owner cut my advertising budget in half and I heard through the grapevine that the team's sale to Kansas City was nearly done. In the middle of all this, I decided to take three or four days off because I had far more important duties to attend to.

Liz and I had been dating for over six months. I had gently won her over, we were deeply in love and my thoughts were turning towards engagement and marriage. We were getting along so well that it certainly felt the right time to ask the most important question of my life.

So, while all the stress of Atlanta Attack was going on, I decided to take time off and surprise my sweetheart Liz. I planned to take her up to the North Georgia Mountains to a lovely old mining town called Dahlonega. I booked a night at a quaint 1850 bed and breakfast inn that reminded me of the house Tara in the movie *Gone With The Wind*. To top it off, the azaleas were in full bloom as we ate a wonderful candlelit dinner on the veranda.

Next morning, after a healthy breakfast, we went horse riding in the mountains. It was a perfect day with the scent of different flowers filling the air. I had a surprise in store, but I had to pretend I needed to attend an Atlanta Attack player appearance later that afternoon. I then concocted another white lie that Liz should be one of the judges at an Atlanta Attack cheerleading competition. Fortunately, she bought both white lies and agreed to come. Little did she know of my real plan.

I could tell Liz was not feeling very enthusiastic about cutting short our romantic weekend and that she was smiling through gritted teeth as we neared our destination. Then as I was driving into the parking area where the player appearance was supposedly happening, she noticed a hot air balloon being inflated in a nearby large field.

Liz looked at me and shrieked with excitement: 'Look someone is going for a hot air balloon ride. I've always wanted to do that. How romantic!' I had made a mental note about a hot air balloon ride six months earlier when Liz had looked on in delight when we watched one float off into the sunset. Back then she had tears in her eyes when it took off. It was the same day I confessed my love for her.

It was time to come clean: 'Lizzie, the hot air balloon is for you my darling,' I said to her. She gazed at me for a few seconds with a confused look on her face: 'Lizzie, there is no player appearance scheduled. I was just fibbing a little.'

Then I drove closer and parked opposite the hot air balloon. I took a deep breath as I considered the enormity of the moment. As I turned off the engine Liz spotted a dozen of our closest friends standing to the side of the balloon with champagne bottles and glasses in hand. Everyone was smiling and it was then she began to figure things out.

After a glass or two of champagne with our friends, we gently lifted off. It was a magical moment. Within ten minutes we were out of sight. It was really something special floating over the foothills of the North Georgia Mountains. We saw a large deer with its fawn get startled by the balloon's shadow as we floated over them. Then they both took off running up a mountain ridge that we were also following.

After about 20 minutes, I asked our pilot to give us some privacy. Being an old romantic I knew I had to do this the right way so I got on one knee and asked Liz if she'd marry me. Thank God without hesitation she accepted. We exchanged some private words and then shared a celebratory kiss. To this point it was the best day of my life.

Soon after the ring ceremony we brushed over the top of a gigantic pine tree where I reached down low enough to grab two pinecones from the top of the tree that were attached together. We saw this as a lifelong souvenir of the occasion.

It was official and now we had a wedding to plan. But that could wait. We were both blissfully happy as we floated over the Appalachian Mountains of North Georgia.

Chapter 49

Hello Married Life, Goodbye Atlanta Attack

A MONTH before our wedding, we purchased a beautiful little cabin nestled on the side of a trout stream. It was so remote that few people had heard of the area, which was mainly used for farmland. Located in the foothills of the Appalachian Mountains, near a sleepy town called Talking Rock, with no traffic lights, our cabin was a hidden gem just over an hour's drive from Atlanta.

We had a fantastic wedding with over 120 guests at our reception. Liz was then playing for an over-30s women's team, so they were all invited, as was my over-30s men's team plus our family and friends. It made for a fun-filled reception, doing the conga, having a good 'dance up' and sharing time with loved ones.

We left the wedding reception in a white horse-drawn carriage and clip-clopped through some well-to-do neighbourhoods and mansions in Buckhead. We were heading towards our overnight stay at the Ritz Carlton before leaving for London on our official honeymoon the next day.

Just before our arrival at the hotel we realised we were starving. We had been so excited at the wedding reception we had simply forgotten to eat. So, we asked our carriage driver if he could go to the nearest fast-food drive-through. The driver selected a famous hamburger place nearby called the Varsity and we had burgers with champagne. Even the horse got in on the act by chomping two cheeseburgers.

Then, in a unique gesture, the entire Varsity kitchen staff of about 25 people came out to wish us congratulations and started serenading us with the old Carpenters song 'We've Only Just Begun'. Another group, who looked like they were down on their luck, drinking alcohol out of brown paper bags, joined in and sang well too. We trotted away with the strains of the Carpenters ringing in our ears. 'We've Only Just Begun'; I can still hear them!

We spent our honeymoon in London and in the south of England seeing extended family before heading to Paris to be totally on our own for the last week. We drifted slowly down the River Seine past the Eiffel Tower and Notre Dame Cathedral having a candlelit dinner on a classy romantic boat. We could not have asked for more. It was an unforgettable honeymoon.

When I returned, I had to make a decision. Atlanta Attack had been an all-consuming project. I was working long hours, and feeling the stress of an under-invested franchise and a disenchanted owner who was close to sealing the deal to move the team from Atlanta to Kansas City, where they would be known as the Kansas City Attack.

With a heavy heart, I resigned from the club. I felt the owner had got tired of indoor soccer and was moving on to other interests. I was more than disappointed as were several loyal front-office staff who had shown a great deal of dedication. We all believed the team would have been successful given one more season. Ironically that was proven when the Kansas City Attack won the indoor title with the nucleus of the team we had put together in their very first season.

About the same time as I resigned from the Attack, Liz quit her job. So, with no jobs to worry about, we moved up to our cabin on the trout stream in the mountains for a few months to plan for the future. We were in our own little world and sharing nature with the occasional heron, otter and deer. We had got off the fast train of living life. It was truly needed and magnificent.

We were both in our mid-30s and wanted children fairly soon. But there was a problem. Liz had known since her teenage days that getting pregnant might be an issue. We went to see a specialist in Atlanta who told us that Liz might qualify to be part of a new trial that could possibly solve our problem. We jumped at the chance.

It meant I had to give poor Liz a daily injection in her thigh for three months and we had to make a four-hour round trip from the cabin to see the specialist three times per week. It was an emotionally trying time because we both wanted a child so badly. Besides the daily injections, Liz had to keep records on her temperature readings four times a day. It was all part of the study.

As we entered the final month of the study, we received terrible news that Liz's father, Bill, was losing his battle with cancer. Liz was very close to her dad who was a lovely man. So, we decided after the third month of injections that we would move to Dallas where her parents, two sisters and their families lived. I would get a job and Liz would spend as much time with her dad as possible.

As the three-month trial drew to an end, we still had nothing to show for it so Liz begged the doctor for a few more days of treatment and we returned to the cabin. The doctor asked us to keep the faith for three more days but that was the only extension he could allow. We thanked him profusely for not giving up on us.

The next hurdle was that I had to fly to Dallas for a very important job interview the following day with a recruitment firm. I did not know if I should go to the interview or not. Liz, bless her heart, said she would administer the final three injections herself and if there was some positive news, she would join me immediately.

I left with a heavy heart the next morning for Dallas. Liz stayed by herself at the cabin and then went to see the specialist for the last time. After a few agonising minutes of 'Ah – ahs' and 'Mm – mms' while the doctor studied her recent temperature charts, he sat back in his chair and according to Liz said: 'It looks like we have hit the jackpot this time. You have one more injection to take 24 hours from now and then you'll both have about a five-day window of good opportunity. So, get out of here and go do what you got to do.' Liz knew exactly what he meant. The clock was ticking and time was of the essence.

Liz did not want to waste any time and had a small suitcase packed and ready to go in the car.

Four hours later I was picking Liz up with my mother-in-law, Patsie, at Dallas airport. My father-in-law, Bill, did not feel quite well enough to travel with us. Patsie is one of the sweetest people you could ever meet. However, her innocence made us laugh out loud on the way home from the airport when she said, 'What do you guys want to do tonight after dinner? Do you want to go out and see a movie?' I couldn't help but laugh out loud when I replied, 'I don't think we'll go out tonight Patsie. I have an important job to do. Maybe you and Bill will want to go out to see a movie.'

Seven months later I had to witness a most heartbreaking sight. It was seeing my Lizzie at seven months pregnant sitting in the front row of the graveside service for her father, Bill, who had lost his battle with cancer. Bill was a good, kind man with so much to live for. He loved his family and was a source of strength and love for many people. He loved to go deep-sea fishing 20 to 50 miles off shore, down at his favourite place on the Texas coast called Port Aransas. He would take as many of the family as he could with him. He was all about family first and ran his leather saddle and horse accessory business second. Everyone loved Bill.

Two months after the funeral, our son Billy was born on 25 August 1992. He was a healthy 7lb 11oz. Our prayers were finally answered. Billy provided the sunshine the whole family needed. The happiness of his birth gave us such great cause for celebration and rejuvenated all of our family's spirits. We also all knew that his Grandfather Bill would always be watching over him as Billy's Guardian Angel.

Chapter 50

'There's No Meat in the Fridge!'

I WAS offered the job in Dallas with a national recruiting firm specialising in placing doctors in hospitals. I did not have a clue what I was supposed to be doing but thankfully the company had an intensive three-month training programme. It taught me much about recruiting, which would stand me in good stead for the future.

Liz had also started an office management job but I could tell she would change as soon as it made sense. That happened following a Monday morning 6am phone call for Liz when Billy was just a few months old and we were still living with Liz's mum, Patsie. The call came from one of Liz's former co-workers at the high school in Atlanta where she had coached soccer and taught PE for five years. I knew the only reason her co-worker would be calling so early in the morning was to see if Liz was interested in going back to teach and coach soccer at the school.

After Liz put the phone down, she could barely contain her excitement. She had been offered and accepted her former position as PE teacher and head soccer coach at Pace Academy in Atlanta.

We were delighted. Our 14 months in Dallas had been necessary for family reasons but we missed Atlanta, our friends and our cabin in the beautiful North Georgia Mountains. We had been homesick for a while but never dreamt such an offer would come our way.

A few days after Christmas we packed up our belongings and headed back to the cabin. It was tough saying goodbye to Patsie but she was excited and pleased for us, which made it less painful to leave her. Patsie was wise enough to realise we all had to move on and this was a great opportunity for us.

Because the cabin was too far for Liz to commute to school each day, we rented a home on the outskirts of Atlanta. Now I had to find another job. For some reason I fancied myself as a residential real estate salesperson. At the second attempt I passed the entrance test and joined a company called Northside Realty whose president was also a prominent political figure in Georgia and in Washington DC, Senator Johnny Isakson.

It was not an easy time at all. The housing market had recently tanked and was at an all-time low with interest rates going through the ceiling. It was tough getting a home listed, let alone trying to sell it. We were going into a recession where everyone was holding on to what they had. The real estate business wasn't working so after six months of due diligence I handed in my two-week notice.

On my last day at the real estate office, I was packing up my stuff when I received a phone call from Liz. She sounded frantic. 'There's no meat!' she screamed. 'I looked in the fridge and there was no meat in there! I mean no meat at all! Just fruit and it kinda made me sick to think about meat. Does that sound familiar to you?'

I'm thinking she's gone nuts. She's losing it. Then she asked: 'When and why did I go off meat before?' I sat bewildered. Then she shrieked: 'I'm pregnant!' Then I realised that the doctor had previously told us Liz's system could well right itself by having Billy.

By now all my co-workers had clicked on what was happening and were virtually pushing me out of the office to get home. They were beaming with joy and clapping ecstatically.

I used to think playing in Soweto was pressure but that was nothing compared to when the realisation dawned on the journey home that I had no job, a seven-month-old son and a pregnant wife. 'Oh shit, I had better get going on something,' I said out loud as I motored home.

We were also worried about something we would later laugh about. Could we find enough room in our heart to love another baby as much as we loved our Billy? That fear quickly subsided when we realised that our hearts would simply grow larger.

Chapter 51

The Waiting Game

WHILE EATING breakfast and trying to feed Billy his bottle, I was leafing through the sports section of the *Atlanta Journal and Constitution*. I read that Life University, the number one chiropractic college in the world in nearby Marietta, was building a new sports stadium and running track.

The president and founder of the college, Dr Sid E. Williams, saw himself as a visionary and believed the new stadium facilities could be used by athletes to practise before the 1996 Olympic Games, which were coming to Atlanta in four years.

I was impressed. I could tell Dr Sid wanted to spread the chiropractic word across the world and what better way to do so? No doubt the world's media would descend on the Life University campus filming these elite athletes. It would make an excellent advertisement for the college as would images of the athletes getting worked on by Life University chiropractors.

Then I had a classic light-bulb moment. Why not use the inner area where all the field events took place for soccer? The only problem I could see was that the college didn't actually have a soccer team. As soon as I could put Billy down for a nap, I called Dr Sid's office and got chatting to his secretary, Jean, who told me her grandson had come to my soccer camp and had a great time. This got me a foot in the door so to speak. I offered to drop in a business plan and she said I should come at 8am the next morning.

I worked through the night on the plan and got to bed at 4am, just four hours before the appointed time. It's amazing how motivated you can be when your wife is six months pregnant, your son is 14 months old and you have no job! I was outside Dr Sid's office at eight o'clock on the dot.

Jean was most accommodating and promised to hand my plan to Dr Sid and to call me if he was interested. Just after lunch, Jean did just that and told me Dr Sid wanted to see me the following Wednesday at 10am. I thanked her, saying her grandson could also bring a friend for free to my next camp. I was hugely optimistic.

I had five days to prepare for the meeting and, to make sure I looked as professional and businesslike as I could, I got a sharp haircut, wore a smart dark suit and tie and polished my shoes until they shone like the sun. I was fired up and ready. I arrived the customary 15 minutes before my 10am appointment. Jean came out on the stroke of ten and said Dr Sid had a few things to do and would I mind waiting a while? Of course I wouldn't!

So, I waited. And waited. And I waited some more. The clock moved slowly towards noon and there was still no sign of the elusive doctor. I was starting to get hungry.

Jean emerged again at 1pm and said it should not be much longer. I smiled. It was only a very slightly forced smile. Then 3pm came and went. By this time I had read and studied everything about Dr Sid's highly successful career in pioneering chiropractic care.

I was starving but dared not leave to go to the school's cafeteria. It was nearly 4pm and I had been waiting for over six hours. Then at 4.15 the all-important door opened. It was Jean. I stood up expectantly, straightened my tie and waited for the invitation to come in. Instead, Jean asked me if I'd seen Dr Sid. I politely answered that I hadn't. Jean grimaced and wondered if he'd left without saying anything, as he was sometimes prone to do.

'I'm sure he'll be back soon,' I said, trying to be as accommodating and flexible as possible. My stomach was rumbling with hunger.

An hour and a half later at 5.45pm – nearly eight hours later than my scheduled appointment – Jean popped her head out and said: 'No one can find him. Sometimes he'll go out and teach a class and not tell anyone.' Jean seemed genuinely irritated by her boss's vanishing act. I said calmly, through a somewhat rictus grin like a ventriloquist's dummy: 'I'm sure he had to go somewhere important Jean. He'll be back.' It was tough to smile but I did, sort of, and then sat down again.

The clock showed 6.15. I was getting dizzy with hunger and starting to shake a little. The executive door slowly opened. Jean had her coat on, preparing to head home, which didn't bode well for my prospects. Obviously embarrassed by her boss's antics, Jean said Dr Sid had asked if I could return at 10am tomorrow. With as much patience and tolerance as I could muster, I said it was fine and would gladly do that.

'Thanks for your patience today, Graham, I'll get you in to see him in the morning,' she said, as we neared her car. I opened her car's back door so she could empty her armfuls of paperwork and I could demonstrate my chivalry and old-school good manners.

She looked at me with a sheepish grin and reiterated her promise: 'Tomorrow, Graham, I'll get you in to see Dr Sid.'

That was a day I'll never get back.

Not to worry. The next morning, I was there at 9.45 and to my relief Jean said that Dr Sid should be in shortly. Then it began again. The waiting I mean. By lunchtime there was still no sign of the great man. I was starting to think he was being discourteous. At that point, my determination kicked in. I needed this job so badly. Liz was six months pregnant and working herself silly at Pace, Billy was nearly 15 months old and the bills were starting to mount up.

Lunchtime came and went. It was now 3pm. I was starting to think Dr Sid might be a figment of my imagination, some kind of hologram who didn't actually exist in the real world. Jean came out to check I was still there. My body was but my mind had left long ago. She said he would be about ten minutes before gently closing the executive door.

Another three hours dragged by. It was now 6pm. I had stood up about three or four times wanting to run out the door in frustration, but I just couldn't do it. I had too much on the line to risk missing this meeting.

At 6.15, Jean came out with the sheepish grin I was becoming accustomed to. She was very apologetic and said with huge embarrassment: 'Dr Sid has asked if you can come back tomorrow at 10am. He has a mini emergency to take care of.'

To say I was exasperated would be an understatement but I answered very patiently that I understood, wished him well with his emergency and that I would be back tomorrow morning. Jean thanked me and closed the door.

I had waited for a grand total of 17 hours and still not exchanged a single syllable with Dr Sid. The next day I was there at my regular time of 9.45am, starting to think I was in the middle of some 'gotcha' TV reality show.

Noon came very quickly for a change. I was lapsing into some sort of robotic, hypnotic state. I felt like a shell. I was brain-dead and numb, feeling like a waxwork in an exhibition. I may as well have been a tailor's dummy for the last three days. I had read all that could be read on Dr Sid and the Life University chiropractic programme and the undergraduate degrees that were offered. I felt like I could take a chiropractic exam and pass with flying colours, I knew that much about it. By 3pm I was starting to get frazzled. It was like a perverse game. A kind of torture to see if I would crack. I had been waiting for more than 22 hours. In seven days' time it would be Christmas Eve. An absurd thought ran through my head that I would be waiting here on Christmas Day while the rest of the nation was celebrating.

At 5pm Jean poked her head out and said: 'Dr Sid said he will be five minutes.'

'That will be lovely,' I replied dizzily with glazed eyes, smiling manically like an imbecile. I wasn't really there. I felt my sanity ebbing away.

Five minutes turned in to an hour and ten minutes. I was now pushing 25 hours and ten minutes on my three-day wait. It was 6.10pm. I walked over to the exit door and looked through the glass double doors like a condemned man peering out into freedom.

It was raining cats and dogs and getting very gloomy. I was on the verge of quitting and had my hand on the door for a split second. This was a form of torture and my spirit was waning. I knew Liz would be home, having picked up Billy from day care, and was probably feeding him right then and wondering when I would be home.

I wondered again whether I should just leave and throw the towel in completely. Right then I thought of Dad. I heard his voice: 'Never give up, son. It doesn't matter what happens. Never give up.' It was the motivation I needed.

'No. Damn it, I'm staying,' I said out loud to no one. 'I'm staying for as long as it takes.'

A bit more waiting, but this time with renewed optimism. Then it happened. The man I was fearing did not exist finally proved he did.

Wearing an expensive suit, with white hair and a face like George Washington, Dr Sid, mirage-like, was walking towards me with his hand outstretched.

'Sorry to keep you waiting Coach Tutt.' He had kept me waiting for three days but I was so relieved it felt like I had only waited three minutes. 'It's nice to meet you Dr Sid,' I said sincerely. Suddenly things were happening.

'I have read your credentials and want you to start Monday. I'll pay you $45,000 a year. That's what I pay my other head coaches. And how many scholarships will you need to win a championship?' was his final comment.

'Eighteen scholarships, Dr Sid,' I replied assertively. Originally, I was going to ask for nine but I had worked out he wanted me and he had pissed me off by making me wait for three full days and I was feeling emboldened, and maybe he felt he owed me one.

Dr Sid grinned and said: 'Eighteen scholarships it is then. Go and see Coach Kaiser on Monday at ten, he's our director of athletics.'

I shook his hand again, thanked him and closed by telling him I aimed to make him proud of his college soccer programme. He slapped me on the back and said, 'Welcome to Life,' before whisking around and leaving as quickly as he had entered. I stood there on my own for a good minute, taking it all in.

I had landed a college head-coaching job that would be challenging, exciting and right down my alley. I threw my hands up in the air and screamed 'yes' about a dozen times before walking in a daze to my car that had been occupying the same parking spot for three full days. On the way home I picked up a large bottle of non-alcoholic champagne for Liz and a six-pack of beer for me. It was time for a long overdue celebration.

Liz was waiting anxiously at the doorway of our rented home, holding Billy in her arms. She instantly knew by my face and the bottle of champagne that I had secured the job. I threw my arms around both of them then dropped to my knees to kiss her belly and our unborn. Without a word being said, Liz and I began to cry and laugh with joy at the same time.

The timing could not have been better. We were just keeping our head above water financially. Now we could really enjoy our Christmas.

Chapter 52

'Life's' a Mess!

AFTER FIVE months and with some extra cash coming in, we eventually found the family home of our dreams, a Tudor-style four-bedroomed house. It was perfectly located at the end of a quiet street with no traffic, making it ideally safe for kids. The back and side garden sat next to an area thick with trees so we felt like we were up in the woods, just like our cabin.

Our house was only a 20-minute drive for Liz to school and a mere ten minutes for me to Life University. We were blissfully happy, with our new son, Taylor, completing our family. Our neighbourhood pool was hardly used so we felt very private swimming and splashing around, playing with our boys. We felt like we had hit the jackpot.

I had known from the outset that developing a Life University soccer programme from scratch was going to be a huge challenge in itself. Yet having to deal with internal college politics would prove even more difficult than I imagined. There were certain individuals in critical positions who simply thought soccer was a 'communist sport' compared with the traditional American games of football, basketball and baseball. I felt that they were threatened by the growing popularity of soccer.

I also knew that other college head soccer coaches faced constant roadblocks. Some individuals at Life could barely hide their resentment of me. I sensed they viewed me as a foreigner representing a foreign sport.

I had to, somehow, confront this blinkered thinking and win them over with kindness, patience and charm and demonstrate that they should embrace soccer and not view it as a threat.

The players I initially recruited were from all over the world, which is exactly what Dr Sid had asked me to do. His thinking was that they would spread the chiropractic word when they returned to their homelands.

This was Dr Sid's vision so I went with a virtually international line-up. The players/students came from England, Scotland, Ireland, France, Germany, Costa Rica, Brazil, Argentina and South Africa.

The next challenge was finding teams willing to play us. I noticed that, when we did, it was often unnecessarily physical. I am convinced that some American referees, favouring their countrymen, chose not to 'see' many off-the-ball incidents and dangerous, late tackles on our international players.

However, our soccer programme triumphed on and off the field in my nine seasons there. Over that time, we recorded 189 wins, 28 defeats and 16 draws. We never won a championship because, in my opinion at least, our players would be too beaten up when it came to the really crucial play-off games.

Going totally with foreign players bit me on the backside somewhat but did the chiropractic world a lot of good, which is what Dr Sid wanted. After they graduated many of the players stayed in the States but some went back to their homelands to 'spread the chiropractic word'.

Dr Sid and I had a good deal of mutual respect for one another. He was different, that's for sure. He had an aura when he entered a room but could also be very unpredictable in his behaviour. It made me feel a little better when I heard he once kept the Mayor of Atlanta waiting over two hours. I'd have loved to have been kept waiting for just two hours. I had the record waiting time of 25½ hours. Jean confirmed as much!

The whole university came to a grinding halt in June 2002 when the school lost its academic accreditation. There were many things that went on that we did not hear about but the writing was on the wall. The school had all but closed its doors when the university went from over 5,500 students to under 1,000 because of the accreditation loss.

Dr Sid and his wife, Dr Nell, had started the school in 1974 with only 12 students. It was said that they did not hire the right professors. It meant the teaching was substandard in some areas and cost them dearly as students' degrees would not be officially recognised when they finished the programme.

Dr Sid's ego, which had taken him a long way, was ultimately his downfall. He was a shameless self-publicist. Just before the accreditation was taken away, he awarded himself a plaque with the title Chiropractor of the Century. The following year his wife was also named Chiropractor of the Century. His ego certainly got the better of him towards the end. He had become disconnected from the day-to-day running of the college and the executive heads driving the bus were not capable enough.

I learned a lot from Dr Sid. I thought he was a great guy, especially one on one, but when it came to more than one person in the room, he would feel the need to be 'on show'. He was also erratic and prone to occasional bouts of bizarre behaviour.

On more than one occasion he would be over 90 minutes late coming to the students' assembly, making them sit and wait. If they left, they would lose their credit hours for not attending. That was tough on the students who were starving for lunch when he rocked up at 11.30am instead of 10am and then talked at them for three hours. The doors were locked and nobody was allowed to leave once Dr Sid started talking.

I really cared for him and I believe he wanted to please everyone but ended up upsetting too many people along the way with some of his antics.

Each of us head coaches from Life University's six sports (basketball, rugby, soccer, ice hockey, track and field) knew we could never have a team photo taken without Dr Sid. If we did, we probably would have been fired. Once, he kept our entire squad waiting for nearly four hours on a blazing hot July summer's day at the stadium.

Sadly, I think his mental health started to suffer, but what a great promoter of chiropractic care he had been. His passion could never be faulted.

When the accreditation bombshell hit, it was no great surprise. I got a knock on my office door in early June 2002 from a minion in Dr Sid's office. He politely told me the athletic department was being closed at the end of the month because of the loss of academic accreditation. Then this faceless creature quietly closed my door and oozed away, giving me no chance to respond.

I sat in my office chair, stunned. The really sad thing was telling my six future overseas players that the college was not honouring their soccer scholarship contracts. I did my best to get them fixed up elsewhere but it was too late in the day for most of them. I felt awful for them and their parents as they had been so excited.

I had also just purchased over $25,000 (about £19,000) worth of uniforms, soccer boots, bags, sweat suits and training equipment. I was ordered by the finance department to send it all back which made our vendors furious.

'Life' was a mess.

The Life Athletic offices were closed at the end of that month. I wondered what was coming next.

Chapter 53

Time for Action

THE SEED for developing an indoor soccer league had been firmly planted in me as a ten-year-old lad when my mum encouraged me to invite my friends – sometimes as many as 16 of them – around to our house to play the legendary game that is Subbuteo.

I'd be surprised if anyone reading this has not heard of Subbuteo. The field is made out of green baize that is laid out flat on a dining table or, in my case, the quarter-size snooker table in our living room. We were always ready for a game of Subbuteo, especially when bad weather forced us indoors. At ten years old I took the title of league commissioner and would regularly arrange a tournament. The trophy was one of my mum's silver-plated egg cups that got passed from winner to winner.

Back to my adult life, and by this point I felt that indoor soccer had proven its popularity at youth, high school, college and professional level but had not been marketed correctly to ensure its commercial viability. When the NASL outdoor league folded in the mid-80s, indoor soccer went down the pan with it.

The Major Indoor Soccer League (MISL) replaced the fertile pro indoor soccer market. It instantly garnered tremendous growth in a short space of time even though it was rumoured to demand outrageous franchise fees and ludicrously high salaries. There was hardly any way a team owner could make a profit with that type of financial structure. The word on the street was that ego and greed got the better of some owners.

I felt the overseas, big-name players meant little or nothing to most of the pro clubs' local communities. George Best's introduction and lack of fanfare at our own Atlanta stadium proved this. In my view the owners' efforts would have been better spent focusing on advertising and promoting talented lads from their own towns.

I was keen to appeal to as wide a market as possible so I came up with the idea of developing a US/Canada men and women's professional co-ed indoor soccer league. It was a bit radical and 'out there' to think a co-ed team consisting of three men and three women could work but I believed in it. When running my indoor co-ed league, at grass-roots level, I had noted how much the fans (that's the players' families and children) were enjoying it.

However, I had to introduce some strict rules to ensure that no woman could be intimidated or injured by an over-zealous male player. The men had to play fair and respect the women on their team and the opposing one. Once this was understood everything fell into place and I found the teams 'policed' themselves and reined in any man who got too aggressive. I also introduced a rule which meant any goal scored by a woman counted double. I didn't listen to any truck from people who said I was reinforcing stereotypes and viewing women as the weaker sex. I wanted to encourage maximum participation and ensure the game was safe and enjoyable for everyone. Could you imagine having a female scoring against a male, at the pro level? That would make the national media spotlight.

My first priority was to find venues that could seat over 10,000 fans and, after a great deal of research, I found five in Canada and 31 spread evenly across the USA.

With 36 teams, I decided on six regional leagues consisting of six teams each, ensuring the travel budget would be manageable. Teams would play each other twice at home and twice away making a 20-game season. The play-offs would be held on a long weekend, making it budget-friendly and good for families.

My next step was to contact the general managers of every arena to rally their support. I was delighted they all wanted to participate and many gave me team ownership leads to contact.

After two years of networking with investors in the 36 cities I felt it was time for a men's and women's back-to-back exhibition games in Atlanta. I billed the event USA All Stars Versus the International All Stars, with a men's game followed by a women's game.

I wanted to make it a co-ed game at first but decided separate games would be less radical and more palatable for the public, and potential investors, to accept. Further down the road I would float the option of the co-ed league.

The exhibition games would serve two purposes. The first was to showcase the excitement of an indoor soccer match to potential investors and the second was to get them interested in joining the league and introducing the idea of dual-sex soccer.

The next challenge I had was finding an umbrella name for the league. I had adopted the Atlanta Attack indoor soccer franchise name several years earlier and at first I considered calling the league Attack Indoor Soccer but I decided the word 'Attack' was too loaded and open to political misinterpretation.

I spent many weeks mulling this over but could not land on a league name I liked. Our son Billy, who was then 11 years old, sensed my frustration. He must have taken this to heart because the next day, in art class, he made a laminated diary divider to give to me and wrote on the back of it:

Billy T. February 24, 2004
Never give up!

I was delighted that he had the insight to see I was frustrated and thoughtfully made me something I could see every day in my diary. I was very proud he recognised my dilemma and at the same time a little embarrassed he had witnessed me so frustrated. But I am glad he did.

I went to bed that night thinking of my son's words. All I knew for sure was that the name had to be strong enough to overarch and 'anchor' all 36 franchises.

At two o'clock in the morning somehow the answer came to me. I'm convinced I had been sleepwalking because I woke up in my office chair at the end of our hallway, a good distance from our bedroom. I just had to take the appropriate 'action' I said to myself, out loud. Then it hit me in a flash, 'ACTION Indoor Soccer League'. It had to be the name for the league. It all fell into place and I knew that each team name should be followed by the word 'action' like Atlanta ACTION … Las Vegas ACTION … The New York ACTION and so on. Because team nicknames are an important part of North American sporting culture the fans could vote on their city's nickname. This would generate additional publicity and spark community fan involvement in each city.

I wanted the league name to relate to each team and give the league a special identification on who we were and our unique co-ed soccer league.

The next day, I realised I needed a business partner, ideally someone familiar with the television industry who could appreciate the indoor game and knew how to make it work on screen with smart production to attract decent television network agreements. I strongly believe the indoor game was made for TV because goals aplenty are guaranteed. I felt the American public wanted a simplified, family-friendly version of soccer with goals galore and no complexities or distractions like offside to interfere with the enjoyment.

Later that morning I found my television partner. I was waiting at a traffic light not far from our home with the word 'action' buzzing in my head. I glanced over towards a small strip shopping centre and there in large red letters was a video production store called Action Video. I had been in it before when they converted my home movies of our boys and Liz to British television standards for Mum and Dad to see in England.

I went in and asked the owner if he knew of a reliable television producer who understood the industry. Without hesitating, the owner recommended a man named Jerry Wilson of Fourth Street Productions.

I immediately called Jerry and requested a face-to-face meeting. Jerry said it would have to be in a week because he was finishing off a television special for the Atlanta Falcons NFL team. This gave me a week to prepare, during which time I put together a complete plan with budget, league rules and structure.

When I met Jerry, I immediately realised he would be my ideal business partner and liked him from the off. Before getting down to business, we talked about how important our families were to both of us.

After sharing my plan, Jerry was sold. I said we would split everything 50/50 but he said no. He reasoned that because this was my vision and dream, I should be a 51 per cent majority owner and ultimate decision-maker and that Jerry would be happy at 49 per cent. This was a wise man talking.

I could not have wished for a better partner. His ideas and professionalism were totally spot on. Jerry shared a brilliant pre-promotional 'infomercial' script for each of the 36 franchises that would introduce teams to their surrounding communities in a professional manner. The infomercial was called *Going Pro with ACTION Indoor Soccer* and each team would have its own personalised version. The format would be based on *American Idol*, except that the players would be filmed and interviewed during their trial period as they endeavoured to make their team. Editorially, he knew there would be some great stories to be told from each and we devised the slogan: 'Home Grown Talent becoming Home Town Heroes.'

A panel of judges would choose the final team, similar to *American Idol* or the *X Factor*.

Each infomercial would carry ticket information, the team's home game schedule, merchandise details and the all-important owner's message to develop a first-class indoor soccer franchise for their city to be proud of. Jerry said he would devise a template of programming to be used in each city to ensure brand consistency.

In March 2006 we were ready to put the men's and women's exhibition games together and I invited all 36 potential Action

Indoor Soccer owners to attend. The venue I rented was the Arena at Gwinnett just 12 miles outside Atlanta with an ideal capacity of 11,200. But it cost us $25,000 (about £15,000) which was a fair sum for me to shell out for two games in one day. But I couldn't resist.

I rented the playing walls – also called dasher boards – and surrounding plexi-glass from a former Atlanta pro ice hockey team and leased the turf pitch from a company in Dalton, Georgia, which was only one hour away. Operationally, at least, we were all set.

Marketing and promotion were clearly going to be absolutely critical. The executive director for Georgia Soccer, Rick Skirvin, lived close by and had always been a close and trusted friend. He ran the day-to-day operations for an organisation boasting nearly 100,000 youth members, 7,000 adult players and around 5,500 referees, all of whom were registered in their organisation. I reached an agreement with Rick that three mass emails would be sent to their members in three stages. The first mass email was sent three weeks before the event. The second, one week out and a final one as a reminder three days before the event. We felt that should get the word out sufficiently and guarantee a decent crowd.

Another ace for Jerry and I was the Arena at Gwinnett which offered us 500 free television advertisements if Jerry could produce a 30-second advertisement of our event. Evidently the Arena had already purchased 10,000 advertising slots for a year and had not used the last 500, which had to be used before the end of September or they would lose them. Our game was in late August so that fitted perfectly. We produced a quality advertisement which we gave to the Arena marketing manager who in turn issued it to a local Atlanta cable station to begin airing two weeks before the event. It was all falling into place.

The last challenge was selecting four quality competitive teams – two men's and two women's. I recruited four highly qualified coaches to form their own teams through multiple try-outs. Once the teams were selected, the coaches had two months to work with them to get to a decent level. Because I was billing the two games as internationals, it was important that one team for both games be all Americans and the opposition team be all from other countries.

I am a firm believer in fate, so when the only feasible Arena date available was Sunday, 27 August 2006 I jumped at it. That would be my 50th birthday so I wrote a $15,000 Arena deposit rental cheque to secure the date and facility. Jerry did not have to put up any money because I insisted I would pay all the expenses at this stage. I knew he would appreciate this gesture and work even harder to make it a success.

With two weeks to go, all was good. Georgia Soccer had already sent the first email out to their members and the TV ads would kick in at any time. Then a massive problem arose. To my huge disappointment, I learned that the second and third emails to the 100,000 members advertising our event did not get sent out at all. It was an awful blow. I was given a particularly lame excuse that there was nobody available to send them out.

Jerry and I felt we were let down.

The second major problem was that the promise of 500 free TV ads also went totally awry. Jerry and I were calmly told that the ads were not going to be aired because of a cable network contract dispute. That news crushed us. Jerry and I were sent up the proverbial creek without a paddle.

We knew it would hurt our attendance and jeopardise the $15,000 I had already shelled out on arena rental. In near panic, I drew 1,500 complimentary tickets four days before the event and walked into various schools and soccer clubs, giving youth tickets away in the hope that parents would buy their own ticket to attend the exhibition games with their kids.

I already had over a dozen potential investors lined up, travelling in from various cities. Originally, I was anticipating all 36 investors, but around two dozen pulled out for various reasons. I learned the difference between a 'wannabe' and someone who could afford to finance a pro indoor soccer franchise with a $300,000 franchise fee rights deposit for the first three seasons.

Because Jerry and I did not want our exhibition matches played in front of a half-empty arena we began the busiest week of our life. We blitzed Atlanta and the suburbs with flyers. Then I gave out some free youth tickets to several soccer-strong YMCAs in the hope their parents would accompany them.

The end result was positive. It worked out pretty well with a decent crowd of nearly 5,000 fans. At least the fans filled most of the lower tier of the Arena seating giving a decent atmosphere. I believe we could have had 10,000 more if we hadn't been let down. We chalked it up to experience and that it doesn't pay to get bitter.

The dozen or so investors were mostly real estate brokers and developers. They appeared impressed and happy to move to the next step of entering the ACTION Indoor Soccer League, which was now open for franchise deposits.

Once again, fate intervened. It all came to a crashing halt when the mortgage crisis and recession hit the country one month later and the stock market took a severe tumble. Big-time national banks were closing their doors. The team of mortgage and real estate investors that I had were flipped on their backs overnight. My investors dried up.

I was totally dumbfounded and felt numb. All the effort Jerry and I had put in, 12-hour days for over three months, had been for nothing. The only option we did have was to tough out the financial crisis and pick up the ACTION Indoor Soccer League when the economy became healthy again. I went back to coaching youth soccer, giving private coaching sessions, and working with the male and female goalkeepers at Liz's school. Plus, it was always fun working with Liz; she was now my 'boss' (as such) by being the head ladies' coach at the high school.

A tremendous spin-off benefit was that Jerry and I became best friends. Having put the indoor league on pause, Jerry and I worked together on second tier indoor soccer projects organising adult indoor tournaments at various locations. One really rewarding project was when we produced a promotional video to raise funds and awareness for physically challenged children who wished to play a form of soccer using special equipment. The charity was called Top Soccer which was a fabulous organisation with volunteers led by a remarkable local woman called Suzanne Conlon. She took the Top Soccer Program nationwide.

But life was to take another cruel turn and tragedy was just around the corner.

Chapter 54
Saint Jerry

ONE AFTERNOON we were up at Jerry's office, when he started to cringe with pain. He took a quick breath and leaned forward with a shallow moan.

'Are you alright, mate?' I said, obviously concerned.

'Sharp pain, down below,' he whispered.

'Jerry, I'll call 911 or take you straight to hospital,' I said, trying to remain calm.

'No. I'll be okay. Just give me a minute. It's been coming and going the last few days. It'll settle in a minute,' he said with some difficulty.

Sure enough, after a few minutes, the pain subsided and Jerry returned to his old self apart from a rather ashen face. He promised me he would call his doctor later. I followed him home, worried he might have another attack. Fortunately, he was okay and waved me off at his driveway.

Jerry was a tough, John Wayne type of guy who never moaned about life's tribulations let alone any physical pain he may have. He was always positive, business savvy, friendly, with a heart of gold. He was a former State High School Championship wrestler and was built 'ram tough' as they say in America.

Jerry had an enduring passion for helping people realise their dreams, which was one of the reasons I wanted to be his business partner.

In our earlier meetings, he had asked me about my head and eye injury but he got watery eyed so I stopped talking about it. Then he told me how he had received a career-ending injury and it cost him a college scholarship. We both understood that we had been robbed of our potential to truly flourish as athletes.

I had a lot of love, respect and trust for Jerry. I knew he cared for me as much as I did him and we became as close as brothers. He was as honest as the day is long and always doing his best for others. He was reliable, creative and was always delivered. He was a man of his word.

I liked it when he used to say these words towards the close of a work day: 'Let's get going, my lovely bride is waiting for me.' You could tell how much he loved his wife of 35 years, Mary Madeline. Jerry was not in the least bit shy about saying how much he loved her. I would share the same feelings about my Lizzie. We were both dedicated husbands and totally devoted to our families.

Next morning at 8am, I called Jerry's cell phone and it went straight to voicemail. That was not like him. I had an awful feeling in the pit of my stomach and immediately called Mary Madeline. She picked up straight away and breathlessly told me, in quick short sentences, that she was at the hospital and Jerry was going into surgery very soon. With that she was gone.

Just after lunch, Jerry himself called and told me the doctors had found something of concern. It turned out that Jerry had pancreatic cancer. He later told me a priest had come into his hospital room and had given him the last rites. I started to laugh but only because he did. The stark fact was that the doctor said his chances of survival were slim. Jerry closed our conversation with: 'But you never know. With the right treatment and prayer, miracles do happen.'

I knew Jerry was trying his best to sugar-coat the situation so I went along with him. Otherwise, we would both have been sobbing our hearts out. I did not want to lose my new-found brother but it didn't sound at all good.

Mary Madeline called me after a second operation a few days later. She asked me to come to the hospital because Jerry was feeling very low and understandably scared. I was there in 15 minutes. Jerry's pregnant daughter was standing beside her mum, which brought back sad memories of my Lizzie being pregnant ten years earlier at her dad's graveside. One of Jerry's fine sons, Brandon, was giving his sister some support. Jerry's other two sons were on their way. We were all hoping for the best but expecting the worse.

Mary Madeline gave me the one-minute low-down. She quietly said the operation had found cancer and it was in more than one place. She then said that Jerry would like to see me.

Reeling from the shock of what I had just heard, I walked quietly into a very dark room. Jerry was deep in thought. We made eye contact and then Jerry started to cry. I held his hand and cried with him until I could regain some sort of composure and then I began a prayer. I was as devastated as the family. Jerry was now fighting for his life.

What happened next was classic Jerry. While undergoing weekly chemotherapy, Jerry noticed that some of the other patients would have to wait several hours for a member of their family or a friend to pick them up to take them home. This bothered Jerry.

He knew from personal experience how awful people felt after having chemo treatment and the last thing they wanted was to wait another five or six hours to go home. So, from his hospital bed, he started a non-profit organisation called Loving Arms. Jerry and Mary Madeline formed a team of volunteers who raised funds for cab rides to and from home for ailing cancer patients. I thought it demonstrated perfectly what a thoughtful, caring man Jerry was.

After nearly two years of chemo treatment and showing tremendous courage, Jerry died in a special care centre on 25 May 2012. The song 'A rainy night in Georgia' was playing on my car radio on the drive home. It was very poignant and fitted the occasion. It was not fair. We had lost a diamond of a man.

One of the most difficult things I had to do was to speak, at Mary Madeline's request, at Jerry's funeral. The speaking was difficult, but it was not at all hard to find good things to say about one of the finest men I ever had the privilege to meet. He epitomised everything we all should strive to be.

Jerry often called me 'the Commish' – short for commissioner and I referred to him, even before he got sick, as 'Saint Jerry'. He just fitted the bill. If you got to know him, even for five minutes, you would feel exactly the same way.

I vowed to Mary Madeline and Jerry's family at the funeral that one day our ACTION Indoor Soccer League, that we had planned together, would come to fruition with the championship trophy named after him, the Saint Jerry Cup. Jerry's values would then be passed on to thousands of people as a great example of how we should live our lives. I couldn't think of any better tribute to Saint Jerry and the future of pro co-ed indoor soccer. Undoubtedly, we had lost a fantastic person who helped so many.

Chapter 55

Swimming with Sharks

AFTER JERRY died, the wind was taken out of my sails. I needed time to grieve and shelved the indoor soccer project because I felt empty and lost without my best friend and business partner.

Because of the long recession between 2007 and 2010, job opportunities had become scarce. I simply could not find a decent college coaching position or even create one because the economy was so bad. In general people were trying to hold on to what they had. Any decent job opportunity that came my way would mean leaving Georgia and, for family upheaval reasons, that was not an option.

The only bright light during this grey period was when I was inducted into the Georgia Soccer Hall of Fame in recognition of my contribution to youth, club, high school, college and pro soccer (indoors and outdoors). It was humbling to be recognised.

As was said at the induction ceremony, I had covered virtually every aspect of the game in Atlanta between 1980 and 2012. Many thought I had retired when I was inducted which made it even more difficult to find a decent soccer job in the Atlanta area. So, I eased back by coaching goalkeepers, the occasional youth team, and just one summer soccer camp for our local church, a small camp of about 75 boys and girls aged five to 12.

I was starting to feel my coaching days were behind me. My body was telling me it was no picnic coaching in 90-degree heat anymore. I was getting ready to hang my boots up.

I knew in my heart, head and gut that the ACTION Indoor Soccer League would be successful with the right selection of team ownerships. It was just a question of finding the right investors!

An opportunity to present and expose my plans to literally millions of people arrived in the shape of *Shark Tank*, a national television show here in America, the US version of Britain's *Dragons' Den.*

The audition for the show was held at the famous Fox Theater in Atlanta, the same location where *Gone With The Wind* had premiered with Clark Gable and Vivien Leigh 60 years earlier. It was cold and rainy on the Saturday morning when I arrived to join the queue at the unearthly time of 4am in mid-January 2013. I had to turn up so early because only the first 200 in line would be guaranteed an audition. Weather-wise it was a bad day. The wind was howling and the rain was lashing down. We hopefuls were all getting soaked to the skin and starting to feel very cold. Even our umbrellas were being turned inside out. January weather can be severe to brutal in the south.

Eventually, after five hours of toe-tapping waiting, at nine on the dot, an official began handing out our audition numbers that were printed on bright-yellow wristbands. I got #8, my lucky number.

The audition went very well, especially when the person conducting my audition said one of the *Shark Tank* investors,

Mark Cuban, loved sports and owned an NBA basketball franchise in Dallas, Texas.

I delivered my pitch to the absolute best of my ability. At the end, the host gave me some papers to sign and then asked me to make my own video and mail it back within five weeks, which I did.

A week later the *Shark Tank* producer called me with great excitement in his voice after receiving the video and advised me to add some additional background information about myself and to make it more personal by mentioning the 'Sharks' by name. Lastly, he said if I could demonstrate that between 20 to 25 cities had already committed to join the league, with each of the 20 to 25 team owners standing behind me and holding a poster board of their city's name printed on it, then he would put me on the show.

The producer was 100 per cent correct. If the Sharks could see my future team owners standing in line across the studio, it would surely be a deal clincher.

I'm still working on this and I'm determined to make it happen. As you may have realised by now, I 'never give up' and the search for team owners continues, to help make my dream a reality. So far, I have five or six cities/team owners interested in joining the league and need another 20 or more to make a presentation on the *Shark Tank* television show. Once there in the studios with the future owners present and lined up showing their commitment behind me, I can visualise each of the five Sharks wanting to own a team simply because of their natural competitiveness making them want to beat each other.

There are additional team owners interested, in Canada and Mexico. Carefully controlled travel expenses and player salaries are crucial to an owner staying in the league. No one wants to lose money. I believe the key to having a successful league is having 36 teams, divided into six divisions of six teams and no more than a seven or eight-hour coach ride for each fixture.

If I can make it happen, I will have helped develop the first of its kind, an International Co-ed Pro Indoor Soccer League.

You can watch my *Shark Tank* video audition tapes online. Just type in 'Graham Tutt Shark Tank' and you'll find them. Details of how cities can enter the league are included towards the end of this book.

Chapter 56

A Source of Pride

WHEN I first arrived in America, which is now over 40 years ago, the game was really still in its infancy. Yet you only have to look at the Major League Soccer (MLS) and Atlanta United to see how far the sport has come over here.

The Atlanta United MLS team has made an incredible impact throughout Georgia and the league. Not only did they win a MLS Championship in their second season, but also averaged over 50,000 fans at home games. The MLS recently announced the team was its top-valued franchise at $330 million and over 70,000 fans turned out for their last play-off games.

I had lunch with Atlanta United's very bright and likeable president, Darren Eales. He has tremendous support from the team owner, Arthur Blank, who has the uncanny knack of making success happen to whatever he touches. Mr Blank is a brilliant businessman who has built an outstanding empire, starting with Home Depot, consisting of hundreds of pick-up and do-it-yourself home stores, the Atlanta Falcons NFL franchise and now Atlanta United. What I admire about him is that he's a true giver and is always giving back to the community.

I can only wish the whole operation continued success. It makes me proud to have played a small part in its development. I cannot help but wonder how many of the 50,000 to 70,000 fans attending their games were influenced by one of us former NASL players. We did our fair share of pioneering soccer in many American cities from the late 60s onwards.

Likewise, between the early 1980s and the present day, I have been blessed with just over 40,000 boys and girls coming through my soccer camps. I've often wondered while watching an Atlanta United game at the sparkling new Mercedes Benz Stadium how many of my past soccer campers were there.

In 2018 Atlanta United honoured us old Atlanta Chiefs players before a game. It was a wonderful gesture of recognition and appreciation and felt fantastic to be in front of a big crowd of 50,000 or more again. I persuaded Liz to walk on the pitch with me. After all, Liz had played her part pioneering the past 30 years by being a high-school ladies head soccer coach.

I always knew the day would come when that many fans would attend matches. We believers always knew the day would come when that many fans would attend matches. The game has now arrived. Really arrived.

Chapter 57

Family Guy

BEFORE WE finish, I'd like to tell you something more about my family, starting with our sons, Billy and Taylor.

Liz and I share the same views on education, believing that a limited education is like having a boat with no rudder. That is why we stretched ourselves financially to give our boys a first-class education. It was worth it, for it set our lads on the right course in life.

Liz and I also felt strongly that our sons should select the college of their choice, not necessarily the one we wanted, simply because it was them who had to study, eat and sleep there. In our case, within 20 minutes of being on the Furman University campus, Billy told us it was the one for him. The same thing happened a year later with Taylor and Belmont University in Nashville.

I think there's nothing worse than 'helicoptering' your kids by hovering over them, making decisions for them all the time. If you do that, they will never be decision-makers. Just make sure they know you are always available to talk things through when they are struggling with an issue or opportunity. Liz and I have been around high-school kids and their parents for over 60 years between us. We have seen first-hand the destruction and havoc parents can wreak with their kids. Let them figure things out. They'll never learn to grow up otherwise.

One thing is for sure, if you are patient, they'll come and ask for your opinion when they are ready. So, we go easy as parents. Liz taught me that. I was guilty on occasion of wanting to do everything for our lads. Fortunately, Liz reined me in a couple of times and I saw the light.

Liz is looking to retire from teaching after 33 years. I know I am biased but she has performed brilliantly during her tenure as a teacher and head soccer coach. She accomplished an outstanding winning record for a small school, with five state championships and multiple play-off appearances. She has always gone the extra mile in her career by serving as a dean, assistant athletics director and PE teacher. That's a lot of work and responsibility to take on.

Everything she did at Pace Academy received her full attention. And just like I saw when I fell in love with her at camp, 30-plus years ago, she did it with dedication, finesse and love. She made coaching soccer look so easy. I am so proud of her and feel lucky to have her by my side. There are 7.6 billion people on our planet and somehow, some way, something brought us together. I believe it was more than fate. Maybe my guardian angel or God had his hand on my shoulder at times when I did not know it. I know he gave me incredible speed when chasing a moving bus at the close of the Windhoek riot game!

I started writing this book five years ago. It took me a while to complete (mostly because I am very slow at typing) but in truth I wanted to tell my story in my own words. I decided to write this book for many reasons. Liz thinks it has served as some form of therapy, a cathartic experience which helped me come to terms with my head injury all those years ago.

It was also about forgiving Tom Finney, whose boot struck my face. I think Liz is probably right. I'm still trying to work through that event, even though it was 44 years ago. It has been tough to forgive someone I spent many years blaming but I thought long and hard about it and realised if I couldn't forgive Tom, well, shame on me. I look at what I have with my wife, family and friends and feel totally blessed. Now I believe the boot in the face was the best thing that could have ever happened to me and I never thought I would be saying that, I can tell you.

For sure, there have been some 'head issues' which I have been able to directly address. There have been plenty of 'what might have been' moments but I still experienced what so many aspiring footballers strive towards but never reach. Only a very small proportion of footballers make the grade and the overwhelming majority fall by the wayside for a variety of reasons and it can be a devastating experience. Some never recover properly and bitterness sadly sets in. Some take refuge in alcohol; others simply drift through life feeling unfulfilled.

The biggest mistake most career-ending injured athletes make is clinging on to the past. The 'I could have been a contender if only' brigade. I get it, but it's not the right road and will only create negativity. I know because I've veered close to this territory myself.

Yet, with the right mindset these former players and athletes can be okay. Even the shortest career in football can teach players a boatload of skills to help them be successful in other walks of life. Without even realising it, they will have learned about teamwork, dedication, determination and discipline. They will understand, better than most, ambition, willingness to learn, honesty, passion and self-confidence. They'll know that nothing comes without hard work and that maintaining a high level of physical health is important. I could go on and on.

Many former players forget or don't realise that these life lessons are already inside them and can be easily transferred to the 'real world.' Just have the confidence to believe in your plan, think it through from start to finish and then take action by following your plan. Again, I can only speak from experience.

Chapter 58

Forgive and Forget

DAD PASSED away in April 2000 aged 83. Mum said that Dad was determined to see in the new millennium and he did. She told me that one of his final wishes was to have his old Charlton scarf wrapped around his neck in his coffin. He also confided in her, just a few months before he died, that when I finished playing at Charlton he found it too difficult to go to any more of their games. Apparently, he did go to watch one game at the Valley when I was playing in South Africa, but couldn't take it. He told Mum he was having too many flashbacks of me keeping goal. It was too much for him and he left The Valley for the last time and before the first half had ended. He had been a loyal Charlton supporter for 49 years. Mum claimed, after he passed, that the pain was too great for him to watch a match without his son between the sticks.

Eventually Mum moved away from London and close to my sister Julie in Sittingbourne, Kent. Mum doted on her grandchildren, John, Mark, Katie and David for the last decade of her 80 years.

I would go home every three or four years to see her but never as much as I wanted to. She also liked coming out to the States to stay with me. She thought life for the average American was on cruise control with so little to worry about.

Mum followed Dad and died in 2002. They were married two years before the end of the war, in April 1943, and were together for 57 years.

It's incredible how much you learn about yourself after your parents die. Their resilience was amazing. There was nothing my mum or dad couldn't handle, and both had a positive way of dealing with the most awkward of things. They always hoped for good things to emerge from tough situations. They both really had the hearts of a loving lion.

The experience of living in three countries has made me grow internally. So, I recommend travel as much as you can because you'll learn more about yourself and it will broaden your horizons.

I remember when Dad came to visit me in Atlanta in 1985. It was the first time he had been on an aircraft and he was 68 years old. I gave him the best vacation I could by taking him down to Florida and seeing Cape Canaveral where all the NASA rockets were launched. As we were waiting for his return flight to London, and I was seeing him off at the gate, he said something which has stayed with me. He looked at the throngs of people milling this way and that throughout the airport and said quietly: 'There are a lot of people in the world, son.'

You could see the penny drop as they say. My dad had never travelled, never really wanted to. But travelling had shown him how busy the world had become in his lifetime.

Incidentally, I still have double vision. But it doesn't stop me from living life to the full.

I do have one request. If you know someone who is struggling, give him or her a helping hand.

It doesn't have to be money. Encourage them with kindness and hope. It costs nothing and makes you really feel good. I've learned that doing good things feeds the soul and makes you sleep better.

Forgive, forget and go forward. That's been a tough one for me personally. For many years I was consumed with bitterness about what happened at Roker Park all those years ago. I couldn't forgive and forget and, as a result, I was emotionally paralysed.

But, over time, I learned to put a different perspective on things. In my mind I forgave Tom Finney and came to cherish what I had, not what I didn't have. If that injury had not happened then my life would have taken a completely different course. I would never have met my soulmate, Lizzie, who I'll cherish until the day I leave this world. I'll be waiting for her patiently at the pearly gates. We would never have had our two fine sons and I might not have had the opportunity to see some truly beautiful parts of the world.

You see, good things can spring from even the worst experiences. I'm nearly 64. I now believe the boot that hit me in the face when I was 19 was the best thing that could ever have happened to me. I have thought about this a lot and, increasingly, I wanted to contact Tom Finney as some form of closure.

Chapter 59
Finding Tom Finney

IN THE summer of 2020, I was approaching my 63rd birthday and I had what I can only describe as a light-bulb moment. As I hope I've conveyed to you, though many years have passed since the injury that finished my professional career in the UK, I've had a nagging sense of unfinished business. Though many happy things have happened to me, there was still something buried in the dark recesses of my mind that I couldn't shake off. It was preventing me from moving on, a kind of albatross around my neck that, every now and then, took me back to that chilly Saturday afternoon in Sunderland in February 1976.

I realised that my inability to forgive Tom Finney had been a spectre hanging over me, a permanent niggle that had been casting a shadow over me for all this time. There is no doubt that the injury was a defining moment in my life. It set in motion a chain of events which brought me to where I am today. For all the wonderful things in my life, mainly related to my family, I am thankful. But the emotional scar ran deep and was always there.

I was grappling for a solution when I heard the thoughts of someone I had never even spoken to, let alone met. They came from Lisa Eastley, the wife of my collaborator and editor on this book, Matt Eastley. Lisa and Matt were having a long weekend away from home and were walking along the coast in southern England when she suggested that I should simply contact Tom Finney, the Sunderland striker involved that day. Lisa thought it would be a weight off my shoulders and enable me to finally, truly move forward and close the door on an event that, in truth, has haunted me ever since it happened. When Matt conveyed his and Lisa's conversation, I knew it was the right thing to do. I had in fact thought about it many times before but now the time seemed right. Writing the book had been such a cathartic experience that I knew this was the closure I needed and I immediately chose to take some steps in reconnecting.

Another important reason for trying to contact Tom was what I had recently learned about the US Congressman and civil rights activist, John Lewis, who had just died at 80 years old. John had walked alongside Martin Luther King in the 1960s on some important civil rights marches.

In 1965, he had led the first of three Selma to Montgomery marches across the Edmund Pettus Bridge. In an incident which became known as Bloody Sunday, state troopers and police attacked the marchers, including John, whose skull was fractured. It was not the first time John had been beaten – he had also been beaten by Klansmen a few years earlier. The thing is John Lewis had forgiven the people who inflicted the savage beatings on him. He believed forgiveness was the best response. He even visited the Alabama State Trooper who fractured his skull and told him he was forgiven.

I dwelt on this wonderful magnanimous gesture by John Lewis. How easy it would have been for him to be consumed by bitterness or revenge. Instead, he decided forgiveness was the best route. And I believe he was right.

It made me even more determined to 'Find Finney' to tell him that I harboured no ill feeling or resentment towards him – everything I hadn't been ready or willing to say when he visited me in hospital in Sunderland. I wanted to let Tom know I had forgiven him and that my life had moved on with a wonderful 30-year marriage, two great sons and a lovely home. Most importantly I wanted to let him know that I bore no malice towards him.

I was also interested to know how Tom himself had fared. It cannot have been easy knowing that he had unwittingly finished someone's professional career in the UK. How had it affected him? Tom hadn't stayed long at Sunderland but he became something of a goalscoring legend at his next club, Cambridge United. Tom was good enough to play 14 times for Northern Ireland between 1974 and 1980 and was still in the World Cup squad which went to Spain in 1982.

After Cambridge, Tom moved to Brentford for a short period before returning to Cambridge and then playing for a number of non-league clubs in Cambridgeshire, later managing Histon.

After that, I didn't really know what had happened to Tom and I'm sure he had no idea what happened to me. So, I resolved to find out. I wanted to contact him and decided the best way to do this was by letter.

I worked hard on the letter, to find exactly the right words. I didn't want to worry Tom or for him to think there was anything sinister or that my intentions were anything less than honourable. When I had my letter, written, signed and sealed, the problem was I had no idea where to send it! Tom could literally have been anywhere in the world.

Finding Tom was no easy task. I sent out a few speculative emails and made a few tentative enquiries, to no avail. It felt like a needle in a haystack. Then Matt Eastley got on the case. Matt's a bit of an expert at finding people and said he'd find Tom within a week.

He was true to his word and, within a couple of days, he had found a strong lead through the brilliantly named 100 Years of Coconuts, an organisation and website responsible for bringing the history of Cambridge United alive. Matt knew that Tom had been featured on the website so figured that the guys behind it would have a contact for him.

So, we got in touch with them. Because of our history and the incident at Roker Park, it was a little delicate to say the least and we also had to assure the gents at Coconuts that they had nothing to worry about.

After a few days they got back to us and agreed to pass the letter to Tom. After posting the letter, there was another delay, while we waited for news. All I wanted to know was whether Tom had received my letter which, we understood, would be passed to him by another former player.

All we could do was wait. I was hungry for news. Days turned into weeks. I drafted another letter to see if that would do the trick. I decided to give it a few more days.

Just when I was about to give up, an email landed in my inbox from a Pauline Finney. To my delight it was from Tom, who was using his wife's email address. My heart was racing as I clicked on it and I was filled with a sense of dread about what it might contain.

You might have realised by now that I'm a bit of an old softie and soon my eyes were filled with tears of joy as I read Tom's words. I won't reveal exactly what they said, as I believe the correspondence between us should remain private, but suffice to say it was everything I could have hoped for: a sincere and genuine response from a true gentleman.

I immediately emailed Tom back, thanking him for his kind words. It really did mean a lot to me and the sense of relief I felt was palpable. I will reveal that I said I hoped that one day we could meet and that I would gladly buy him a pint. Probably a Guinness – he's an Irish lad, you know!

Since then, my outlook on the world has changed. Life was already wonderful in so many ways but contacting Tom and receiving such a heartfelt email back from him has made it even more so.

As you know, I never give up and maybe, just maybe, that kick to the head at Roker Park all those years ago was the best thing that ever happened to me.

I think so. What do you think?

Postscript

CONTACTING TOM Finney was a special, important moment for me and one that has given me true closure from an incident that scarred me emotionally perhaps more than I realised. That's all in the past now because all I'm concerned about is the future. I still have an unfulfilled dream and that is to establish an international co-ed indoor soccer league.

My *Shark Tank* audition provided me with the confidence that this concept could really fly and become a genuinely popular family attraction across the States.

I have a good foundation to build on, with, so far, six cities and other potential owners expressing strong interest in joining the league. I am still looking for more.

I am determined to follow my ACTION plan.

My best,
Cheers,
Graham (my friends call me Buster).
graham.tutt@comcast.net
www.grahambustertutt.com

PS – And please remember 'NGU' … 'Never Give Up'.

Photograph: David Berry